2250

COPING IS NOT ENOUGH!

THE INTERNATIONAL DEBT CRISIS AND THE ROLES OF THE WORLD BANK AND INTERNATIONAL MONETARY FUND

COPING IS NOT ENOUGH!

THE INTERNATIONAL DEBT CRISIS AND THE ROLES OF THE WORLD BANK AND INTERNATIONAL MONETARY FUND

Morris Miller

DOW JONES-IRWIN
Homewood, Illinois 60430

ISBN 0–87094–933–0

Library of Congress Catalog Card No. 86–71358

Printed in the United States of America

1 2 3 4 5 6 7 8 9 0 B 3 2 1 0 9 8 7 6

To Claire,
who has made of love
"an ever-fixed mark
that looks on tempests and is never shaken."

Shakespeare
Sonnet CXVI

This book had its genesis in a talk on the debt crisis delivered in mid-1983 in Toronto at the annual meeting of the International Association of Financial Analysts. The following summer a revised, updated version on the same subject was given at Aspen, Colorado, at a seminar of the Aspen Institute.

In early 1985 I sent a copy of the talk to my friend, Murray Rossant, director of the 20th Century Fund, and also enclosed a copy of my valedictory comments to the board when leaving the World Bank as executive director. In those comments I addressed some critical remarks and cautionary advice about the role of the World Bank in relation to the debt crisis and other international issues that go beyond the traditional bank-to-country relationship. Mr. Rossant challenged me to write a book on the subject of the debt crisis as seen by someone from my double vantage as a former staff member and as executive director of the World Bank. Caring as I do about the World Bank as a genuinely international institution in which I have spent a substantial part of my professional life, and concerned as I am about the global debt situation and how it is being handled, I made a commitment to write the book.

My intention has been to reach three audiences: those in the national and international organizations and in the financial community on both the lending and borrowing side who I could assume are knowledgeable about the subject in its many ramifications, students, and the concerned public who read about the problem in bits and pieces in their daily newspapers or periodicals but would welcome a way of bringing it all together. Bridging these audiences has posed a problem I thought might be resolved by footnotes, which can be helpful to those unfamiliar with the relevant organizational and procedural aspects—without disrupting the continuity of the argument for those who have little need for footnote explanations and amplifications. Thus, I would hope the treatment is "popular" without too much sacrifice of detail needed to support the line of argument.

In writing this book I was supported in ways that were helpful beyond measure by my wife, Claire, whose devotion and understanding was boundless and whose advice was invaluable. I'm also deeply indebted to the dedication and the analytic and editorial skills of my son, Riel, who allowed me without complaint to divert him from pressing work on his doctoral thesis. I had, as well, the research assistance of Jody Holtzman and Bruce Tate and for the time I was serving in my capacity as Executive Director, the staff of that office and my alternate, George Reid of Barbados. I've also profited from the helpful advice of my colleagues, Arthur Domike of the Economic Development Group and Marcel Cote of Secor Inc., and of others who were kind enough to read and comment on earlier drafts: Isa Bakker, Scott Douglas, Arshad Farooq, Shereen Benzvy Miller, Mark Schachter, David Schwartzman, and my many former colleagues at the World Bank and the IMF who provided statistical and other documentation as well as perceptive and critical comments. Lastly, I must add the inspiration and counsel of Murray Rossant whose editorial talents and tact are beyond compare.

None of those who have helped in various ways should, of course, be held responsible for the views expressed.

Morris Miller

CONTENTS

CHAPTER ONE

The Challenge of the Debt Crisis

We must not deceive ourselves. There are no easy solutions, and none of us can escape our responsibilities. . . . Everybody has to make some contributions.

James A. Baker III, U.S. Secretary of the Treasury[1]

"If you had absolute power, if you had to play God, how would you solve the debt problem?" First, I would refuse to play God in a world that spends billions of dollars on armaments . . . And I would be frank with the bankers and tell them: 'like Dante in hell—abandon all hope.'

Alan Garcia Perez, President of Peru[2]

---

[1] Speech before the World Bank/IMF Annual Meeting, Seoul, South Korea. *Time* (October 21, 1985) used this quote to head a story on the meeting, titled: "Baker Steers a New Course: The U.S. launches an ambitious plan to defuse the Third World's debt bomb."

[2] Quoted from an interview in *Business Week* (September 30, 1985). At the time of the interview an annual report was being issued titled, "World Military and Social Expenditures, 1985," by Ruth Sivard, a former official of the U.S. Arms Control and Disarmament Agency (ACDA). It revealed that the annual global expenditure now exceeds $800 billion. This is a conservative estimate; the ACDA report shows military spending to have been close to $970 billion in 1984. In that year official development assistance (ODA) was much less than $40 billion. (See page 243).

FALSE HOPES AND THE EMERGENCE
OF A TRIPLE-HEADED CRISIS

Midway through 1984 an optimist coined the term, "the Great Debt Crisis of 1982–84." It was then—and it still is—rather premature to fix a terminal date. "The Great Debt Crisis of 1982–" might be a more appropriate label. The time span is still open-ended. Furthermore, the single-focused characterization of the crisis, which until recently has been narrowly spotlighted only on the debts of developing countries, has to be broadened. Commentators, now talk of "the second debt crisis" and even "the triple debt crisis," referring to the U.S. budget deficit, which now exceeds $200 billion, and the trade deficit, which in 1985 surpassed all previous records to reach more than $150 billion. The combined effect has been to bring the United States, for the first time in 70 years, back into the ranks of debtor nations.[3] If present trends continue, by the end of the decade, the U.S. net foreign debt will exceed the combined debt of the developing countries.

The nature and treatment of the second and third facets of debt crisis differ markedly from the first because the

---

[3] C. Fred Bergsten, director of the Institute for International Economics, Washington, D.C., spoke and wrote of the second debt crisis early in 1985: "The Second Debt Crisis is Coming," *Challenge* (May-June 1985). Professor Gerald Epstein of the New School for Social Research has written about the third debt crisis by counting the U.S. budget and trade deficits as separate but related phenomena: "The Triple Debt Crisis," *World Policy Journal*, (Fall 1985). This broader perspective brings into the picture other elements of the current situation, which is being called "a debt explosion": Flow of Funds data for 1985 issued by the U.S. Federal Reserve show the combined debt of households, corporations, and governments jumped from $4.3 billion in 1980 to $8.2 trillion at the end of 1985. During 1985 it rose 15 percent, which is much faster than the 2.3 percent rate at which the economy grew in that year. This disparity is symptomatic of a serious, deep-seated problem because deficit spending of this magnitude (in both absolute and relative terms) is normally very stimulative. For a popular treatment of this debt phenomenon, see "The Casino Society," *Business Week* (September 16, 1985).

U.S. foreign debt is denominated in U.S. dollars and thereby subject to U.S. manipulation. Nonetheless, the situation can be characterized as one big global debt crisis, "crisis" being defined as "an unstable condition (with) an abrupt or decisive change . . . impending."[4] While the U.S. facet of the global debt crisis is sufficiently serious to rouse fears of breakdown and talk of "debt balloon bursting," the term *debt crisis* has become part of our lexicon with reference to the Third World's indebtedness alone. It is serious enough to merit the spotlight. A few salient statistics can set the stage:

> Rounding the numbers to simplify the picture, imagine a situation in which the total foreign debt owed by both government and private citizens of the developing countries or less developed countries (LDCs) amounts to about $1,000 billion or $1 trillion and that the annual interest and principal repayments due on this debt amounts to about $175 billion. Imagine too that for the average country this level of payment would absorb about one third the net foreign exchange earned from exports and, in the case of some countries, actually would exceed the total of such earnings.[5] Accordingly, unless there is a substantial unexpected increase in the flow of borrowed capital, investment capital, and foreign aid, many of the debtors would face a situation of being unable to meet

---

[4] The American Heritage Dictionary defines crisis as "a) a crucial point or situation in the course of anything; turning point, b) in political, international or economic affairs, an unstable condition in which an abrupt or decisive change is impending, c) in pathology, a sudden change in the course of an acute disease, either towards improvement or deterioration, d) in literature, the point in a story or drama in which hostile forces are in the most tense state of opposition."

[5] Debt service payments as a percentage of total export earnings (the debt service ratio) of several countries can illustrate the severity of the problem. In 1985 percentage figures for five countries were as follows: Argentina - 136 percent; Peru - 87 percent; Mexico - 67 percent; Brazil - 47 percent; Nigeria - 37 percent. After the most recent reschedulings, Argentina's obligations were reduced to 24 percent, Peru's to 22 percent, Mexico's to 35 percent, Brazil's to 39 percent, Nigeria's to 17 percent.

TABLE 1-1   Growth of Long- and Short-Term Debt of Developing Countries (1970–86)

US $ billions

Country Group	1970–73	1973–80	1981	1982	1983	1984	1985[a]	1986[b]
DRS reporting countries[c]			662	737	793[e]	828[f]	865	920
Long-term debt[d]			490	547	622[e]	665[f]	708	755
From official sources			177	195	215	232	250	273
From private sources			313	352	407	433	458	482
Short-term debt[g]			158	170	140	129	120	⎰ 165
Use of IMF credit[h]			14	20	30	33	37	
Other developing countries[i]			67	72	78	80	85	90
Long-term debt[d]			43	46	52	52	56	60
From official sources			16	19	20	23	24	26
From private sources			27	27	32	30	32	34
Short-term debt[g]			23	25	25	27	28	⎰ 30
Use of IMF credit[h]			1	1	1	1	1	
Total			729	809	871	908	950	1010
Memo item								
% Growth of total liabilities	18.3	21.3	15.3	11.0	7.7	4.2	4.6	6.3

a. Data for 1985 are preliminary.

b. Data for 1986 are estimated.

c. Includes data for 104 developing countries for which standard and complete reporting is made through the World Bank's Debtor Reporting System (DRS).

d. Debt of original maturity of more than one year.

e. Reflects the rescheduling of $22 billion of short-term debt to banks into long-term debt during 1983.

f. Reflects the rescheduling of $25 billion of short-term debt to banks into long-term debt during 1984.

g. Debt of original maturity of no more than one year. Data are estimated from information on bank claims on developing countries as reported by the Bank for International Settlements and are amended to take account of information on short-term debt reported by individual developing countries.

h. Excludes loans from the IMF Trust Fund; they are included in medium-term and long-term debt.

i. Includes data for developing countries that do not report through the DRS and for those that either have reported incomplete data through the DRS or report in a form that does not admit publication in the standard tables. Excludes debt of the high-income oil-exporting countries and includes estimates for developing countries that are not World Bank members but are included in the global analysis underlying the *World Development Report*.

the payments and would need to call for rescheduling, of their debt. This would result in new agreements to pay about $125 billion with the remaining $50 billion added to the foreign debt outstanding.

Thus, as one can readily see from Table 1-1 and Chart 1-1, the external debt burden of the developing countries has continued to increase. By the summer of 1982 the total outstanding debt of the developing countries amounted to approximately 750 billion. By the end of 1984 it stood at $900 billion; during 1986 the total passed the trillion-dollar

CHART 1-1   Less Developed Countries' Debt (1980–86)

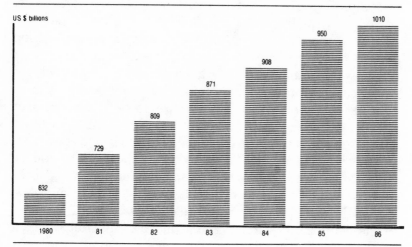

US $ billions

threshold, a number that is more than 10 times greater (in constant dollars) than the Third World debt of 1931 at the nadir of the Great Depression.[6]

Over the past decade, the momentum of the buildup of the developing countries' external debt has been unprecedented, having increased more than fivefold. However,

---

[6] For succint treatments comparing the 1930s and 1980s see Angus Maddison, *Two Crises: Latin America and Asia 1929–38 and 1973–83* (Paris: OECD, November 1985), and the *World Development Report 1982* (Washington, D.C.: World Bank), box 2.2, pp. 20–21: "Though there are obvious similarities between the 1930s and the 1980s—recession, a fall in world trade, the growing problem of debt, a reverse flow of capital from the developing to the developed countries—the magnitude of events in recent years bears no resemblance to what happened in the 1930s." This dampened effect is attributed to the fact that "international cooperation through the Bretton Woods institutions and among governments has permitted a much more effective defense against the spread of some of the worst problems of the recession." Maddison's study also lends support to the decisive roles played by the institutions of the present postwar era.

since 1983 the rate of increase has been slowing. From an annual rate of more than 21 percent in the 1973–80 period, it has decreased in 1985 to less than 5 percent. Observers who see some glimmer of hope for the resolution of this problem focus on this deceleration in the rate of change, particularly with regard to those major debtors categorized as problem debtors: the rate of increase in their debt has decelerated from a 22 percent yearly average over the 1971–81 decade to 4 percent by 1983[7] and even more sharply in the case of the debts of Latin American countries, as shown in Table 1–2. Cold-turkey withdrawal would be an apt metaphor for the treatment applied to these debtor countries and to many of the countries with smaller debts.

While the optimists point to a lower rate of increase in the debt, the pessimists see as more significant the concurrent higher rate of increase in political and social tension in the debtor countries. Over time, tolerance of the prevailing situation declines, especially when there are no tangible signs of an end to the tunnel of despair. This psychological trend may not be measurable, but it manifests itself as an acute problem in those countries where a high percentage of their export earnings must be devoted to meeting their debt servicing obligations and imports must be cut back to a traumatic degree. The situation has been further exacerbated by the drying up of commercial bank lending to these countries, which fell from about $50 billion

---

[7] These are countries that owe at least $15 billion in medium- and long-term debt to external creditors and are therefore a problem for the creditors. At the end of 1983 the following countries were in this group: Argentina, Brazil, Chile, Egypt, India, Indonesia, Israel, Korea, Mexico, Turkey, Venezuela, and Yugoslavia. Some of these countries have not required rescheduling and are managing their debt without special help or extraordinary measures; other countries that have smaller debts in absolute terms are, however, in a different type of problem category in the sense that they do have problems contending with their debt but pose no threat or serious problem for the creditor banks and thus the international financial system.

TABLE 1–2   Latin America: Total External Debt (end of the year balance in billions of dollars)

Country	1978	1979	1980	1981	1982	1983	1984[a]
Latin America	150.9	182.0	221.1	275.4	315.3	340.9	360.2[b]
Bolivia[c]	1.8	1.9	2.2	2.5	2.4	3.1	3.2
Ecuador	3.0	3.6	4.7	5.9	6.2	6.7	6.9
Mexico	33.9	39.7	49.3	72.0	85.0[bd]	90.0	95.9[bd]
Peru	9.3	9.3	9.6	9.6	11.1	12.4	13.5
Venezuela[e]	16.4	23.1	26.5	29.0	31.0	33.5	34.0
Argentina	12.5	19.0	27.1	35.7	43.6	45.5	48.0
Brazil[f]	52.3	58.9	68.3	78.6	87.6	96.5	101.8
Colombia	4.2	5.1	6.3	7.9	9.4	10.4	10.8
Chile[g]	6.7	8.5	11.1	15.5	17.1	17.4	18.4[h]
Uruguay	1.2	1.7	2.2	3.1	4.3	4.6	4.7
Growth of debt (percentage)		20.6	21.5	24.6	14.5	8.1	5.6

SOURCE: ECLA, on official information basis; Brazil and Venezuela: on the International Payment Bank data basis.

[a] Preliminary figures.

[b] Figures noncomparable to those of the years before 1982 because of the inclusion of the debt of commercial banks of Mexico.

[c] Corresponds to public debt.

[d] Includes the debt of commercial banks. Valuation based on the information given by the Secretary of Estate and Public Credit.

[e] Includes the public debt plus the short- and long-term nonguaranteed debt with financial institutions that give information to the International Payment Bank.

[f] Includes total debt in the middle- and long-term plus the short-term debt with financial institutions that give information to the International Payment Bank.

[g] Long-, middle- and short-term debt, excluding the debt with the IMF and short-term credits for foreign trade operations.

[h] Up to September.

per year in 1981 to less than $5 billion by 1983, and by the decrease in direct foreign investment, which dropped from $17 billion to $8 billion during the same period. Furthermore, in the rescheduling process, these countries have also had to submit to terms that shifted the maturity and rate structure of their debts. This change has reduced the amortization component and, *pari passu,* increased the interest payment obligations. Because the debt burden of these countries is most meaningfully measured by the interest component of the debt service, this change has increased the debt burden by a greater degree than is reflected by the increase in the total aggregate debt outstanding.

Though average interest rates on new loans obtained by the developing countries in 1985 have dropped from 11.4 percent in 1981 to about 8 percent today, it can be said the debt servicing burden increased for many debtors from 1982 to 1985 when considering the changing composition and "harder" terms of a larger size of their debt and the worsening terms of trade—the prices of their exports relative to the prices of their imports. This is shown in Chart 1–2, which depicts, for a representative sample of developing countries, the interest payments on the out-

CHART 1–2   Changes in Debt Servicing Burden (Real interest payments as a percentage of current account earnings for 18 debtor countries for 1982–85.)

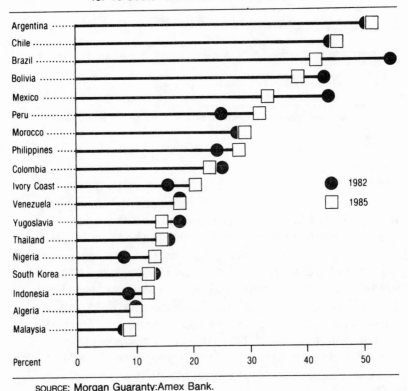

SOURCE: Morgan Guaranty:Amex Bank.

standing debt as a percentage of current account earnings.

The more distressful aspect is the inequity of the present process of coping with this situation. This is symbolized by the fact that, under prevailing arrangements, the debtor countries have to contend with a situation where the net transfer is negative, that is, from the poor to the rich nations. The net transfer on long-term debt had been more than $20 billion in 1982. By 1984 the transfer was *from* developing countries, or minus $3.3 billion. This phenomenon has been dubbed "the transfer paradox."[8] This process is projected to continue well past 1990. The sense of inequity that this phenomenon engenders has raised the emotional pitch and reduced the degree of tolerance for the way the prevailing situation is being managed.

THE INDIAN SUMMER OF 1984 AND THE LOSS OF ILLUSION

For about two years after the panic period of the summer of 1982, an aura of imminent doom hung over the global

---

[8] Mario Henrique Simonsen, formerly a Brazilian minister of finance and now professor of economics, Graduate School of Economics, Rio de Janeiro: "The most dramatic consequence of the debt crisis was the perverse change of sign in the international flow of funds. Developing countries, in spite of their traditional standing as capital importers, are now forced to transfer abroad a sizable proportion of their export earnings . . . Latin American countries raised their average surplus/ export ratio to 27.5 percent in 1983, transferring abroad $29.5 billion . . . (Such) net resource transfers benefit mainly the United States, whose huge external gaps have no parallel in contemporary economic history . . . This leads to a challenging political question: how stable is a world that, although repudiating colonialism, requests debtor developing countries to transfer abroad 25 to 30 percent of their export revenues . . . Many of the political leaders in the main debtor countries question whether (sustaining this) will lead to the eventual payoff of the external debts (which), of course, creates a serious potential for confrontation": From the "The Developing-Country Debt Problem," *International Debt and the Developing Countries, a World Bank Symposium*, eds. G. W. Smith and J. T. Cuddington, The World Bank, Washington, D.C., 1985, pp. 108–109.

economic scene. The debtor countries appeared able to meet interest payments through rescheduling exercises that involved the rollover of more than $200 billion, but it was admittedly a fragile situation on both sides. The creditors were clearly engaged in involuntary lending. They saw themselves held hostage by desperate debtors. But, in this process, the overcommitted bankers were maintaining the face value of their loan receivable assets and were buying time to build up reserves against bad debt losses. The debtors hoped for a favorable conjuncture of events. The sun broke through the storm clouds in 1984 to induce a sense of euphoria: the crisis was downgraded to the status of "problem," which was quite manageable without significant far-reaching changes in policies or institutional arrangements.

The circumstances that contributed to this optimistic assessment, however, make it clear that the 1984 conditions could not be counted upon as a basis for diagnosis or treatment of the debt situation. It was an exceptional year with the main factor being the growth of the U.S. economy, which attained a rate of almost 7 percent, and of the other industrialized countries as a group, of almost 5 percent. This was accompanied by an increase in exports of much more than 8 percent on a global basis with the value of exports of primary commodities rising more than 10 percent (despite a price drop of more than 2.5 percent). The current account deficits of the most heavily indebted developing countries were reduced sharply. This favorable outcome on the export side was further improved by a second factor, the concurrent reduction in their imports. The policy of import compression was politically feasible in the aftermath of the crisis atmosphere of mid-1982.

However, with 1985 the growth of the global economy reverted back to earlier conditions. The average growth rate of all the industrialized countries slowed to less than 3 percent and in international trade to less than 4 percent, less than half the rate of 1984. Exports of non-oil-exporting developing countries went on expanding but at about one third of the pace of 1984. Commodity prices, which did not respond to the 1984 boomlet, dropped a further 13 percent (in constant dollars) to reach a level in real terms that has not been experienced since the Great Depression of the 1930s. By the middle of 1985 the realization began to dawn on the public and the policy makers that 1984 was an exceptional rather than a normal year. Talk of debtor revolt was heard once again. The crisis atmosphere had returned.

Though this time there is little trace of panic, there is greater cause for worry. Two elements in the present situation make the prospects less hopeful. The first might be called the after-shock syndrome: having survived the first big wave without capsizing, there remains a dangerous residue of that sense of euphoria. This time, however, the underlying circumstances are even more threatening:

- Primary commodity prices have not risen in response to the global recovery surge. They show little prospect in the near future of breaking out of the deep cellar into which they've slumped.
- Protectionist pressures have increased. The exports of the major debtors are being further constrained as resistance grows stronger in the industrialized countries to bar or reduce imports from the Third World of such items as textiles, shoes, sugar, copper, and so on. This is a political fact of life in the United States, which absorbs about 70 percent of Third world exports, and in Europe, which accounts for 30 percent of the market for Third World goods.[9]

---

[9] In the export surge of 1984, the United States absorbed more than 95 percent of Latin America's exports. The Japanese market has accounted for less than 10 percent of Third World exports to the developed countries. Any significant change in this situation must overcome even more barriers than tariffs, quotas, and subsidies to indigenous producers.

- The amount of net new funds made available in 1984 to the developing countries was down to about $50 billion, half the 1982 level, despite the herculean efforts of the debtor countries to reestablish their "creditworthiness." Even after the 1984 improvement in their current account surplus, new money has not been forthcoming. Thus, the pace of rescheduling remains at crisis levels with about $30 billion needing to be rolled over in 1986, according to International Monetary Fund (IMF) estimates.
- Several leaders of the hard-pressed debtor countries have openly begun to question the asymmetric impact of the process that puts the full burden of adjustment on their shoulders. With greater frequency political leaders have opted by threat or action to declare noncompliance with the terms of rescheduling agreements, putting their own needs for development and political stability ahead of repayment and related obligations that have come to be regarded as crippling, inequitable and unsustainable.

A second new element has also radically changed the nature of the debt crisis, namely, the passage in 1986 of the United States from creditor to debtor status and the increased interdependence between the U.S. economy and that of the Third World. At the time of the onset of the debt crisis of the developing countries the United States had a net investment income of more than $30 billion on net foreign assets of about $150 billion. In the twinkling of a historic eye, only three years, the financial credit balance that the United States has enjoyed for more than seven decades from investment abroad has turned into a net deficit and an inconsequential trade deficit, which totaled only about $20 billion over the decade of the 1970s, exploded into a deficit of almost $150 billion in this last year alone, an increase of 7,500 percent. Both the magnitude and the suddenness of this change give cause for worry. But *what is more troubling is that this new situation severely constrains the United States in its options for assisting with the Third World's debt.* The increased interdependence makes this clear. From 1973 to 1983 U.S. exports to the developing countries rose sixfold (much faster than U.S. GNP growth) to account for almost 40 percent of its total exports at the end of this period. With one-quarter of U.S. overseas investment in these countries (over $50 billion) and much of it linked to multinational firms, a high proportion of that trade was captive and therefore highly profitable, which rebounded in some measure to improve the average income of the American people. This export volume also provided employment, which has been estimated to add up to one job out of every six in the industrial sector. However, in the three years since the debt crisis broke in mid-1982 and forced the developing countries to cut their imports drastically, it is estimated that the fall in total exports to developing countries accounted for a loss of about 2 million work-years in the United States. For the industrialized nations as a whole (which includes the United States), exports to developing countries had been rising since the mid-1940s to a point where, by the end of the 1970s, this Third World market accounted for over 25 percent of their total exports. In 1983 their exports to the developing countries fell almost $50 billion, which translates into an estimated loss of about 9 million work-years in Europe. Thus the reduced ability of these countries to purchase U.S. goods and services aggravates the U.S. trade deficit and as the United States takes steps to remedy its own plight through reducing its imports, this action, in turn, aggravates the plight of the Third World debtors. There is, thus, an immeasurably greater danger of breakdown in the debt repayment process.

Under the circumstances, the assessments made in late 1984 and early 1985 about the debt crisis look quaint. With the focus largely on the survival of the banking system, dozens of articles were published that reflected a buoyant mood, tinged with only a hint of caution that the worst might not be over, even if the first shock wave had been surmounted.[10] Realism has returned since mid-1985 with almost daily reminders in the press that the debt crisis is still in a critical phase, leading one commentator, the economic consultant/banker Geoffrey Bell in an article in the *New York Times* of August 25, 1985, to declare "a simple and troubling fact—the next year will be the most dangerous since the international debt crisis began in 1982."[11] As if to give credence to these ominous words, the press has been full of stories of aborted agreements, repeated negotiations, and ultimatums as political leaders declare they will unilaterally set the limits to their debt repayments and challenge the prevailing process for handling this issue.

THE NEW-BORN CONCERN AND THE MUCH-VAUNTED BAKER INITIATIVE

A significant and long-overdue recognition of the critical nature of the current global financial situation was given

---

[10] Gary Hector, "Third World Debt: The Bomb is Defused," *Fortune* (February 18, 1985); Nicolas D. Kristof, "Debt Crisis Called All But Over," *New York Times* (February 4, 1985).

[11] Geoffrey Bell, in "Only the World Bank Has the Means," refers to "high stakes" and "critical points" as developing countries are hit by a combination of adverse factors such as no new lending, falling commodity prices, slowing demand for their exports, and a 'feedback factor' as some debtors harden their positions and set precedents that are seen to be successful and gaining in popularity as tactics vis a vis the creditors. L. Glynn, in "Is the Debt Crisis over? Don't Kid Yourself," *Institutional Investor* (May 1985), cites these same conditions with special reference to Latin America, particularly Brazil and Mexico, and asserts: "Far from being solved, in fact, the LDC debt crisis of 1982–84 may simply have been contained (and) there may be good grounds to worry that the current calm is simply the eye of the storm."

by U.S. Secretary of the Treasury James A. Baker III in the waning months of 1985. In two gestures—more than three years after the crisis broke—the United States took actions reflecting a belated acknowledgment that there is an international financial problem serious enough to call for *coordinated* international action.

The first step was to convene a meeting in early September 1985 of the finance ministers of the five leading industrialized nations (otherwise known as the Group of 5, or G-5 for short) in the Plaza Hotel in New York. The second was the highly publicized speech of Mr. Baker delivered at the October annual meeting of the World Bank and IMF in Seoul, South Korea. This was followed in early 1986 by a second meeting of the Plaza Group and by President Reagan's State of the Union message to Congress in which he referred to the unsatisfactory state of the global monetary system and commissioned a study to consider the need for a major international conference on the subject. These statements and actions reveal a new sense of awareness about the debt problem and the related international economic and financial situation and a willingness by the United States to play an active interventionist role. In line with the new policy posture, at the World Bank/IMF annual meeting in Seoul, Secretary Baker proposed that the following steps be taken to address the debt crisis situation:

a) From the commercial banks, an additional commitment of $20 billion over three years (mainly from the 100 largest of the 550 banks now involved).

b) From the World Bank and the Inter-American Development Bank, an additional disbursement of $9 billion over the next three years, and from the IMF, an earmarking of the $2.7 billion due to flow back over the next six years to its Trust Fund, which had been set up in the 1970s for the benefit of the poorest countries suffering from chronic balance of payment problems.

c) From the developing countries, especially the 15 being singled out to receive these additional resources,
commitments to adopt policies that are more market-
oriented and attractive to foreign investors, and that
constrain of consumption through the reduction or
elimination of subsidies and imposition of taxes and
wage restraining measures, in effect, to undertake
structural changes that would increase the role of
the private sector while reducing the state's role and
would increase the trade surplus so interest payments could be met.

d) From the United States, a conditional promissory
note: virtuous actions by others might be rewarded
with consideration of support for a general capital
increase for the World Bank and for the forthcoming
replenishment of the bank's "soft window," the International Development Association (IDA).

The U.S. administration had belatedly found virtue in
intervening to increase commitments by commercial banks
and to increase the lending programs of the international
financial institutions. There was, however, nothing offered
beyond exhortation to induce commercial bankers to be
more forthcoming. Nor was anything offered to enable the
World Bank and other sister institutions to significantly
expand their lending.

The most doubts about the Baker initiative related to
the "adequacy" of the amounts specified, the $29 billion
that would be forthcoming over the next three years, that
is, $10 billion per year. This amounted to less than one
quarter of the interest due from the 15 countries designated
as beneficiaries and less than half of the lost export earnings of the developing countries that can be attributed no-
tionally to the fall in commodity prices and the slowdown
in the industrialized countries' rate of growth in the last

year.[12] Its adequacy or inadequacy can be most concretely gauged in relating it to one or more of the 15 countries. Mexico can serve as an example.

At the time of the Seoul meeting when the price of oil was about $25 a barrel, it had been estimated that if Mexico was to be able to meet its debt obligations *and* its own requirements for a rate of growth of 5 percent, in the first year it would need about $2.5 billion of the $10 billion from commercial banks and more than $1.5 billion from multilateral and bilateral sources. The spectacular drop in the price of oil in the early months of 1986, cost Mexico more than $6 billion in anticipated export earnings, a development that added $3 billion to the estimated need.[13] In that event, Mexico's requirement would account for about half or more of the total annual amount of commercial bank lending of $10 billion that the Baker initiative would hope to allocate to 15 countries.

Looking at the minimal capital required by all 15 countries, to attain any reasonable target rate of growth the amount would be so far in excess of the $10 billion per year as to provoke wonderment. The World Bank and IMF estimates provide a basis for judgment.

---

[12] This "loss" has been estimated at $65 billion. See "The Poor Man's Gift," *Economist* (November 30, 1985).

[13] In March 1986 the Mexican finance minister announced this country would seek $6 billion in new loans from foreign lenders or $2 billion more than it had planned to borrow before the drop in oil prices. There were reports that Mexico would need as much as $10 billion. A downward adjustment was effected on the basis of a further planned reduction in imports amounting to $1.5 billion, a projected increase in nonoil exports of $0.5 billion and the postponement of a planned $1.2 billion replenishment to foreign reserves, now estimated at only $5 billion, an amount that would cover import requirements for four months. Almost $1 billion was to be saved by virtue of the actual and anticipated reduction in U.S. interest rates and the LIBOR (London inter-bank rate), which affect the variable interest portion of the Mexican debt.

Leaving aside aid and foreign investment flows, the World Bank has estimated net borrowing requirements of developing countries under a low-growth scenario (which assumes a target of an average annual real growth of 4.7 percent) to be about $50 billion by 1990. The IMF has estimated about $31 billion in 1986, rising by 5.5 percent until 1990, requiring about $35 billion to $50 billion per year over the next few years. The Baker initiative list of 15 countries would account for roughly half of that estimate. If aid flows to them continue at present levels of $3 billion per year and net World Bank lending at about $1 billion ($3 billion less repayments of $2 billion), the residual new lending requirements can be seen to be far higher than is envisaged in the Baker initiative. Even a fully favorable response from the private banking community of about $7 billion per year over the next few years allows no margin for error, that is, for a faster rate of growth for these developing countries, nor would the Baker initiative help assure other poorer debtor countries of comparable treatment. In all likelihood, as a result of the Baker initiative, commercial bank lending would be more redirected than augmented.

It is difficult to imagine commercial bankers need a reminder that they have a great deal at stake in "staying the course." As Table 1–3 shows, they have been making that extra commitment of financial resources as part of the debt rescheduling process. Nonetheless, soon after Treasury Secretary Baker spoke, a chorus of the banking community could be heard lauding the initiative and pledging support "in principle." However, almost all those bankers who expressed a supportive view of the Baker plea have done so in a highly qualified way. There is a great deal of skepticism about whether U.S. government intervention can succeed in extracting a greater commitment for the designated 15 countries without the United States making a commitment of its own, such as pledging to provide some form of guarantees or special tax or regulatory induce-

TABLE 1-3 Debt Outstanding of 15 Countries Designated in Baker Initiative (1985)

Country	Foreign Debt in Billions	1985 Interest		Debt Owed to U.S. Banks in Billions	Debt Owed to IMF and World Bank in Billions
		in Billions	Estimated % of 1985 GNP		
Brazil	$103.5	$11.8	5.8%	$23.8	$8.5
Mexico	$97.7	$10.0	6.3%	$25.8	$5.9
Argentina	$50.8	$5.1	7.9%	$8.1	$2.2
Venezuela	$32.6	$4.1	8.1%	$10.6	$0.1
Philippines	$27.4	$2.1	6.2%	$5.5	$2.6
Chile	$21.9	$2.1	12.9%	$6.6	$1.1
Yugoslavia	$20.0	$1.7	3.6%	$2.4	$2.7
Nigeria	$18.0	$1.8	1.9%	$1.5	$0.6
Morocco	$14.4	$1.0	8.2%	$0.9	$2.0
Peru	$13.9	$1.3	10.8%	$2.1	$1.3
Colombia	$13.9	$1.3	3.3%	$2.6	$1.8
Ecuador	$7.9	$0.7	6.0%	$2.2	$0.5
Ivory Coast	$6.3	$0.6	8.7%	$0.5	$1.4
Uruguay	$4.9	$0.5	9.8%	$1.0	$0.3
Bolivia	$4.2	$0.4	10.0%	$0.2	$0.3
TOTAL	$437.4	$44.5	Average 7.3%	$93.8	$32.6

SOURCE: *Fortune* (December 23, 1985), Copyright by 1985 Time Inc. All rights reserved.

ments. It would appear that most of the applause for this initiative has been evoked by the belated indication of U.S. administration awareness of the seriousness of the problem.

Other bankers have voiced dismay and resentment. One member of the banking community seemed to speak for many in noting that the private banking community is being asked to break one of the key rules of prudence, namely, in lending to borrowers who need the additional loans to meet interest payments on existing loans. Another observed:

> It is astonishing that reasonable people in the official circles in Washington and the other political and financial capitals can imagine that this will work . . . The disastrous record of private financing for economic development shows that this is no place for (private commercial) banks.[14]

One of the outspoken champions of the Baker proposal, former World Bank President Tom Clausen, has expressed a common viewpoint in stating that the initiative is often mislabeled as "The Baker Plan." It is more akin to a concept that had yet to be fleshed out. Treasury Secretary Baker himself has tried to clarify the issue: "The people who have labeled it a plan have missed the point. It is a principle, an initiative, or a concept—and I haven't heard of an alternative except writing down the debt."[15]

---

[14] The tenor of the response of many in the U.S. financial community appears to be well-reflected in the comments of an editorial writer in the *Journal of Commerce* (December 9, 1985) who referred to "the suspicion that the Baker plan—no matter how praised—in principle, is floundering. . . . Barring some breakthroughs soon, the Baker plan may make Treasury look more like misguided amateurs than sagacious professionals in the complicated world of high international finance."

[15] Mr. Clausen, in an interview in the *Los Angeles Times*, (January 28, 1986), is reported to have said the so-called Baker Plan should more properly be dubbed the Baker Initiative: "If you look at it, where's the plan? Intellectually, it is sound as a concept, which is all it is."

Secretary Baker's comment was reported in the *Washington Post* (March 13, 1986) as testimony before a congressional subcommittee. Sec-

The bankers who have lent verbal support to the Baker plea have yet to be asked to ante up much money. The reason is simply that the political leaders of the major debtor nations have been hesitant about meeting the conditions called for in the Baker initiative. The disappointment and puzzlement this initiative evoked from the developing countries is reflected in the comments of two ministers: the Brazilian minister of finance, Dilson Funaro, considered the Baker proposal "too timid and two years too late," and the minister of finance and planning of Pakistan, formerly director of the policy planning division of the World Bank, Mahbub ul Haq, characterized the Baker proposal as an invisible entity, an idea that never materialized: "It is a little puzzling as to what or where the Baker plan is; it is a celebrated U.S. initiative that never was." A party was announced, but it is not surprising that nobody came.

Some fundamental questions underlie the critical judgment:

- First, could the recipient countries accept the conditions without doing violent injury to sovereign pride and to social and political constraints that political leaders must recognize? Acquiescence would involve foreign entities—in the guise of private bankers or experts from the international financial institu-

---

retary Baker added an interesting comment regarding the write-down of debt: "That would only cause a serious 'hit' to our banks and the loss of some democratic countries in Latin America." None of the members of the subcommittee seems to have sought an explanation on the last point.

Congressman Stan Lundine, a Democrat from New York and chairman of the House subcommittee on international finance, has also expressed his support for the Baker initiative, "but the Baker plan is not really a plan, and there is not enough money in it . . . (to meet the dangers of the debt problem which) we all know is a ticking bomb we haven't been willing to face up to," in the "Baker Debt Plan Criticized as 'Unfocused' ", *Washington Post* (March 4, 1986).

CHART 1–3 Net Transfer (actual and projected) of Debtor Developing Countries (1983–90)

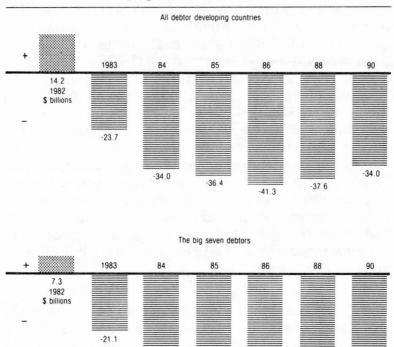

All debtor developing countries

| | 1983 | 84 | 85 | 86 | 88 | 90 |

+

14.2
1982
$ billions

−

-23.7
-34.0
-36.4
-41.3
-37.6
-34.0

The big seven debtors

| | 1983 | 84 | 85 | 86 | 88 | 90 |

+

7.3
1982
$ billions

−

-21.1
-28.7
-29.2
-28.2
-33.4
-39.9

---

tions—meddling in the basic decisions related to macro-policy such as the desirable path of development, its speed and distributional characteristics, and the degree of dependency. These are the types of decisions that give sovereignty meaning.

• Second, how many of the developing countries would be able, under any reasonable assumptions, to export their way out of the debt trap? A single statistic reveals the ominous answer to that question: After the 1984 boomlet, exports of the developing countries to the United States fell 2 percent while the exports from the major industrial countries to the United States rose by 14 percent. There is the problem of severe infrastructural weaknesses in their economies. To count on the response of private investors under such circumstances is especially foolhardy. This is troubling enough in the best of times, but in a period when these countries are experiencing negative capital transfers, as depicted in Chart 1-3, the skepticism is even more justified since the environment for starting and operating businesses becomes particularly difficult and risky.

• Third, would playing the designated roles seriously damage or enhance the reputation of international agencies, such as the World Bank, the regional banks, and the IMF? As a condition for receiving loans the Baker proposal would require recipient countries to agree to accept, as axiomatic, that "private is good and public is bad." Should the international financial institutions become the blatant instruments for the imposition of this ideology their analysis and advice would quite understandably be called into question. This is hardly an academic point when there already exists considerable criticism and skepticism on that score, and not exclusively from the left of the political spectrum.[16] The issue is espe-

---

[16] From the left there are such statements as those delivered by the Peruvian minister of economy and finance, Luis Alva Castro, at the Joint Discussion of the Annual Meetings in Seoul, October 10, 1985 (as quoted from Press Release No. 56): "We affirm that the IMF has not performed the role asigned to it under its Articles of Agreement. . . . In our view, for the Fund to be of any use it should adopt clear and symmetrical rules regarding adjustment. Both the deficit and surplus countries should be subject to international discipline of a general

cially relevant at this time when, in response to the need for quick disbursements, the World Bank and the regional development banks are being pressured to devote a much higher proportion of their lending to the "structural adjustment" type of loans at the expense of the traditional emphasis on project lending. If carried much further, this trend would likely open a Pandora's box of problems for these institutions and for those who rely on them to play their roles without bending to current ideological winds.[17]

The most serious injury likely to be inflicted by the Baker initiative is that it may put off consideration of measures more commensurate with the magnitude and seriousness of the problem. While the Baker initiative reveals a welcome recognition that warning signs need to be posted and some corrective and preventive action taken, there is still too little appreciation of how perilously thin is the ice on which the players are skating. When the troubling

---

nature. There is no point in applying discipline to some but not to others. . . . The right of veto that the U.S. has retained to the present day (in the IMF) should be eliminated. If this is not done, the Fund will continue to serve that country's imperial policies."

From the right there are statements such as those by Peter Montagnon, Euromarket correspondent of the *Financial Times (U.K.)* who observed in a column (August 27, 1985) that "throughout Latin America a third year of crisis has provoked increasing doubts over the IMF's actual competence and its ability to prescribe the right medicine." It is a view heard with increasing frequency.

[17] There is potential for serious damage to these institutions if such changes are made in response to the timetable and criteria of the Baker proposal. This danger is even greater when these institutions are pressured to lend directly through private channels (as has been recently authorized by the Asian Development Bank Executive Board) and to promote private bank lending by offering the World Bank's guarantees (as was done in the case of loans to Chile and Uruguay in late 1985). The meaning and implications of this shift are explored in Chapter Seven, which focuses on the role of the international financial institutions.

condition is permitted to fester and to continue to inflict incalculable hardship, anxiety is welcome and wise. Any lessening of anxiety about the debt crisis with its hardships and asymmetry makes the present situation more fragile and dangerous and polarizes views as to what should be done, how soon, and by whom.

THE ACCENTUATED DANGER OF THE PRESENT PHASE OF THE DEBT CRISIS

A perceptible change in tone and in substance occurred in the months before the October 1985 World Bank/IMF annual meeting in Seoul. There was a more than usual confrontational juxtaposition of the views of the developing countries, as represented by the "Group of 24," with that of the industrialized countries, as represented by the "Group of 10."[18] The stance taken by the G-10 represented one extreme. The basic premise was that the prevailing approach to the debt crisis is basically sound but needs to be bolstered by greater financial commitments from others, principally the commercial banks and the international financial institutions. Neither the United States nor Japan, to take two of the principal parties in that group, indicated a willingness to make a dramatic gesture commensurate

---

[18] These groups are informal "rumps" of the Interim Committee of the IMF, the G-24 being 24 ministers from the Group of 77 with eight chosen as representatives from three different geographic groupings from among the developing countries and the G-10 being the finance ministers from the major industrialized countries.

To ease the international debt situation the G-24 called for global cooperation to reduce exchange rate fluctuations, to expand liquidity through the creation of more Special Drawing Rights (SDRs), and to increase concessional foreign aid. The G-10 position was diametrically at odds with the diagnosis and with the suggested cure in all its aspects, contending that the floating exchange rate system is adequate and requires no change, rejecting the notion of expanding international liquidity through the creation of SDRs, and making no commitments with regard to expanding aid flows.

with the magnitude and urgency of the situation. In sharp contrast, in the statement of the G-24 and in the speeches of almost all of the developing country ministers—particularly those by the Pakistani and Peruvian spokesmen—this view was challenged both as to the feasibility and the equity of the prevailing process of debt rescheduling. The basic premise underlying this position is that there is a potential gain for all parties in a debtor-creditor or developing country-developed country relationship through trade and capital flows involving a substantial net transfer of resources *from* the developed *to* the developing countries.[19]

The underlying rationale for the mutual advantage in this flow from richer, developed industrialized countries to the poorer developing countries (apart from sheer non-economic compassionate reasons) rests on the logic of what might be called the "debt cycle hypothesis." This hypothesis holds that (a) the developing countries as debtors have a rate of return on investment on average higher than in creditor countries and (b) at their stage of development, they must achieve a real rate of growth of exports higher than the real rate of interest they have to pay for borrowed

---

[19] There is a school of thought, generally labeled "Marxist" and "leftist radical," that would challenge this. This position in all its permutations and combinations is sketched out in an article by Keith Griffin (Oxford University) and John Gurley (Stanford University), "Radical Analyses of Imperialism, The Third World, and the Transition to Socialism: A Survey Article," *Journal of Economic Literature* (September 1985). See especially, pp. 1105–1116 on "Underdevelopment in a Historical Context" and pp. 1116–1120 on "Foreign Aid and International Financial Agencies." As the authors note, the two fundamental assumptions of so-called radicals in these studies on international finance is that "the integration of LDCs into the world capitalist system would reduce, perhaps even eliminate, their development possibilities . . . (and that) LDCs could achieve development only within a socialist mode of production—and (for some) only within a self-sufficient socialism." The authors note in critically appraising these views that "radicals, like everyone else, can be misled by the initial propositions that they take for granted."

funds.[20] Thus, at the "young debtor" stage, a country's account deficit and debt burden are expected to grow rapidly until at a later stage of development, the country is capable of rapidly increasing its export earnings and thereby enabled to finance both interest payment and amortization. The accompanying Table 1–4 reveals that even under very adverse conditions, the financial rate of return in the capital markets of many developing countries are higher than those in the United States and even Japan.

Obviously, something has gone wrong when the transfer is running in the opposite direction. The question is how basic or superficial is this failing, and the answer or remedy follows from the diagnosis of the cause. Apart from the accepted assumptions of mutual interdependence and the necessary and desirable direction of the net flow of resources, the divergent views as to what must or should be done stem from different assumptions about the global economic situation and the appropriate role of the participants.

There is, however, a new element in the equation arising from the greater economic and financial interdependence, namely, the threat of a domino-effect breakdown in present

---

[20] The "debt cycle hypothesis" is clearly and schematically elaborated in the *World Development Report 1985* (Washington, D.C.: World Bank) pp. 47–48, Box 4.1. In this schema the rate and direction of international capital flows change over time as countries develop at different speeds and as rates of saving, capital stock accumulation, and rates of return on investment change in the developmental process. Countries can revert to different stages: "during the latter half of the 1970s, many developing countries thought to be 'mature debtors' (the second stage in a five-stage cycle from 'young debtor' to 'mature creditor' status) reverted to the early debtor stage, importing capital and running mounting trade deficits (while in the 1980s, many of these same countries moved to the third, or early creditor, stage, reducing net debt by running huge trade surpluses, the mirror image of what has occurred in some industrialized countries as, for example, the U.S. (which) recently reentered the early debtor stage of the debt cycle, incurring debt at an accelerating rate while increasing its trade deficit."

TABLE 1-4 Return on Investment in Emerging Markets (1976–83)

(percent)

Country Group	1976	1977	1978	1979	1980	1981	1982	1983[a]	Average Annual Change, 1976–83[a]
Emerging markets									
Argentina	147.0	-43.6	79.9	233.6	-72.2	-54.5	66.2	124.5	18.7
Brazil	1.3	11.9	-6.0	-12.5	4.1	9.0	-19.9	97.4[b]	6.6[b]
Chile	103.4	146.3	56.3	131.6	92.7	-48.3	-52.1	-18.4	27.7
Hong Kong	40.0	-11.0	18.0	80.0	71.0	-16.0	-42.0	-8.6	9.2
India	34.1	13.7	51.2	21.1	42.3	23.8	-5.9	6.0	22.0
Jordan[c]			53.4	27.7	21.5	35.0	8.0	-7.0	19.9
Korea	72.4	114.2	23.7	-13.0	-26.5	40.2	7.9	7.4	21.5
Mexico	19.1	22.3	127.8	96.3	17.7	-46.8[d]	-79.8[d]	170.2[d]	-0.6[d]
Singapore	14.0	6.0	52.0	-12.0	29.0	15.0	-1.0	29.2	15.0
Thailand	0.4	187.7	43.2	-40.7	-12.9	-19.2	21.1	9.7	12.3
Zimbabwe	13.2	3.1	-6.9	178.7	30.4	-56.7	-32.4	-7.9	0.8
Industrial countries									
United States	23	-8	6	14	29	-4	21	20	13.5
Japan	25	15	52	-12	29	15	-1	23	16.8
Cumulative return									
Capital International world index[e]	114	116	136	152	192	184	205	250	12.1
IFC emerging market index[f]	134	196	304	514	645	593	412	617	25.5

NOTE: The returns depicted are calculated as follows. Assume a U.S. investor has $100 to invest in an emerging market. After conversion to domestic currency, the proceeds are placed in a basket of actively traded stocks. Dividends may be paid on the investment during the year, and capital gains may also be secured if the market price of the stock rises. These two sources of income are converted back to U.S. dollars at yearend exchange rates to yield a return denominated in U.S. dollars. This return is expressed as a percentage of the original $100 investment.

a. Returns for 1983 are up to the end of November for Argentina and to the end of December for Brazil, Hong Kong, India, Jordan, Mexico, Singapore, Thailand, and Zimbabwe.

b. Based on preliminary data for 1983.

c. Jordan's stock market opened in January 1978, hence data are not available for earlier years.

d. Based on *Capital International* data for 1981–83, including net dividends.

e. Based on *Capital International* data; January 1, 1976 = 100.

f. Returns in emerging markets included in this table, except for Hong Kong and Singapore, on a market-weighted basis (1980 for 1975–80; individual years for 1981–83); January 1, 1976 = 100.

arrangements for contending with the debt situation. The leaders of many major debtor nations are finding it increasingly difficult—to a point of impossibility or suicidal danger, politically speaking—to service even the interest portion of their debt obligations without inciting widespread civil unrest and radical political upheaval. The potential threat that a full debt servicing might pose for a fragile democratic regime would not likely move the creditor banks or their supporting central banks and governments to change their policy on the debt and related issues. But if this situation should deteriorate to a point where widespread defaults or moratoriums followed and with that the threatened collapse of some major banks with profound implications for the banking system, the situation becomes dangerous and calls for action.

There are basically two schools of thought as to what needs to be done in response to this situation:

- On the one side, there are those who see the recent events related to the debt crisis as a one-time shock, an unfortunate nonrecurring (or rarely recurring) conjuncture of events from which recovery is a matter of time and patience—mixed with a bit of, wisdom or common sense. They see the problem as "transitional" meaning its resolution does not call for significant changes in policies and the prevailing institutional arragements for managing the crisis, which is now proceeding on a case-by-case basis.

- On the other side, there are those who see the present situation as unsustainable, inequitable, and, therefore unstable. Given the magnitude and dynamic of the debt situation and the deep-seated and structural nature of changes that underlie it, the problem is perceived to be systemic and more accurately described as a crisis rather than a liquidity problem. Thus, if we are to achieve appreciably

higher levels of and more favorable conditions for
the net transfer of capital from developed to developing countries, significant changes are needed in key
economic and financial institutions and the way they
operate, that is, in "the rules of the game."

To assess the proposed solutions and what they imply
with respect to necessary and desirable policy and institutional changes over the years ahead requires a better appreciation of the complex nature of the present debt crisis
situation. The origins or roots of the crisis must be understood. Diagnosis must come before the cure. We need to
know whether the appropriate treatment is of the bandage
and chicken soup variety or some form of surgery and life-
style change. The appropriateness of treatment depends
on how superficial or how deep (structural) are the causes
or sources of the present malaise. To do this we need to
identify and understand the historically new patterns and
institutional arrangements that facilitated and abetted the
buildup of the debt load to a point where it was no longer
sustainable and called for extraordinary emergency measures.

Chapter two, therefore, recounts the story of how the
foreign debt of the developing countries became a problem
of crisis proportions and identifies the underlying structural changes that facilitated this buildup to a crisis. There
then follows in the subsequent four chapters a review of
proposed initiatives, including Bretton Woods II. This lays
the ground for the seventh chapter in which consideration
is given to the role the major international financial institutions might play. The final chapter provides a wrap-up and
an indication as to what steps might be taken to help assure
a more promising future.

The *Economist* suggestively described the situation in
which we find ourselves by reference to a classical analogy:
"The participants seemed to be unaware that they closely

resembled the prisoners in Plato's legend of the cave, looking at shadows and believing that these were the real
world."[21]

There is a great deal at stake in finding our way out
of the cave—soon. But by which path? If we are to find
our way onto that path there is an urgent need not to
confuse shadow for substance, wishful-thinking for hard
reality.

---

[21] "Power of the Bankrupt: The Nonaligned Turn from Political
Shadows to Economic Substance," *Economist* (March 19, 1983), p. 65.

The Roots of the Debt Crisis

*The 'wallflower' theory of finance (envisages) banks sitting like maid-
ens at an old-fashioned ball waiting to be asked for a dance. Presumably an alert wallflower will recognize a bad loan or an irresponsible
country when she sees one. The alternative view (would) emphasize
"loan-pushing" and subsequent pulling, (at which time) with all
lenders on the run, the country has nowhere to borrow and no one
can be repaid. . . . Bankers forgot the sections in their elementary
economics courses dealing with the fallacies of composition.*

Professor Lance Taylor[1]

*Some people who borrow money prefer to cloak what they are doing
in euphemisms. The thickest cloak of all was used in the 1970s:
'recycling.' How simple it all seemed: on one side, billions of petrodollars piling up in banks; on the other, countries with big deficits to
finance. Recycle the cash from one to another, and the problem would
be solved. Actually, it was created.*

Rupert Pennant-Rea[2]

THE BUILDUP TO A FALL

Surprise marked the onset of the crisis in that summer
of 1982 when Mexico met with a rebuff from private bank-

---

[1] Lance Taylor, professor of economics, Massachusetts Institute of
Technology. "The Theory and Practice of Developing Country Debt: An
Informal Guide for the Perplexed," *The Debt Problem: Acute and Chronic
Aspects—Journal of Development Planning* (no. 16, 1985), ed. Carlos
Massad, United Nations, N.Y., pp. 204–205.

[2] "Everybody's Business—International Monetary Reform: A Survey," *Economist* (October 5, 1985).

ers in its attempts to refinance its debt on a business-as-usual basis. This was compounded when a few months later, Brazil unilaterally declared its inability to service its loans and threatened to declare itself insolvent if its requests for rescheduling were not agreed to by a certain date. There then dawned the sobering realization that the international financial system had become hostage to its major debtors. Panic followed.

The story of the buildup to the events of 1982 is familiar. What is not familiar is why the conditions and decisions that contributed to the crisis were allowed during the 1970s and early 1980s with seemingly little awareness on the part of the decision makers of the fragility and dangers of the situation.

From the perspective of the borrower, the period beginning in the late 1960s and early 1970s had features that made it very tempting to borrow. Real interest rates were exceptionally low (with the average real rate from 1973 to 1980 only about 0.5 percent in the Eurocurrency markets) and, at times, negative.[3] At the same time, most of the developing countries were enjoying higher prices for their primary commodity exports. The economies of the developing world were averaging a rate of growth in excess of 5 percent a year and their export earnings were rising at a rate of 20 percent a year, almost in line with the rate of increase in their borrowing. The current account deficits of the oil-importing developing countries rose initially after the 1973 oil price rise to about 5 percent of their collective gross national product (GNP) and by 1978 these deficits

---

[3] For example, in 1978 prices for Chile's exports rose by 27 percent while LIBOR was 11 percent. This made the "real" interest rate − 16 percent. When these prices dropped, as in 1982 by 9 percent and LIBOR had risen to 13 percent, the real rate was 22 percent, a swing of 38 percent. L. A. Sjaastad, "Working off the debt in Latin America," 1984 (mimeo), cited by L. Taylor, *The Debt Problem,* p. 212. This case is not exceptional in terms of the change in circumstances over this period.

were down to pre-1973 levels, or about 2 percent. Thus, few developing countries had qualms about borrowing to cover both the increased price of the imported oil and the greater quantities of imports needed to sustain such growth rates.

From the lenders perspective the outstanding factor was the change on the supply side that occurred over the decade of the 1970s, particularly after the first oil shock of 1973. Members of the Organization of Petroleum Exporting Countries (OPEC) found their collective surplus, which had been barely more than $1 billion per year in the five years before 1973, jump in 1974 to almost $70 billion. At the same time the oil-importing developing countries found their pre-1973 average annual collective surplus of $13 billion turn to a deficit of about $37 billion in one year.

The private banking system rose to the challenge, the commercial banks acting as the intermediating agents in the process of petrodollar recycling. The volume of bank lending expanded exponentially. Longer-term private commercial bank lending to developing countries quadrupled between 1970 and 1975, from $3 billion to $12 billion, and doubled again to almost $25 billion by 1980. The annual expansion rate was more than 30 percent so by the end of the 1970s, commercial bank lending had expanded to a point where commercial banks were responsible for almost two thirds of the total flow of capital resources to the developing countries, as shown in Table 2–1 and Chart 2–1.

Toward the end of 1976 or soon after, the lenders became nervous, suspecting the lending should have begun to wind down at some point. This was the period when, in real terms, oil prices were leveling off and negative or near-negative interest rates made borrowing exceedingly tempting. The nervousness was offset by both the temptation and the bandwagon effect, so it was only toward the very end of the 1970s that the spigot was turned down.

TABLE 2-1 Net Resource Receipts of Developing Countries from all Sources in Selected Years (1970–83)

(billions of dollars)

Type of Receipt	1970	1975	1980	1981	1982	1983
Official development assistance	8.1	20.1	37.5	37.3	34.7	33.6
Bilateral	7.0	16.2	29.7	29.4	27.2	26.1
Multilateral	1.1	3.9	7.8	7.9	7.5	7.5
Grants by private voluntary agencies	0.9	1.3	2.3	2.0	2.3	2.2
Nonconcessional flows	10.9	34.3	59.4	70.5	60.4	63.9
Official or officially supported flows	3.9	10.5	24.5	22.2	22.0	19.6
Private export credits	2.1	4.4	11.1	11.3	7.1	5.5
Official export credits	0.6	1.2	2.5	2.0	2.7	2.1
Multilateral flows	0.7	2.5	4.9	5.7	6.6	7.0
Other official and private flows	0.2	0.8	2.2	2.0	2.6	3.0
Other donors	0.3	1.6	3.8	1.2	3.0	2.0
Private flows	7.0	23.8	34.9	48.3	38.4	44.3
Direct investment	3.7	11.4	10.5	17.2	11.9	7.8
Bank lending[a]	3.0	12.0	23.0	30.0	26.0	36.0
Bond lending	0.3	0.4	1.4	1.1	0.5	0.5
Total	19.9	55.7	99.2	109.8	97.4	99.7
Memo items						
Short-term bank lending	..	..	26.0	22.0	15.0	−2.0
IMF purchases (net)	0.3	3.2	2.6	6.2	6.4	12.4

[a] Excluding bond lending and export credits extended by banks, which are included in private export credits.

SOURCE: OECD 1984, World Development Report, 1985, World Bank.

CHART 2–1 Net Capital Flows and Debt (1970–84)

Net flows to developing countries

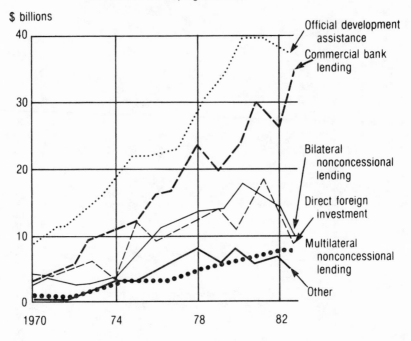

$ billions

Official development assistance

Commercial bank lending

Bilateral nonconcessional lending

Direct foreign investment

Multilateral nonconcessional lending

Other

Debt outstanding and disbursed

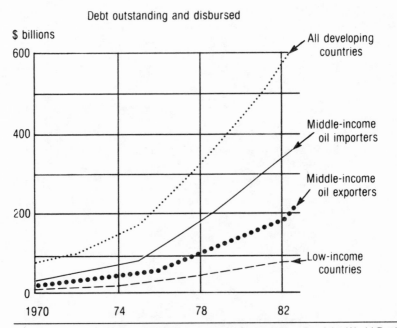

$ billions

All developing countries

Middle-income oil importers

Middle-income oil exporters

Low-income countries

SOURCE: For net flows: OECD *Development Co-operation*; for debt: World Bank data.

The flow from commercial banking sources then fell even more quickly than it had risen. Net transfers of short-term lending went down by a third after 1980 to a level of about $15 billion in 1982 and to minus $2 billion in 1983. The flow of medium- and long-term transfers to low-income African countries fell by almost a half from their already low levels but because their borrowing had not been so dependent on commercial banks, the net transfer remained positive. The countries hardest hit were the major borrowers, principally the large Latin American debtors.

Both lenders and borrowers had been playing the odds, counting on a continuation of rising commodity prices, a depreciating dollar, and low or negative real interest rates. When these conditions abruptly changed, the tempo of the debt rescheduling process quickened. Commercial bank lending had to be continued, if necessary on an involuntary basis. Reschedulings that had averaged 5 a year between 1975 and 1980 jumped to 13 in 1981 and by 1983 had doubled again. From a level of less than $4 billion in 1980, the amounts involved in the rescheduling exercise rose to more than $50 billion by 1983, a twelvefold increase. By 1985 the number of rescheduling agreements had increased slightly to 31, but the amounts involved had risen to about $120 billion, more than double that of 1983.

Two policy decisions were the straws that broke the proverbial camel's back:

- The first decision came when the OPEC ministers delivered the "second oil shock" in 1979 by boosting oil prices to five times the 1973 level in real terms. This reversed the trend of falling real oil prices that had followed the initial 1973–74 price increases and gave added inflationary impact to the second round of price increases, which had been building up over the decade, especially since the 1973–74 jump in oil prices.

- The second straw was the famous 1979 decison by Paul Volcker, chairman of the U.S. Federal Reserve System, who delivered what has often been referred to as the Volcker shock: an extremely contractionary monetary policy. The centerpiece of that policy was an unprecedented rise in nominal and real interest rates, as shown in Charts 2–2 and 2–3. The intended effect was achieved. The value of the dollar rose spectacularly and the inflationary pressures subsided. The cure was bought at a high price, a corrective recession with the heaviest economic and social costs in both absolute and real terms borne by the debtor developing countries and, to a lesser extent, the other industrialized countries that were forced to follow suit in raising interest rates. (France resisted for a time but succumbed after futile and costly resistance).

CHART 2–2 Long-Term Interest Rates in the United States (1965–84)

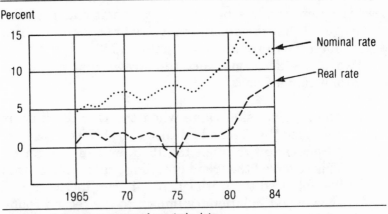

NOTE: Data are averages of quarterly data.

SOURCE: OECD *Financial Statistics* and *National Accounts;* Federal Reserve Board statistical releases.

CHART 2–3   Trends in Interest Rates: New Long-Term
Commitments to Public Borrowers (1975–83)

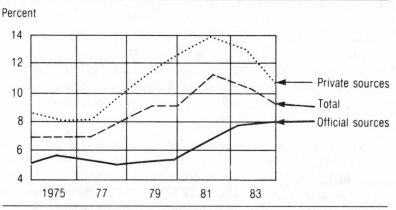

Percent

NOTE: Data are the weighted average interest rates on new loans at the time of commitment. For loans on variable interest rates, interest actually paid will vary with changes in market rates.

Both in 1973 and 1978, OPEC pushed on the accelerator. The United States in 1979 slammed on the brakes and the rest of the world, like unbuckled passengers, went through the windshield. The debt crisis arrived.

UNDERLYING ASSUMPTIONS: SUBJECTIVE AND OBJECTIVE FACTORS

The Subjective Perspective

These policy decisions cannot be explained away as capricious or arbitrary. Decisions that have such far-reaching ramifications can be understood only with reference to the institutional context in which the crisis was nurtured. Because the prevailing "system," or "international order," is characterized by the preponderant economic and financial power of the major industrialized countries—and of the United States in particular as the reserve currency country—the spotlight must be focused mainly on their policies and on the underlying dynamics of the institutional changes that have given rise to the present global condition.

The climactic events of 1931 shed some light on the roots of the current debt crisis. This period was character- ized by a rash of defaults, mainly of German, Eastern Euro- pean, and Latin American debts. Writing about this period as backdrop for an analysis of the present crisis, one author observed:

> Then as now the developing countries of Eastern Europe and Latin America were overwhelmed by a world recession that turned domestic policy shortcomings into a crisis. So too Ger- many, although its *difficulties originated in the decision to fight the war of 1914–18 by borrowing from its citizens, rather than taxing them. The squandering of a generation's savings left Germany excessively dependent on foreign capital, which flooded in and then out.* Yet the German experience merely represented in an extreme form the root of debt difficulties wherever and whenever encountered, which consists of will- ing the end without the means.[4] (Emphasis added.)

The parallel with the United States is extremely suggestive, particularly, firstly, with respect to the policies of relying on large capital inflow rather than fostering domestic sav- ings and proceeding only as fast as such savings allow and, secondly, the policies of allocating unprecedented amounts of resources for military purposes rather than for pro- ductive endeavors.

Reference to policy mistakes and motivations of the principal borrowers and lenders and their political counter- parts is much too facile and misleading to explain either

---

[4] M. S. Mendelsohn, *The Debt of Nations*, New York: (Twentieth Century Fund, 1984), pp. 29–30. He refers, in this context to "events which had economic consequences rather than causes."

past or present crises. They are not explained by assertions such as that articulated by an executive director of the Inter-American Development Bank, who has said, "Stupid bankers made stupid loans to stupid countries."[5] This is a view often repeated, as though it sufficed to explain anything significant. While such analyses may contain an element of truth, they hardly help understanding to point to such attributes as the greed, naivete, biases, stupidity, or "invalid mind-sets" of the major players on the world scene. Eschewing demonological explanation is not to excuse the borrowers who gambled recklessly on continuing inflation and negative interest rates, who devised policies that dissipated the incoming capital in speculative and nonproductive uses and encouraged and permitted the flight of capital to a degree that would have wrought incalculable damage to their economies under the best of circumstances. The question must still be asked, however: were the officials of the borrowing countries any more or less competent and prudent in other eras? Why did their behavior—assuming

---

[5] Jorge Sol, "Origins of the Debt Crisis," summary report of meeting on the international debt crisis, September 26, 1984, *World Development Report 1985* (Washington, D.C.: World Bank), pp. 5 and 143.

The dangers and temptations of personifying the problem rather than searching for the contextual circumstances of policy decision making is exemplified in a recent speech by a major international civil servant. The speech, titled "The Growth of Debt and the Need for Fiscal Disciplines," alludes to psychological and ideological traits as causal factors: "An attitude of fiscal laxity on the part of policymakers, a certain nonchalance [about] fiscal deficits" and "insidious abandonment of traditional principles in favor of fiscal activism that [has] made full employment and the expansion of the welfare state programs predominant objectives of economic policy." What does he have in mind? The culprit is not military expenditures. The finger is pointed at "the prevailing mood of the [present] time [which has] created high expectations of the role that governments should play with respect to income maintenance, job creation, and income distribution (and, as well, the provision), almost as a natural right, to cheap or free health care, transportation, communications, and so forth."

it was roughly comparable and rational in the context of the times—lead *at this particular point in time* to such a disastrous outcome?

Former Brazilian Minister of Finance Mario Henrique Simonsen poses the question and provides "a plausible explanation":

> Who is to be held responsible for the debt crisis: commercial banks that behaved as imprudent lenders, or debtor developing countries that misused the borrowed external funds?
>
> This is the fashionable debate in witch-hunting circles, where every crisis provides a unique opportunity to practice their favorite sport. The debate reflects nothing but poor logic.
> . . . *A plausible explanation for the debt crisis must rely on either some external factor or the inadequacy of the recycling system, or both.* [6] (Emphasis added.)

Some Objective Factors

While there are always objective reasons for major decisions that are sustained over time, the difficulty—and controversy—is to arrive at consensus as to what the factors are, how they play their role, and with what impact. Attention has often—too often—been focused on what might be called trigger events, occurrences that are natural in origin (usually of a disastrous nature such as major earthquakes, volcanic eruptions) or are technological and political developments that have led to the booms and busts, mania and panics, and other such phenomena. With regard to the current debt crisis, the tendency is to identify as the main culprit the financial impact of OPEC's price shocks of 1973–74 and 1979–80.

---

[6] "The Developing Country Debt Problem," *International Debt and the Developing Countries, A Symposium,* Washington, D.C.: (World Bank, 1985), p. 117.

Singling out these types of factors or sets of phenomena does not provide an adequate account of the basic causal origins of crises when they are only symptomatic of a more profound problem. The adverse impact on the oil price rise was felt almost immediately by all oil-importing countries, but most poignantly by the oil-importing developing countries. Over the 1973–83 decade they added an estimated $250 billion to their import bill for oil.[7] This shock entailed painful adjustments for the oil-importing countries. But questions arise: Was the shock manageable? Need this sudden change have led to the sharp global recession and the ensuing debt crisis of 1982? If there were other options for petrodollar recycling, why did the process take the form that it did, which turned out to have been a disastrous course? The spotlight should not be on the petrodollar phenomenon *per se* but on the manner in which it was handled and on the institutional context within which this process took place. Two features of that context need to be singled out:

- The rise of the unregulated Eurocurrency market and commercial bank lending to developing countries with commensurate institutional changes in

---

[7] While this aspect of OPEC impact is self-evident, out of the glare has been the connection between U.S. energy policy decisions (such as the oil import quota) of the 1950s and 1960s and OPEC's capacity to control the price of oil, that is, to become an *effective* cartel. Through a series of policy decisions heavily influenced by the oil lobby, OPEC was indirectly strengthened over the postwar decades by a series of U.S. policy decisions to a point where OPEC was able to administer the well-publicized series of oil price shocks in 1973 and in 1979. This is well described in *The Control of Oil*, by G. Barnes, former adviser to the congressional committee concerned with these matters. He sets out the condition that enabled the cartel to acquire teeth and traces the U.S. administration and congressional decisions on oil import and pricing and related taxation policies, which date back half a century, and directly links them to decisions made on behalf of the multinational oil companies.

lending procedures and criteria and concomitant relative decline in the importance of the capital flows from international financial organizations, private investors, and bilateral aid programs.

- The increased trade interdependence between developed and developing countries and the relative decline in the position of the United States from its absolute dominance in almost all economic and financial spheres from the days of Bretton Woods to today.

Both of these elements of global change have a significant common characteristic: they both contribute to or reflect a loss of control. The process in each case has spanned decades and, rooted in structural rigidities associated with or a consequence of these changes, will not be easily or quickly overcome. Each element merits elaboration.

THE EUROCURRENCY INTERMEDIATION AND SYNDICATION PHENOMENA (AND OTHER MANIFESTATIONS OF "THE CASINO SOCIETY" SYNDROME)

Regarding the first factor, in retrospect it seems clear that the rise to starring roles of the Eurodollar market and commercial bank lending to the developing countries had great significance in the buildup to the debt crisis. The rapid growth of the twin phenomena of the Eurodollar market and of syndication made it possible—and evidently too easy—for the commercial banking system to recycle petrodollars in response to the demand of the developing countries. As is evident from Charts 2–4 and 2–5, from 1973 to 1980, syndicated Eurocurrency lending to the developing countries increased 1,200 percent from less than $4 billion to almost $50 billion. The process has been aptly described by a London banker, Minos Zombanakis, as a lending orgy.

CHART 2–4 Stock of International and Eurocurrency Loans
(1973–82)

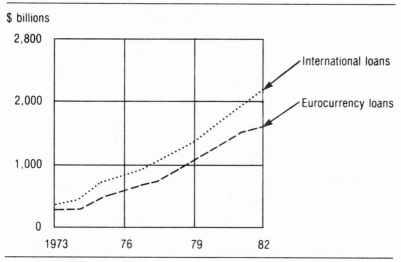

$ billions

NOTE: Data indicate stock at the end of the last quarter of each year.
SOURCE: BIS *Quarterly Report* 1974–85.

In the syndication process the major commercial banks took the lead—and the fees that go with that role—while the smaller banks jumped enthusiastically, but blindly, onto the syndication bandwagon. By 1980 these banks that had never before ventured into international lending accounted for about one third of the total volume of such loans. "Follow the leader" was the big game in town for bank lemmings, big and small.

Few bankers seemed to be able to resist the temptation to get on the syndication bandwagon once it got rolling in earnest after 1974. This was made possible by the technical and organizational strengthening of the network of interbank deposits, which by 1983, had expanded so rapidly that it accounted for more than 40 percent of the volume

CHART 2–5 International Bank Lending (1973–84)

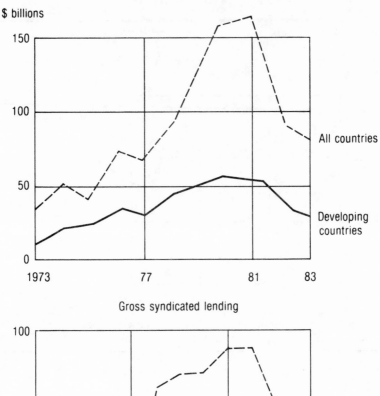

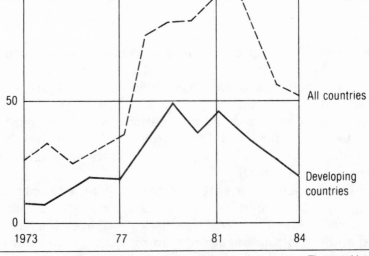

NOTE: International bank lending is measured here in two ways. First, total international lending is measured net of loan repayments for a defined set of reporting banks (in this instance, banks reporting to the Bank for International Settlements). These data, after 1976, are adjusted for the valuation effects of exchange rate movements. Second, a major element of international lending—syndicated loans—is measured on a gross basis, no allowance being made for repayments. Only published syndicated lending is covered by the data, however.

SOURCE: IMF, *International Capital Markets: Developments and Prospects, 1984.* For syndicated lending: OECD *Financial Market Trends.*

of Euromarket deposits and 50 percent of the Asian dollar market. As the main depositories of petrodollars, the major banks were eager to lend both directly to countries and indirectly to the interbank system. By virtue of this indirect process, very few of the hundreds of smaller banks that participated could obtain—or even cared to obtain—any knowledge, let alone any measure of control, over how the funds were to be used by the borrowers.

The banks plunged into these international financial waters knowing there was some danger in doing so because with regard to the international lending that drew heavily on the available Eurocurrency, there were no reserve requirements and no analogue to central bank control. The banking community forcefully and openly opposed any international collaborative approach to examine the implications of this lending mania. Prominent bankers even went on record to oppose the calls being made by some for safety nets that were being then proposed by some nervous political leaders.

The principles of Gresham's law ("bad money drives out good money") were clearly operating. Particularly after 1974, the commercial bank syndicates had access to a form of financial marketing centers that enjoyed the Greshamite advantage of "international monetary indiscipline" to use a felicitous phrase of Dr. Raul Prebisch.[8] It was an institutional arrangement that operated with no constraints on the borrowers and lenders who were caught up in a frenzy of delusions that the conditions then prevailing would continue *ad infinitum*. It should have occasioned no surprise that the process took on the attributes of what is known

---

[8] Raul Prebisch, former executive secretary of the Economic Commission for Latin American and the Caribbean (ECLA), in "International Monetary Indiscipline and the Debt Problem," *The Debt Problem: Acute and Chronic Aspects*, pp. 173–76.

as a Ponzi scheme and built what one knowledgeable banker, Lord Harold Lever, has described as a house of cards. The rules of the financial game had made collapse or crisis not only a possible outcome, but a probable one.

It seems hard to imagine that the zealous borrowers and loan-pushing lenders could expect that the "debtors' paradise" conditions prevailing in the 1960s and early 1970s would continue indefinitely. Politicians who enjoy an uncertain and generally short life span have an understandable (though regrettable) tendency to discount the future very heavily. To a certain extent, this mode of thought was rationalized by the recurrence of an old theme that became fashionable in the late 1970s and early 1980s, namely, the neo-Malthusian limits-to-growth psychology. This theory stressed the finiteness and, therefore, the likely shortages and ever-rising prices of the globe's resources that would enable the borrowing countries to earn enough to service their debts.[9] There were apparently few who had similar fears about the limits of the recycling process since, for about five or six years after the first oil shock, there seemed little cause for worry.

This aura of complacency was not disturbed by the collective memory of previous financial crashes. That memory is very short, as all histories of such crashes attest. Certainly forgotten were the dire warnings of the 1960s from the authors of the Pearson Commission Report, *Partners in Development,* and by others.[10] They had pointed out—even at that time when the debt problem was minuscule

---

[9] The Club of Rome with its bible, *The Limits to Growth,* by Dennis and Daniella Meadows, Jorgen Randers, William Behrens (New York: Universe Books, 1972), had become very popular. The roots of this recurrent psychological/intellectual virus, known as "Malthusianism" or "the chicken-little syndrome," need not be explored here, but it may suffice to note it is not by accident that the prevailing mood of the times should be so downbeat while the bankers and borowers were so upbeat—and such risk-takers.

relative to today and real interest rates were much lower—
that there was no way of avoiding a debt crisis within a
decade unless the gross flow of capital transfers (aid, commercial bank lending, direct private investment, and so
on) continued to accelerate and unless donor nations provided an ever-increasing volume of aid and/or softer terms
for such aid. The day of reckoning was put off for several
years by the frenzy of lending or petrodollar recycling,
which far exceeded the capital transfer rate of 8 percent
a year, but the writing was on the wall all the time. Few
cared to read the warnings. But then many play the odds
in casinos, hoping to come out ahead.

A recurrent and very relevant question: Were there
options, other forms of capital transfer, that could have
responded to the challenging conditions posed by the surfeit
of petrodollars and the need for financing the more expen-
sive oil and development? In earlier times this financial
intermediation process would have included bond financing
and direct foreign investment; more recently, in the decades
after World War II, the financial sources would have also
included official development assistance (ODA) with a very
high grant element and lending by international financial

---

[10] The Pearson Commission Report, *Partners in Development* (Washington, D.C.: World Bank, 1969,) passim. The report noted that by 1967
Latin American borrowers had to devote about seven-eighths of their
current loan proceeds to servicing debts incurred in the past and that
within 10 years, by 1977, most developing countries would have to use
all of their new loans to service past debts unless the total inflow of
receipts exceeded 8 percent per year or unless a higher proportion of
new loans were on soft terms with a high grant element. See also Charles
R. Frank Jr., "Debt and the Terms of Aid," *Assisting Developing Countries* (Washington, D.C.: Overseas Development Council, 1972,) p. 31,
in which he asserted, "Any attempt to finance large capital flows to
an average LDC over a period of 10 to 20 years, except on soft terms,
results in debt service payments which soon threaten to become unman-
ageable." The inexorable logic of compounding and exponentiality underlies these warnings.

institutions on soft and hard terms, as well as the IMF's newly minted special drawing rights (SDRs). Some of these sources were constrained by reliance on "market" rather than governmental modalities from attaining their full potential to respond adequately (in terms of speed, volume, and conditions such as rates and maturities) to the liquidity requirements posed by the oil shocks. There clearly were other options open but not chosen. It is relevant to understand why the "easy road" was taken.

"THE SHRINKING OF AMERICA" AND GLOBAL IMPLICATIONS

A veritable transformation in the international economic and financial scene has occurred since the end of World War II, a phenomenon the *Economist* (October 5, 1985) refers to as "the shrinking of the U.S." This change in the relative position or power of the U.S. economy underlies the rationale or pressures for the policy decisions taken during the postwar decades. This change had special significance for the debt crisis because the U.S. economy, by virtue of its size in terms of output and trade, was expected to and had formally assumed obligations to play a pivotal role in the global economy as the reserve currency country with all that implied in terms of exchange rates, interest rates, and so forth.

At the time of the Bretton Woods agreement in 1944, the United States could boast an industrial capacity almost twice as great as that of the rest of the major western industrial nations combined. Over the two decades after the end of World War II, the U.S. economy continued to enjoy undisputed economic predominance. However, during the 1960s this economic and technological superiority began to be challenged. By the mid-1970s the relative position of the U.S. economy in the global picture had undergone a qualitative and quantitative change in two respects: not only were other industrialized nations now serious competitors, but the United States also had become more dependent on the very global markets in which it competed.

In terms of output and trade, the U.S. economy's slippage has been dramatic, dropping from about 40 percent of global output in 1950 to about 22 percent by 1978 and from 16 percent global trade to 11 percent during the same period, as shown in Charts 2–6 and 2–7. In the early 1950s, the combined exports of the other major industrial nations did not match that of the United States alone; yet within two decades their exports exceeded U.S. exports by 250 percent.

Declining productivity is the factor behind this change in the relative position of the U.S. economy: during the first two decades after Bretton Woods, the productivity of

CHART 2–6 World GNP

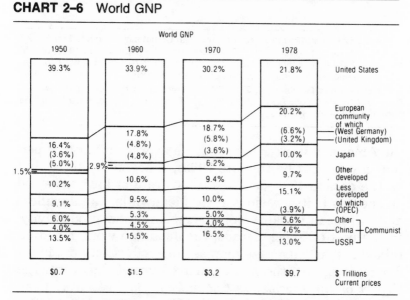

SOURCE: Peter G. Peterson, *The U.S. Competitive Position in the 1980s—And Some Things We Might Do About It* (Dallas, Texas: The Center for International Business, 1980), pp. 9 and 32.

CHART 2–7   World Exports

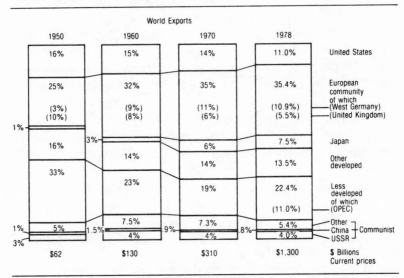

World Exports

	1950	1960	1970	1978	
	16%	15%	14%	11.0%	United States
	25%	32%	35%	35.4%	European community of which
	(3%)	(9%)	(11%)	(10.9%)	(West Germany)
	(10%)	(8%)	(6%)	(5.5%)	(United Kingdom)
	16%	3%	6%	7.5%	Japan
		14%	14%	13.5%	Other developed
	33%	23%	19%	22.4%	Less developed of which
				(11.0%)	(OPEC)
	5%	7.5%	7.3%	5.4%	Other / China — Communist
	1.5%	.9%	8%		
		4%	4%	4.0%	USSR
	$62	$130	$310	$1,300	$ Billions Current prices

NOTE: Exports within the six nation European Community accounted for 31 percent of total EC exports in 1950. 35 percent in 1960, 48 percent in 1970, and 52 percent in 1978 (nine nation European Community). In 1978, Soviet exports to Communist countries accounted for 60 percent of total exports.

SOURCE: Peter G. Peterson, *The U.S. Competitive Position in the 1980s—And Some Things We Might Do About It* (Dallas, Texas: The Center for International Business, 1980), pp. 9 and 32.

---

the American worker increased an average of about 3 percent a year, but by the late 1960s, it began to fall so that by the decade 1973–83 the average rate of increase stood at one tenth its previous rate. Meanwhile, the Japanese and European workers were increasing their productivity. In the post oil-shock decade, the Japanese worker had attained a yearly average increase in productivity of almost 3 percent against the American average of 0.3 percent. The *Report of the President's Commission on Industrial Competitiveness* (also known as the Young Commission after its chairman) observed, "Since 1960 our productivity growth has been dismal—outstripped by almost all our

CHART 2–8   Historical Productivity Growth (Real GDP Per Person Employed)

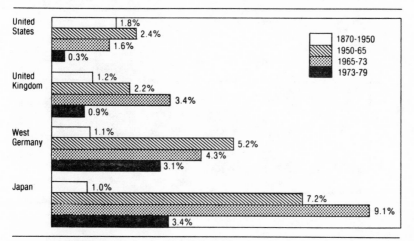

SOURCE: Peter G. Peterson, *The U.S. Competitve Position in the 1980's—And Some Things We Might Do About It* (Dallas, Texas: The Center for International Business, 1980), p. 14

trading partners (with) Japanese productivity growth (averaging over the 1960–83 period) a rate five times greater than our own."[11] This is shown in Charts 2–8 and 2–9.

Manufacturing productivity is perhaps the most relevant factor in comparing the competitive position of differ-

---

[11] "Global Competition: The New Reality," (The Report of the President's Commission on Industrial Competitiveness), Washington, D.C., 1985, V 1, p. 11. The report points out that the trade deficit cannot be explained away by the strong dollar because the deficit dates back to the early 1970s when, despite a 15 percent depreciation of the dollar, the trade deficit actually increased. The deficit began to soar from 1981 onward, increasing from about $40 billion in that year to its present level of about $150 billion, a 400 percent change. In this four-year period this change was accompanied by the soaring value of the dollar which rose about 40 percent against other major currencies.

CHART 2–9   Productivity (Real Gross Domestic Product per Employed Person) (average annual percent change, 1960–83)

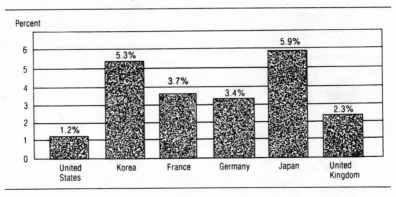

ent economies because manufactured goods are generally tradable and comparable in this global market world. From 1977 to 1983, the Japanese led all other OECD nations in terms of that key indicator, the annual growth rate of manufacturing productivity, with a 3.9 percent rate, followed by France at 3.5 percent. The United States limped along at less than one-third that rate, 1.2 percent; and Canada crawled at 0.9 percent. The performance of all major European economies was more than twice that of the United States. If only the private sector is considered, the U.S. decline is even more serious, with the annual average productivity growth rate falling from 3.3 percent during the two decades after World War I to 1 percent from 1977 to 1984. In the last three months of 1985, the U.S. Labor Department reported that U.S. productivity plummeted 3.1 percent, which resulted in a barely perceptible productivity growth rate of only 0.2 percent, but manufacturing productivity fell at a 1.5 percent annual rate in the fourth quarter. The process has been described as a "headlong slide into industrial oblivion."[12]

Over the decades, this situation has been compounded by a powerful but subtle structural change in the global economic relationships of the United States to other OECD countries, especially Japan. This change is dramatically reflected in one salient statistic: the U.S. economy has become the world's largest exporter of farm and forest products and other primary commodities while the Japanese have become the world's largest exporter of manufactured goods. With terms of trade favoring the higher value-added processed manufactured products, the United States has found itself facing a deteriorating trade balance with a consequent depressing effect on the U.S. dollar. Net dollar obligations to foreigners began to increase exponentially, from $1 billion or $2 billion per year in the mid-1950s to $3 billion to $4 billion in the 1960s, rising to more than $10 billion by the early 1970s. As a result of petrodollar recycling (with oil prices and debts being denominated in dollars), the number jumped to more than $40 billion in 1976 and continued to surge.

---

[12] *The Wall Street Journal* (February 10, 1986). Peter Behr, *Washington Post* (February 20, 1985) refers to the "crucial piece of bad news (which) concerns the economy's poor performance on productivity in the 1980s. Much of the manufacturing sector's productivity improvement (which has not been strong enough to offset the terrible performance in the nonmanufacturing sector through January 1985 and apparently since then) has come from plant shutdowns and layoffs rather than from investments that increase employes' productivity. . . . The Young Commission concluded that the competitiveness problem was not confined to an over-valued dollar and a record budget deficit."

Professor Robert B. Reich, *The Next American Frontier,* (New York: Times Books, 1983), pp. 117–118, wrote of the absolute decline of American productivity since 1979 and of the drop in the proportion of U.S. manufacturing capacity employed in production, which averaged 80 percent during the 1970s and fell to less than 70 percent by 1982. "The decline (in productivity) is particularly startling when compared with the performance of several other industrial countries."

An important contributing factor in this process has been the high proportion of this capital outflow devoted to military expenditure, which has been estimated to total more than $140 billion for the Vietnam War alone and more than $50 billion in military aid in the two decades after the end of World War II.[13]

These foreign exchange expenditures, in large measure, helped account for the transformation of the "dollar gap" of the immediate postwar years in the "dollar glut" of the late 1950s.

All of these trends had a cumulative impact over the subsequent decade that undermined the U.S. capacity to adhere to the basic assumption on which the Bretton Woods agreement was founded—confidence in the dollar as a reserve currency. With the U.S. economy under severe financial strain the the late 1960s and early 1970s, President Nixon in 1968 decided to restrict gold sales to individuals from the U.S. reserve and in 1971 to unilaterally close the gold window entirely and thereby abandon the Bretton Woods agreement.[14] It also led to another set of policy decisions, which is of even more direct relevance to the debt

---

[13] While this type of foreign exchange expenditure has had little or no compensating productivity benefit (in a real or welfare sense), it has had a stimulative effect on the U.S. economy as part of the phenomenon that has been called military Keynesianism by Professor Robert Reich and pentagon capitalism by Professor Seymour Melmon. See Robert B. Reich, "Toward a New Public Philosophy," *Atlantic Monthly* (May 1985), pp. 76–79; Seymour Melman, *Pentagon Capitalism: The Political Economy of War* (New York: McGraw-Hill, 1970). Also, Senator William J. Fulbright, *The Arrogance of Power* (New York: Random House, 1966): "What I fear is that (America) may be drifting into commitments which, though generous and benevolent in intent, are so far-reaching as to exceed even America's great capacities. It is my hope that America will escape those fatal temptations of power which have ruined other great nations."

[14] This aspect is considered in Chapter Six where the focus is on the concept of a new Bretton Woods and an understanding of what went wrong with the original one.

crisis—the decision in 1979 by President Carter and Paul Volcker of the U.S. Federal Reserve Board to pursue a severely contractionary monetarist policy that precipitated the debt crisis in the summer of 1982. The U.S. policies pursued in the 1960s and 1970s to contend with a deteriorating trade balance had a direct and powerful impact that contributed to the debt buildup over those years.

SEARCHING FOR THE WAY OUT AND ONTO THE HIGH ROAD OF GROWTH

From the very onset of the panic phase of the debt crisis there was a wide range of proposals put forward, many of a purely emergency nature. Primarily, the focus during this period was narrowly centered on avoiding default. In practical terms, the method adopted for coping with repayment problems has treated every case as if it were unique and isolated from all others. Each time the fabric of financial interaction has begun to tear, a customized patch has been fashioned and hurriedly stitched into place with the hope that, in the meantime, the whole garment would not fall apart.

William Cline, the strongest academic advocate of this approach, has called it "crisis management on a case-by-case basis." It is a label given to a procedure that is reactive and limited in its objectives, which are to avoid default, hasten the return to "normal" conditions, and minimize the costs of adjustment on both the debtors and the creditors.

Other proposals have come forward in great profusion in reaction to a widely held perception that the case-by-case procedure has proved unable to address some fundamental weaknesses in the international financial system, which have permitted or abetted the current crisis. Others stress it has proved to be unfair, placing the major burden of adjustment on the debtors. These proposals, which could be categorized as case-by-case plus, seek to restructure the debt burden through institutional and policy arrangements that require agreement, if not cooperation, among both debtors and creditors but that fall far short of a broader systemic approach.

A third approach advocated by many questions whether the constraints inherent in the system are appropriate from the point of view of "the public interest" and whether the heavy load of debt rests on a sufficiently strong foundation both on the banking system side and on the debtors' side. The advocates of proposals in this group range across the political spectrum but have one element in common, namely, the belief that the global financial system is in need of change and that the status quo is an inappropriate goal. Though there is a range of views as to what institutional or policy modifications might be necessary and desirable, the advocates of the approach would place some key aspects of the rules of the game on the table for consideration and modification. Since this would call for international agreements or understandings, this has been labeled, a Bretton Woods approach.

Each of the three categories of proposals being put forward for coping with and it is hoped overcoming the debt crisis rests on different asumptions, both as to the scope and nature of the debt crisis and as to its cause or causes. Each will be examined in the following chapters to identify their key features as a basis for making judgments about their efficacy, equity, and sustainability. We can then consider what role the international financial institutions might play in any initiative designed to get the global economy out of the debt ditch and back onto the high road of development.

CHAPTER THREE

The Case-by-Case Approach:
Sand Castle Modeling

The international debt situation is spinning out of control and poses a clear and present danger for the entire international financial system comparable to the one preceding 1929. Only drastic action by Western governments impelled by a realistic sense of urgency will head it off. . . . Promises that the crisis can be handled with business-as-usual methods do not help.

Eliot Janeway[1]

It is misguided to see the debt problem as primarily the result of excessive or irresponsible bank lending; the analysis shows the overwhelming role of exogenous shock in the world economy in creating the current situation (oil price shocks, sharply rising interest rates, and declining export prices and volumes caused by global recession). . . . Broadly, the debt problem is one of illiquidity, not insolvency, and if sufficient financial packages can be arranged to tide over debtor countries temporarily, they should be able to return to a sound financial footing within two to four years.

William Cline[2]

---

[1] "The Prince of Pessimism Says the System Could Topple," *Washington Post* (August 14, 1983).

[2] Senior Fellow at the Institute for International Economics, *International Debt and the Stability of the World Economy,* #4 Policy Analyses in International Economics, IIE, Washington, D.C., September 1983, pp. 122–23.

THE CASE FOR THE CASE-BY-CASE APPROACH

Managing the debt crisis on a case-by-case basis would merit scrutiny if for no other reason than that it is the current approach and appears to be successful—so far. That assessment of success is, of course, a relative concept. By the criteria of its first objective of staving off defaults by major debtors, the system is coping. Consideration of alternative approaches is deterred by the logic of the old maxim that rationalizes the established order of things: "if it works, don't fix it."

There is, furthermore, a persuasive argument for the current approach in the incontestable observation of Nicholas Hope, the World Bank's director of the External Debt Division: "We have to take the world as it is: reality dictates that we recognize the factor of sovereignty and the great diversity of circumstances of each case." There is no denying the diversity. The range spans countries that are desperately poor and whose debts are extremely burdensome yet owe insignificant amounts in international terms, to others that are newly industrializing countries (NICs) with debts so massive their creditors are hostages to them, compelled to negotiate an agreement acceptable to both parties. There are also countries, such as India and China that have levels of external debt that are "easily manageable" and enjoy "creditworthy status," which means they have more options to borrow than they choose to exercise.

The most powerful support for the case-by-case approach lies in the way it addresses three major problems posed by the debt crisis: 1.) how to reduce the debt servicing burden so debtors can cope, 2.) how to keep commercial bank lending from drying up, and 3.) how to give the commercial banks time to build up loss-reserves so they could cope. The case-by-case process operates to meet these problems in the following way:

a. The interest burden can be reduced in the rescheduling negotiations through relending part of the interest due, thereby increasing the debt but also providing temporary debt relief. This is the expedient for avoiding breakdown when debtors find it difficult or impossible (politically suicidal) to keep running trade surpluses large enough to pay all interest due.

b. Smaller banks that want to withdraw from the consortia they joined with such abandon during the 1970s can be dissuaded from doing so through the judicious application of direct pressure and persuasion. This tackles the so-called free rider problem where the smaller banks that want out would, if they could, leave the larger banks to carry the load. Higher rates or spreads on the rescheduled loans help keep the incipient wagon-jumpers from jumping off.[3]

c. Massive write-downs by the heavily committed major banks can be avoided or delayed. This process enables them through rescheduling both to keep existing loans to sovereign borrowers on their books at full value and to gain the time necessary to build up reserves against such losses in the event that the worst comes to pass.

THE KEY UNDERLYING ASSUMPTIONS

Undermining the tranquil unanimity surrounding the case-by-case perspective are doubts about its fundamental assumptions, including the values implicit in the process. Our

---

[3] For a description of the interest rate differentials exacted in the debt rescheduling process and rationalized as a way of resolving or aborting the "free rider" problem, see "The Nature and Effects of 'Involuntary' Bank Lending," *The International Monetary System and Financial Markets: Recent Developments and the Policy Challenge*, UNCTAD document, TD/B/C.3/194, December 18, 1984, pp. 29 to 30.

focus, at this point, will be on the empirical aspects of the case for the current approach to the debt problem. We will consider a series of models that contain within them a host of empirical assumptions about the interrelationship between OECD economic growth and LDC net foreign exchange earnings via trade and LDC net capital inflows via investment, aid, and borrowings. Examining some of these key relationships will reveal how solid or shaky is the model on which the empirical justification of this process is based.

The "Growth Rate" Assumption: How Strongly Does It Pull?

Probably the fundamental assumption of the case-by-case approach is that rapid growth in the industrialized world will provide the basis for a normalization of debtor-creditor relations. This can be summed up in a maxim: "A rising tide floats all boats." However, great difficulties face anyone venturing an answer as to the foreign exchange required to enable the various debtor countries to grow at a satisfactory rate while, at the same time, servicing their still-expanding debt burdens. It is virtually impossible to know the relationship between changes in the GNP growth rates of the industrialized countries and changes in the amount of foreign exchange that would become available to debtor countries through exports, direct foreign investment, and official aid. The difficulty of projecting the likely relationships between growth and other key variables stems from the substantial indeterminacy of several critical factors:

- The price and income elasticities of demand and of supply for the exportable goods and services of a very diverse group of developing countries.
- The amount and terms of additional medium and

long-term commercial bank lending that will be
made available under various "concerted lending"
agreements that now account for the greater part
of additional bank lending and that, by their nature, involve decisions that do not have any ascer-
tainable relationship to price and other market signals.

- The movement of real interest rates (involving the
direction and speed of nominal rates and prices) and
the length of maturities of new and renegotiated
loans (influenced to some degree by new institutional
elements such as the availability of and receptivity
to World Bank co-financing, political risk guarantees, and so on).

World economic conditions have been changing so fast
and so erratically, that past and even current relationships
provide a questionable guide to future behavior. The best
way to drive home this point is by considering certain clear
cases of today's large crop of unknowns. We could start
with the linchpin relationship between gross domestic product (GDP) growth rates in the industrialized countries and
the exports of the developing countries. Perhaps the most
comprehensive exercise on this issue is the work of William
Cline, who has come out strongly in support of the case-
by-case approach, which, he asserted in early 1983, "is a
coherent strategy that has shown favorable results so
far."[4]

---

[4] "International Debt: From Crisis to Recovery?" paper delivered
at the American Economic Association Annual Meeting, April 1983,
AEA papers and Proceedings, May 1985, p. 186. The fuller treatment
of this subject is contained in Cline's major work on this subject, *Systemic
Risk and Policy Response,* (Washington, D.C.: Institute for International,
Economics, 1984). In this work Cline tries to take account of "alternative

Cline's model assumes that for every percentage point in the growth of the gross domestic product (GDP) of the OECD countries, export volume can be expected to increase by 3 percent (i.e., an export elasticity of exports of 3.0) and that export prices can be expected to move procyclically, that is, rise faster than the inflation rate. These key relationships led him to conclude that "a 1 percent rise in OECD growth causes approximately 1.5 percent rise in real export prices in the current year and a similar rise in the following year." Professors Rudiger Dornbusch and Stephen Fischer of Massachusetts Institute of Technology have found that the same elasticity for nonoil-exporting developing countries is closer to 2.0.[5] The World Bank reading of the statistical record, as cited by Shahid Javed Burki, director of the International Relations Department of the World Bank, reveals an export elasticity of 1.3 with the figure 3.0 with respect to manufactured products.[6]

Burki goes on to cite the ahistorical behavior of commodity export prices, noting, "this is the first post-recessionary period in which revival of economic activity in devel-

---

studies" (pp. 169–75) and concludes, "In sum, several recent quantitative studies provide additional evidence of the prospective path of developing-country debt. . . . The broad implication of this whole set of studies is that the debt problem is manageable as one of temporary illiquidity, with (several caveats and admonitions)," pp. 174–75.

[5] R. Dornbusch and S. Fischer, *The World Debt Problem: Report to the Group of 24*, UNDP/UNCTAD Project INT/81/046 (UNCTAD/MFD/TA/31), p. 33.

[6] "Flows of International Finance and the International Financial System," *The Bank's World*, March 1985, pp. 13–14. From a speech delivered earlier in Delhi. "In the decade before the first oil shock, the volume of developing countries' exports increased at an annual rate of 6.5 percent while the industrial countries' GDP grew by 4.9 percent.

oped countries has not resulted in an increase in commodity prices." He adds:

> Elasticities (in 1984) comparable to the earlier period . . . should not be interpreted as encouraging for the future, coming as they did at the tail end of a long recesson during which trade in volume actually declined (and) . . . export expansion was obtained by a remarkable compression in demand in developing countries (especially) in Latin America, which registered the most impressive increase in the levels of exports.

The same tone of skepticism is expressed in a recent paper prepared by the secretariat of the U.N. Conference on Trade and Development which noted that: "there is still substantial disagreement as to the relationship between developing countries' export earnings and economic growth in the OECD area."[7]

The terrain hardly provides solid footing at a time when the universe is changing rapidly in fundamental ways and when the nature and rates of change differ so greatly among nations. This is so especially among developing countries, which, by virtue of stage of development, size, and other factors, vary greatly in their dependence on foreign funds and technical know-how and have different capacities to respond to export and import-substitution opportunities. There is a further complication when about half of developing country exports are estimated to be connected with multinational firms. In such cases there are even more serious problems in estimating such elasticities and setting

---

These numbers translated into an export elasticity of 1.3 for the developing countries with respect to GDP increase in the industrial world. Export elasticity for manufactures was nearly 3.0."

[7] UNCTAD's paper, *The International Monetary System and Financial Markets: Recent Developments and the Policy Challenge*, (TD/B/ C3/194,UNCTAD) Geneva, December 18, 1984, p. 33.

norms for such critical ratios as export earnings to debt servicing.

Given all these considerations there would thus seem to be good reason to be skeptical about the empirical support for the view that recovery in the industrial world would suffice to produce commensurate growth in the Third World.

Estimating the Required Rate of Growth for Global Recovery: Shots in the Dark?

Despite the many uncertainties in estimating the global rate of growth required to make the developing country debt manageable, many intrepid souls have dared to put forward such estimates.

These estimates range from 2.5 percent to 4 percent (with Sub-Sahara Africa receiving special treatment).

- Jacques de Larosiere, managing director of the IMF, speaking for his organization, has stated with hardly any reservation, "with a growth rate (among OECD countries) of 3 percent over the next few years, the financial problems of the developing countries are manageable provided (also that) adjustment efforts are sustained worldwide."
- William Cline, of the Institute for International Economics, gives his support to this particular number: "The analysis indicated that a critical threshold of 2.5 to 3 percent was required for OECD growth to avoid stagnation or severe deterioration in external deficits and debt/export ratios for debtor countries.";
- The World Bank seems to have accepted the 3 percent figure.

- The Economic Commission for Latin America (ECLA) puts the minimal rate at 4 percent.[8]

The more modest of these global estimates implies the need for a U.S. growth rate in excess of 5 percent a year. The attainment in 1984 of a growth rate of almost 7 percent in the United States acted as an engine of growth for the other industrialized countries, enabling them to attain a growth rate of almost 5 percent.[9] This 1984 recovery also gave a critically timed boost to exports of the problem debtor countries, especially some in Latin America, which did so well as to evoke such terms "miraculous" and- "bravura performances" and brought on a temporary euphoria.[10] Many believed the results were so favorable

---

[8] Regarding Mr. Cline's statement, *Systemic Risk,* p. 186, he notes: "A return to higher OECD growth would *(not might!)* increase export volume and *prices* . . . and a decline in the dollar from its seriously overvalued level would *raise* the dollar value of the export base." (Emphasis added.)

Regarding the position of the World Bank, see *World Development Report 1985,* passim. Regarding the G-24, see "World Growth Must Top 4 percent to Abate Debt," *CPAL News* (March 1986), p. 3. "The effects of the (global) economy's performance seem to indicate that the rate of growth must be 4 percent to allow for a solution to the debt crisis." This is based on a new study by ECLA titled "Economic Development: Evaluation and Prospectus, 1985–1995."

[9] "The OECD estimates that one-third of the growth in Western Europe in 1984 could be traced to the American recovery and the high value of the dollar . . . There is a real question as to how long the United States can continue to provide such a Keynesian stimulus to the rest of the world . . . (and tolerate a situation where) between 1981 and 1984 imports captured 42 percent of the growth of domestic spending.": Professor Lester Thurow, "America, Europe and Japan: a Time to Dismantle the World Economy," *Economist* (November 9, 1985).

[10] For Latin America as a whole the increase was about 10 percent while for Brazil it was 23 percent and Mexico, 35 percent. The kudos for the Brazilian and Mexican achievements are cited in L. Glynn's article. "Is the Latin Debt Crisis Over? Don't Kid Yourself." *Institutional*

that the strategy could be considered coherent and justified. The debtors had to severely reduce imports, borrow more to pay the interest, and increase their dependence of this export boom on the United States, which absorbed almost 90 percent of the increase in Latin American exports while running a trade deficit of more than $100 billion. All this argues hardly a sustainable trend either in terms of the rapidity of U.S. growth rates or the nation's openness to imports from the developing countries. A brief patch of sunshine does not make a summer.

After its brief 1984 spurt, the rate of increase of the U.S. GNP slowed dramatically in 1985; dropping from 5 percent to 2.8 percent in 1985. The median consensus of forecasters indicates that in 1986, even taking to account the oil price drop, the U.S. and European economies are likely to grow less than 3 percent and that U.S. imports will likely grow by less than 4 percent (compared with the increase of 27 percent in 1984).[11] For Latin American countries, the indicators point to yesterday's ephemeral current account surplus turning into today's deficit of almost $10 million—despite the continued application of severe import constraints.

Investor (May 1985). The subtitle reads, "The region may be paying its bills, but reports about the end of the debt crisis are greatly exaggerated."

[11] "The international 1986 world economic outlook envisaged an income gain for industrialized countries of three quarters of 1 percent due to lower oil prices, with 1986 growth in the United States at 2.9 percent and 3.6 percent in 1987. The more typical outlook is reflected in such articles as "The Global Recovery is Losing its Oomph," *Fortune* (November 11, 1985). The prospect is still slower growth and dangerously excessive dependence on the United States, whose trade deficit is forecast to get worse. "For at least two years, economic seers have been alerting the world to the dangers inherent in a (global) recovery dependent on a single country. Unless other nations begin to assume the role the U.S. has played, the global recovery could screech to a halt in 1987."

To underline this point, the current news about one of the troubled economies, Mexico, can be taken as illustrative. Its situation continues to give cause for worry. In 1985 it experienced a drop in exports of almost 10 percent while imports rose almost 20 percent (consumer goods by 27 percent). The result: a 36 percent drop in Mexico's trade surplus to less than $8 billion. Add to this the fall in export earnings due to the drop in the price of oil and a reduced volume of sales (from 1.5 million barrels per day in late 1985 to barely more than 1 million by early March 1986) and the tally is a loss of almost $1 billion in the first quarter of 1986 and as much as $7 billion for 1986. Those revised estimates indicate that Mexico in 1986 will earn about half of the $13 billion it had expected from oil exports. This has given rise to a call for some extraordinary measures of assistance, including an emergency package of export and trade credits and longer-term forward commitments by the United States to purchase Mexican oil which, in total could add up to between $6 and $7 billion. Another factor in the equation might be an extraordinary aid and investment program by countries, such as Japan, that have been the main beneficiaries of the oil price drop and have large trade surpluses.

Reliance on the growth rate of the industrialized developed countries and the impetus this would provide for the growth of developing countries has proved to be a chimera. The growth assumption appears to be a very weak foundation on which to base a debt management policy and no foundation at all on which to base a policy for longer-term development. This judgment is reinforced when two closely related key factors are considered, namely, what has been happening with respect to *commodity prices* on which the developing countries largely depend for their export earnings, and what has been happening with respect to *protectionist barriers* in the developed industrialized countries.

TABLE 3–1 Change in Export Prices and in Terms of Trade (1965–85)

(average annual percentage change)

Country Group	1965–73	1973–80	1981	1982	1983	1984	1985[a]
Change in export prices							
Developing countries	6.0	14.7	−2.5	−6.1	−3.7	−1.0	−11.1
Manufactures	5.1	10.9	−5.0	−1.9	−3.2	−2.8	1.2
Food	5.8	8.0	−12.1	−17.4	5.8	6.5	−12.8
Nonfood	4.0	10.3	−13.5	−8.1	12.3	−6.9	−15.9
Metals and minerals	1.8	5.8	−10.5	−9.5	3.4	−6.1	−5.9
Fuels	7.9	27.2	12.5	−3.2	−12.4	−2.1	−2.5
Industrial countries							
Manufactures	4.7	10.9	−6.0	−2.1	−4.3	−2.3	1.2
Change in terms of trade							
Developing countries	0.5	2.0	0.5	−1.1	−0.6	1.0	
Industrial countries	−0.5	−3.5	−2.1	2.0	2.1	−0.2	

[a] Estimated.

SOURCE: World Bank

Commodity Prices: What Has Happened to The Procyclical Pattern?

One of the other basic assumptions of the recovery model of the case-by-case approach is an expected procyclical rebound of commodity prices. The current levels of commodity prices, however, have remained stubbornly depressed. The weighted index of primary nonoil commodity prices in terms of U.S. dollars is about 6 percent below the low point reached in the 1982 recession. Between 1979 and 1982 commodity prices had already dropped 44 percent in real terms (nominal prices deflated by the U.S. GDP deflator), their lowest level in 30 years. In 1983 they rose slightly but have fallen back since mid-1984, dropping in 1985 more than 11 percent below the 1984 level.

The nonoil commodity price movements have displayed a pattern that is far from being procyclical, as Table 3–1 and Charts 3–1 and 3–2 reveal. For the first time, the major

---

CHART 3–1   Indexes of Real Commodity Prices (1965–84)

Index (1980 = 100)

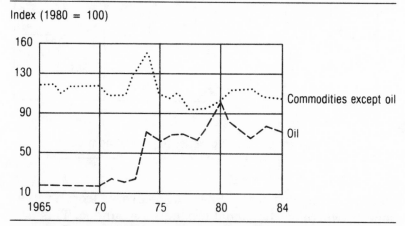

NOTE: Data are nominal prices deflated by the IMF world export unit value index.
SOURCE: World Bank data.

CHART 3–2   Primary Commodity Prices

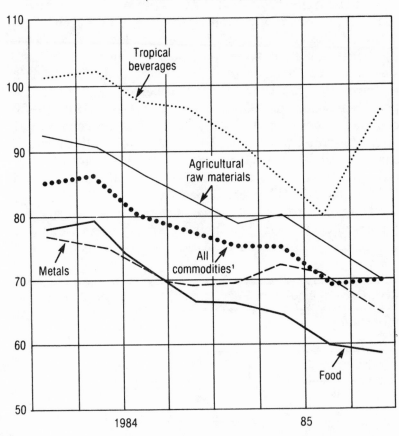

(1980 = 100; in US dollars)

¹Index comprises spot prices of 30 primary commodities.

primary commodity prices have not recovered from a recessionary trough as the global economy rebounded. This has prompted questions about the impact of scientific and technological changes that have given rise to substitutes for such commodities as copper (fiber optics and laser technology) and sugar (aspartame and saccharine) on a scale that is playing havoc with market prospects.

The fall in commodity prices has been a mixed blessing for the United States. Though 70 percent of U.S. exports are manufactured goods, the United States has become the world's largest exporter of farm and forest products. Americans are feeling the full impact of the globally depressed prices of these commodities. The beneficiaries of this trend in the terms of trade have been those countries exporting a higher percentage of manufactured goods, in particular Japan, which has become the world's largest exporter of the more technologically sophisticated products. The developing countries have been the victims by ricochet as U.S. policy makers have grappled with the nation's growing trade deficit problem. Searching for means to improve the trade balance (and protect constituents from international competition), they have turned to increasing import quotas and tariffs and subsidy programs for producers of sugar, dairy products, and other primary commodities. All of this has further depressed world prices for these commodities. The prospects for a drastic change in this situation are not bright so long as this protectionist pressure is strong.

Protectionism: The Wild-Card

Quite clearly, unless the debtor countries can earn sufficient foreign exchange through exports, there is no hope of avoiding breakdown in the debt renegotiating process. The developing countries already face a formidable array of quotas and other nontariff barriers, as Table 3–2 indicates. The "World Development Report 1985" estimates nearly one-third of the developing countries' agricultural exports and about one-fifth of their manufactured goods exports face such restrictions in entering the U.S. market, and there is mounting pressure to make these barriers even higher. In the first half of 1985, U.S. imports from the developing countries fell by 2 percent from the previous year, an ominous trend that can be attributed to the protectionist factor.

There are now several hundred protectionist bills before Congress, and the situation there has been described as "a brushfire of bipartisan support for tough trade bills." The dynamic in this protectionist movement can be gleaned from the fact that in 1979, 62 petitions were filed with the U.S. International Trade Commission (ITC); by 1983 it had tripled to almost 200. In 1980, about 20 percent of goods produced in the United States were shielded from foreign

TABLE 3–2   Percentage of Industrial Countries' Imports Covered by Nontariff Barriers

	Imports From	
Importer	Developed Countries	Developing Countries
United States	13.0	5.5
Japan	19.2	5.4
Switzerland	22.6	48.8
Sweden	1.0	7.0
Norway	8.2	10.9
Austria	15.0	8.1
European Community[a]	15.1	11.8
Denmark	9.4	19.2
Ireland	15.0	9.5
France	20.1	7.1
United Kingdom	14.9	14.3
Italy	12.5	7.0
Germany, Fed. Rep.	12.6	8.5
Netherlands	16.1	19.8
Belgium and Luxembourg	19.2	29.7

NOTE: This table is based on detailed information on nontariff barriers available in UNCTAD. The figures measure the value of imports affected by nontariff measures in relation to total imports. Import figures are from 1980, whereas the information on nontariff barriers applies to 1983. If a country's import restrictions are rigorous, it imports little and few of its imports are affected by restrictions. Thus, these figures provide little basis for comparison among countries in the total amount of restrictions.

[a] Weighted average; excludes Greece.

competition by voluntary agreements; by 1983 this had risen to more than 35 percent. Dr. Paula Stern, chairman of the ITC, recently observed, "The U.S. trade law system is being tested by an avalanche of requests for import relief. Our case load grew by 88 percent between 1981 and 1984, and so far this year it is up by 26 percent."[12]

Though the Reagan administration has indicated its wish to buck the pressure and, in some instances (as in the cases of shoe imports from Brazil and copper from Chile), it has done so, reliance on that resistance would be a rash act of blind faith given the sensitivity of the congressional system to special interests such as the dairy, sugar, textile, and tobacco lobbies. What is being contemplated has been aptly described by a U.S. congressman as "a sledgehammer approach to a problem that requires a scalpel."[13] Nor has the European Economic Community shown any receptivity to calls for more open trading arrangements, a regrettable posture but hardly surprising under prevailing conditions of high unemployment and sluggish growth. This situation is likely to get worse before it gets better. In any case, there is enough uncertainty about the timing and degree of protectionism to have it regarded as a wild card, which should unnerve even the most intrepid observer identifying the conditions that would enable the debt crisis to be resolved.

Capital Flight: Rubbing Salt in the Wound

Another factor at work in this process is the phenomenon known as capital flight, which has been characterized as

---

[12] *New York Times* (August 23, 1985).

[13] Congressman Steven Hofman, executive director of the House Wednesday Group, in commenting on the Trade Emergency and Export Promotion Act of 1985 (the Gephardt-Rostenkowski-Bentsen bill), which would impose a 25 percent import surcharge that could not be targeted to apply to any specific country but would be in force until 1991, in a letter to the *New York Times* (August 10, 1985).

"the great ripoff of the 20th century." This has greatly
exacerbated the debt problem. Instability, turmoil, poverty,
and further austerity have reinforced the decline of already
troubled economies by frightening off both foreign capital
and indigenous capital. Policy mistakes and weak administrative and legal controls in the debtor countries, including
overvaluation of the currency, have contributed to the
mammoth proportions of the capital flight, whether legally
permitted or not.

Capital flight accounts for an unquantifiable leakage
from the debtor countries and constitutes a large percentage of the reverse transfer of resources from the poor countries to the rich. The exact magnitude is difficult to pin
down because of the often illegal nature of the process.
But it is estimated that in some years in some countries
this capital flight is almost equal to the increase in the
outstanding foreign debt. The governor of the Bank of England, Robin Leigh-Pemberton, has estimated: "Virtually
all the debt incurred by Latin America in these four years
(1980–1984) can be regarded as having been used, in effect,
either directly or indirectly to finance capital flight."[14]

Focusing on the 15 countries targeted in the Baker initiative, Gary Hector, in an article in *Fortune* (December
23, 1985, titled, "Nervous Money Keeps on Fleeing"), cites
an estimate that last year's capital flight was about $8.7
billion, an amount countered by $9 billion heading the other
way, and estimates this year the debtor countries could
suffer a net loss of capital from this source alone. He writes
that the situation in this respect is getting worse because:

> The outrush of capital, while below the frenzied volume of
> a few years ago, is doing more damage than ever to the econo-

---

[14] *Financial Times (U.K.)* (January 28, 1986). His estimate is $80
billion for those years. *Business Week* (October 3, 1983), p. 133. The
countries involved included Argentina, Egypt, Indonesia, Mexico, Nigeria, the Philippines, and Venezuela.

mies of the heaviest borrowers (since in former years, such as) in 1981 and 1982, the estimated $50 billion (which) moved out . . . was more than offset by some $80 billion of newly borrowed funds coming in from banks alone.[15]

Business Week puts the figure at more than $70 billion for seven of the largest debtors from 1980 to 1982, the years when their combined debt rose by more than $100 billion.

The extreme seriousness of this phenomenon can be detected by a perusal of specific country cases. Table 3–3, based on estimates compiled by the World Bank, shows Venezuela during the four years ending in 1982 as experiencing a capital flight of 137 percent of its foreign borrowing, Argentina 65 percent, and Mexico 48 percent to list only the most flagrant cases. (The Philippines ranked in that notorious company with about 50 percent during the five years up to 1984.)

Capital flight did not start with the modern era or even with the past decade, but it seems to have become relatively more important in the late 1970s and early 1980s than it was in the early 1970s. The situation took on the dynamic of a vicious circle. Capital was being increasingly siphoned off by legal and illegal means into real estate speculation

---

[15] The author notes that "rough estimates and anecdotal evidence suggest the biggest outflow since the debt crisis heated up a few years ago have been from Mexico, Brazil, Venezuela, Nigeria, and Argentina." He then cites estimates of Morgan Guaranty Trust Co. of New York for the capital flight losses in 1984 of several Latin American countries: Mexico, $4 billion (half of the 1983 loss); Venezuela, $2.7 billion; Brazil, $2.2 billion (a 40 percent increase over 1983), "worrisome amounts" from Uruguay and Peru. The article sketches the methods used to achieve these capital movements, most of which are illegal.

For another popular treatment of the subject see L. Glynn and P. Koening, "The Capital Flight Crisis," *Institutional Investor* (November, 1984), pp. 109–19; Michael R. Sesit, *The Wall Street Journal* (December 3, 1984). For a full fledged treatment of the subject see John T. Cuddington, *Capital Flight: Estimates, Issues and Explanations*. March 1984, revised June 25, 1985, (Washington, D.C.: World Bank) (mimeo, unofficial).

TABLE 3–3   Capital Flight and Gross Capital Inflows in Selected Countries (1979–82)

Country	Capital Flight (billions of dollars)[a]	Gross Capital Inflows (billions of dollars)[b]	Capital Flight as a Percentage of Gross Capital Inflows
Venezuela	22.0	16.1	136.6
Argentina	19.2	29.5	65.1
Mexico	26.5	55.4	47.8
Uruguay	0.6	2.2	27.3
Portugal	1.8	8.6	20.9
Brazil	3.5	43.9	8.0
Turkey	0.4	7.9	5.1
Korea	0.9	18.7	4.8

[a] Data are estimates. Capital flight is defined as the sum of gross capital inflows and the current account deficit, less increases in official foreign reserves. For some countries (notably Argentina and Venezuela), the estimate may overstate capital flight to the extent that unreported imports and normal portfolio investment abroad are included.

[b] Defined as the sum of changes in gross foreign debt (public and private) and net foreign direct investment.

SOURCE: World Bank data.

and other nonproductive activities fed by inflation conditions and into foreign assets by the policy of maintaining an overvalued currency (fueled by inflationary pressures), which fed speculation that the value of the currency would drop dramatically. Then policy makers took steps that reinforced the uncertainties.[16]

This is illustrated most clearly in such cases as that of Argentina, which had its borrowings used primarily to finance capital flight rather than productive domestic investment. "The most interesting aspect of the Argentinian public external indebtedness," writes Professor Rudiger Dornbusch, "is that it appears to be matched, one-for-one

---

[16] John T. Cuddington, *ibid,* pp. 6–7.

TABLE 3-4 Some Aspects of Argentina's Financial Condition (1978–82)

Item	1978	1979	1980	1981	1982
Real exchange rate (1978–83 = 100)	92	68	66	78	109
Inflation (December to December)	176	160	101	105	165
Real interest (passive rate)	−15.6	−9.5	−4.4	6.6	−26.2
Budget deficit (percent of GDP)	10.1	9.0	11.3	16.4	17.2
Excluding debt service	1.8	2.4	7.2	8.2	5.3

SOURCES: Cavallo (1983), Data Resources, Inc., *International Financial Statistics,* and *Indicadores de Coyuntura.*

or better, by increased private holdings of external assets. But because the authorities have no access to these assets, there is nevertheless an acute debt problem."[17] The lack of any effective restrictions on capital outflow, in the environment of a blatantly mismanaged exchange rate policy, virtually invited the massive purchasing of foreign assets as a hedge against the anticipated depreciation. The massive deficits and rampant inflation made depreciation a certainty; the only question was the timing of a breakdown in the borrowing and rescheduling process, which, in Argentina's case, was brought on sooner by the Malvinas misadventure of 1982. Table 3–4 provides a few indicators of Argentina's financial instability in terms of the key factors influencing the exodus of capital.

The salient factors could be replicated in varying de-

---

[17] Rudiger Dornbusch, "External Debt, Budget Deficit and Disequilibrium Exchange Rates," *International Debt & The Developing Countries, A World Bank Symposium,* pp. 227, 229. Professor Dornbusch makes an interesting related point in observing that "expansionary policies yield the political tempation to overvalue the real exchange rate . . . (which calls for) IMF-supported adjustment programs involving stringent demand controls. An intriguing question is how an IMF program would deal with the current U.S. fiscal deficit. . . . If developing countries shared the United States' seignorage—that is, if they could pay off their foreign liabilities with their domestic currencies—the international debt problem would never have emerged."

grees in the case of almost all the major debtor countries, except for some, exemplified by South Korea, where the capital was largely channeled to productive investments enabling the debts to be serviced with current and future export earnings and private capital inflows. Where there is instability and fear for the future, the lack of effective regulatory constraints on capital mobility is a prescription for financial disaster. But the external environment has to be congenial for the mismanagement to persist for so long.

The capital flight situation has been exacerbated by U.S. policy, especially the policy of encouraging such capital movement into the United States through measures related to tax exemptions and anonymity rights for those who choose to place their capital in U.S. government bonds and other financial instruments and dollar-generating assets. This action has made a mockery of the pious admonitions by the U.S. administration to debtor countries afflicted by the capital flight virus to staunch this outflow and to reattract the foreign holdings of their nationals. The ironic twist is that these countries were being urged to rely on the market and not on regulations at a time when the U.S. interest rates were being maintained at unprecedented real levels and when the United States was relying on capital inflow to finance its fast-growing budget deficit and counter the adverse trade balance.

This gulf between ideology and reality has not gone unnoticed. The transfer paradox of capital flow from poor countries to rich ones has become even more distressing and further strained the political climate between the developed and developing worlds. This aspect of the global situation has prompted consideration of measures to force the repatriation of such capital flight. To cite but one example, Albert Hart, professor of economics emeritus of Columbia University, has proposed procedures be established to counteract the flight of capital transferred abroad through illegal means.[18] He notes, "The Mexican crisis, in particular, calls for innovative treatment of 'personal' assets acquired by diversion of loan proceeds and other government funds. . . . Specifically, a program of restitution would fit admirably into a new rescue package for Mexico that must soon take shape."

The application of the ethical principles that underlie this proposal would open a Pandora's box of issues that would be very difficult to resolve:

- If the U.S. were to attempt the task of helping debtor countries recoup some of the clearly illegal export of capital, wouldn't other countries become the havens for such funds?

- If the debtor country's policies made capital flight a compellingly logical action for any prudent investor (because, for example, of a policy of gross and unsustainable overvaluation of currency and concomitant rampant inflation), should the recipient country in which this capital is placed be held responsible and be expected to take action against those who acted "rationally" in their own interests in the light of their own country's policies?[19]

---

[18] In a letter to the editor of the *New York Times* (February 20, 1986), under the heading "On Getting Back International Ill-gotten Gains," Professor Hart observes, "There is plenty of room for argument over the famous radical proposition 'property is theft.' But suddenly we are realizing to what extent our society operates on a twist of that proposition which so far as I know nobody advocates: 'theft is property.' It is comforting that in several areas steps are being taken to apply the principle that the right use of funds acquired by theft is to hand them back to the proper owners. But many more such steps are called for."

[19] The issue is especially difficult when the regime from which the capital is fleeing is not merely ill-advised in its policies, but is also governed in the interests of a privileged group or against the interests of particular groups and is both dictatorial and life-threatening, say as

The issue may be worth pursuing for reasons of principle, but because as an operational option, it is fraught with
great difficulties, it is unlikely to yield significant results
in checking, let alone reversing, the flight of capital. Reliance will have to be placed mainly on the ability of the
debtor countries to attract back the capital held by their
own nationals in foreign accounts and other assets. Pedro-
Pablo Kuczynski, former minister in a previous Peruvian
administration and now co-chairman of First Boston International and managing director of the First Boston Corporation, has ventured to suggest the tide is turning with
regard to capital flight:

> A portion of the $25 billion or so that fled Argentina in 1979–
> 82 is ready to return, attracted by the new positive environ-
> ment as well as by rather high interest rates, (it) will be
> the first clear sign that the Latin American economies are
> really on the mend.[20]

It is not clear how much the wish may be father to the
thought. It would appear that for the immediate future
the prospects are not encouraging even under the best of
circumstances—and the circumstances are now far from
congenial. These countries are struggling under the debt
overhang that darkens the future, at least as far as the
near horizon, which is as far as investors can see.

MODELING AND REALITY

All of the separate assumptions that underlie the rationale
for managing the debt crisis on a case-by-case basis could

---

in Hitler's Germany. Under such circumstances it may not be legal to
transfer money abroad. But does a "higher morality" apply that calls
for survival through escape and through having some financial foothold
abroad after escaping the oppressive state?

[20] *International Herald Tribune* (January 27, 1986).

conceivably mesh in such a way as to yield a satisfactory outcome. But the odds are heavily weighted against this happening without benefit of an overall global perspective and framework of policies. There are sufficient conceptual and methodological uncertainties and ambiguities underlying the case-by-case model in all its various aspects to make one skeptical. When the spotlight focuses on the empirical aspects such as estimating the minimal capital requirements, the sources likely to be available and by what means and on what terms, this skepticism turns to serious doubt. When to this list are added trends in exchange rates, the terms of trade, protectionism, capital flight, and the reaction of political leaders to them, the doubt will likely turn to conviction that modeling the possible outcomes of the global debt crisis is akin to building sand castles.

The next chapter focuses on aspects of the real world with which the modelers must work if their exercises are to be regarded as relevant and helpful.

CHAPTER FOUR

The Case-by-Case Approach: Welcome to the Real World

It (the Mexican rescue) is not a perfect way, but it is flexible, and it has worked so far. Looking back from his central vantage point at what has happened to date, de Larosiere cites Talleyrand: "In history things get arranged—but badly."

Joseph Kraft[1]

Solving debt problems is mostly politics, not economics, yet today, unlike in the 1920s and 1930s, the problem is made to look as if it were solely an issue of economics.

Rudiger Dornbusch[2]

FINANCIAL FLOWS, FINANCIAL SHORTFALLS: IS THE GAP BRIDGEABLE?

The exceptional movement of capital during the 1970s is one of the critical factors that gave rise to the debt crisis. The sharp reduction in capital flows is one of the lending side adjustments that precipitated the crisis; the subsequent necessary reduction in imports on the debtors' side

---

[1] Syndicated columnist Joseph Kraft, *The Mexican Rescue*, (New York: (The Group of 30, 1984), p. 66.

[2] Professor of economics, M.I.T. at a conference on the global debt crisis. February 1985.

(since exports could expand only with a lag even under the best of circumstances) has been one of the most wrenching features of the adjustment for the debtors. The critical task is to arrest the decline in capital flows to the debtor countries and then to revive that flow to levels that can enable resumed growth. Estimation of the capital needed by the debtor countries to both service their debt and to grow and the assessment of the sources of such capital is an essential exercise in assessing the feasibility of the model on which the case-by-case approach is based.

The "Capital-Needs Estimate" Game

One of the key assumptions underlying the case-by-case approach is that the capital flows will soon resume a level and direction that is consistent with global growth.

Four estimates indicate the rough orders of magnitude of the financial gap in aggregate terms. Each estimate is based on different sets of assumptions, but taken together they indicate the range of the gap, which several authoritative sources deem to be realistic:

- The Commonwealth Secretariat's *"Report on the Debt Crisis and the World Economy"* also known as the Lever Report (after its chairman, Lord Harold Lever), estimated the gap for oil-importing countries of $75 billion to $100 billion by 1987 and $100 billion to $120 billion by 1990. This is spelled out in Table 4–1.
- The Brandt Commission Report (1983) *Common Crisis: North-South Cooperation for World Recovery,* estimated the need of the developing countries to call for a transfer of $85 billion to restore their import capacity to 1980 levels, on which basis they could hope to attain a minimally acceptable rate of investment and growth.

TABLE 4–1   Nonoil Developing Countries: Financing Gap and
the Financing Flows: Some Projections
(in billions of dollars)

	1983ᵃ	1984ᶜ	1987	1990
Financing needs:	62	63	75 (100)ᵇ	100 (120)ᵇ
Of which:				
(a) Current account deficit	56	50	63ᶜ	86ᶜ
(b) Change in reserves	6	13	12ᵈ	14ᵈ
Financed by:				
(i) Official sourcesᵉ	36	37	42	47
(a) Transfers	13	14	–	–
(b) Long-term borrowing (net)	23	23	–	–
(ii) Direct investment (net)ᶠ	8	9	12	16
(iii) Borrowing from commercial banks (net)ᵍ	20	21	24	28
(iv) Use of fund creditʰ	10	7	8	10
(v) Othersⁱ	−12	−11	−7	−5
Residual (Unmet financing gap)	–	–	(21)ʲ	(24)ʲ

NOTES: ᵃ Actual (IMF)

ᵇ Assumed (see text)

ᶜ IMF projections

ᵈ Figures assumed (see text)

ᵉ Projected for 1987 and 1990 on the assumption that they remain constant in real terms
(corresponds to IMF's assumptions)

ᶠ Assumed to grow at 9½ percent a year between 1984 and 1990 (corresponds to IMF's
assumptions)

ᵍ Derived by assuming that bank lending will increase at 5 percent a year during 1985 to
1990

ʰ Figures for 1987 and 1990 are assumptions

ⁱ Includes unrecorded capital outflow; this is assumed to decline by the end of the decade

ʲ On the assumption that the financing needs will equal $100 billion in 1987 and $120
billion in 1990.

SOURCE: *The Commonwealth Group of Experts, The Debt Crisis and the World Economy,*
Commonwealth Secretariat. London, 1984, p. 73.

- Rimmer De Vries, senior vice president of Morgan
Guaranty Trust Inc., has put forward an estimate
of a financial gap of roughly $60 billion per year
or $180 billion over three years for the 21 most heav-
ily indebted countries, even assuming a 7 percent
net increase in commercial bank lending. In subse-

quent testimony he has estimated the financial requirements of the four biggest Latin American debtors as $16 billion through 1991 if they are to have any hope of bringing their current account balances to acceptable levels.[3]

- The World Bank estimates that the 12 biggest developing country exporters of manufactured products would need $18 billion per year of new bank loans from now to 1990, if they are to reach a per capita target of 4 percent growth rate.

Particular cases highlight the difficulties ahead in meeting the minimal requirements for additional capital. In Latin America the ABM trio (Argentina, Brazil, and Mexico) illustrates the challenge of estimating and meeting this target gap.

- In 1985 *Argentina* received more than $4 billion from commercial banks and $1 billion from the World Bank and the Interamerican Development Bank, an amount roughly matched by the flight of capital. Though Argentina was thus enabled by this infusion of capital to meet its interest obligations on its $50 billion foreign debt, the austerity program that made it the current model debtor resulted in a drop in per capita income of 4 percent that year, to a level about one fifth below the 1980 income level. Unrest is reported to be growing as the outlook is clouded by falling prices for the nation's exports and by serious damage to its key export crops, grains, which account for nearly half of its export earnings.

---

[3] Rimmer de Vries, "Global Debt: Assessment and Prescriptions," statement before the Subcommittee on International Economic Policy of the Senate Foreign Relations Committee; reproduced in *World Financial Markets*, New York: (Morgan Guaranty Trust, February 1983).

- *Brazil* is less desperate despite its foreign debt of more than $100 billion. The oil price drop is expected to benefit Brazil by shaving its expenditure on that item by about $3 billion in 1986, but Brazilian finance officials are working frantically to reschedule their debt tranches as they come due and talking ominously of default.[4] But because of Brazil's program to curb rampant inflation, running at an annualized rate of more than 500 percent in early 1986, the growth rate is expected to tumble to 3 percent in 1986 from the 1985 rate of about 8 percent. With the richest 10 percent of its population absorbing half of the national income—which Mr. Funaro characterizes as one of the world's worst income distributions—the challenge is to impose the austerity that comes with this dramatic fall in income growth in an equitable way to stave off political and social upheaval and breakdown. The capital required to achieve this is difficult, if not impossible, to gauge because the factors involved in making such a calculation are not amenable to quantification. "How far," Mr. Funaro asked his *Forbes* questioner, "can consumption be reduced for a population working at a minimum wage of $35 a month?"

- The *Mexican* case has been touched upon earlier but merits mention in this context. In early 1985 it was estimated that by 1987 the financial requirements of Mexico would be as high as $4 billion annually, after taking into account the largest-ever multi-year rescheduling agreement of more than $20 billion in debts falling due up to 1990. In light of

---

[4] "Don't Push Us Too Far: Again there is talk of default—Is the debt crisis about to flare again?" *Forbes*, (February 10, 1986), an interview with Brazil Finance Minister Dilson Funaro.

the difficulty occasioned by the oil price drop, the rescheduling of Mexico's debt became necessary earlier.

- Estimates of Mexico's requirements now range from $6.5 billion in new outside financing to $10 billion, of which about $3.5 billion to $5 billion would have to come from commercial banks, which is roughly the amount Mexico was able to borrow in 1983. The banks were balking when the request was less than $3 billion.[5]

The case of Subsahara African countries provides another example of a financial gap exceeding all possible foreseeable sources. This group of countries incurred a debt that in relative terms imposes an even greater burden than for the Latin American countries. From 1977 to 1983 their outstanding and disbursed debt has grown from about $7 billion to $58 billion, a rate of increase in excess of 20 percent a year, which far exceeds the growth of their export earnings and GDPs. Estimates of the debt outstanding range from a low of $92 billion (an IMF figure) to a high of $170 billion. Thirty of these countries have a debt three and a half times their annual export earnings, the servicing

---

[5] The situation has been giving rise to questions of equitable sharing of responsibility for resolving the situation by the officials who are engaged in raising the required capital. Thus Mexico's Finance Minister Jesus Silva Herzog has warned that "something has to give; the debtor nations are paying dearly for a problem for which responsibility clearly must be shared." In a February broadcast to the Mexican people, President Miguel de la Madrid announced Mexico's financial crisis "requires sacrifices by the creditors who have been coresponsible in the process of indebtedness . . . The creditors must make an effort equivalent to that of the Mexican people: Agence France Presse (February 24, 1986.) Mr. Silva Herzog has mentioned such measures as capitalizing part of the interest to lower Mexico's annual payments of $10 billion to $12 billion in interest alone and of obtaining guarantees that Mexico will have a certain level of funds for development purposes each year.

of which absorbs on the average about 40 percent of their export earnings and is projected to rise to 44 percent by 1987, of which about 20 percent will be for interest alone.[6] For many countries the debt service obligations exceeded total export earnings.

The region has had to contend with a "scissor effect": net capital inflows falling from an annual average in 1981–82 of almost $11 billion to about $5 billion in 1985, at a time when its debt servicing had gone up from about $4 billion in 1981 to more than $10 billion. The outcome has been an increase in the foreign exchange financing gap of $12 billion. Given foreseeable sources, the region faces a shortfall of about $2.5 billion a year for the next several years.[7]

Seen in human terms it is not hard to appreciate the commentary of the *World Development Report 1984* (page 31) that "for Africa the 'debt crisis' had a different meaning": per capita real incomes down by about 5 percent from the already low 1981 levels, food production increasing at half the rate of population growth, and excessive dependence on fuelwood making the ecology fragile and droughts frequent, widespread, and exceptionally severe.

The World Bank estimates that one-half to three fourths of the African population subsists in "absolute poverty— (a condition) where people are too poor to obtain a calorie-

---

[6] The problem has been exacerbated by the changing nature of the debt, which, as a result of rescheduling conditions and new lending, has been increasingly shorter term and at higher rates. About one twelfth of the debt between 1974 and 1983 was at variable commercial rates with the average real interest rates in the 1973-83 period increasing from 2 percent to more than 6 percent. Over 25 percent of this debt is concessional, which should be contrasted with the situation 10 years before when about 44 percent was on "soft" terms.

[7] A. W. Clausen, "Don't Forget Africa," *Washington Post* (April 29, 1986).

TABLE 4–2   Selected Condition of Life Indicators
for 12 Countries

	Life Expectancy at Birth (years)	Percent Adult Illiterate M/F	Infant Mortality Rate
Ethiopia	40	92/96	146
Zaire	47	23/61	111
Sudan	48	62/86	123
Indonesia	49	22/42	92
Nigeria	43	54/86	145
Ivory Coast	47	42/76	126
Ecuador	61	18/24	81
Chile	66	6/9	33
Brazil	63	25/28	76
Mexico	66	13/19	55
Argentina	70	4/6	41
United States	74	1/1	11.4

SOURCES: Infant mortality rate and life expectancy from *World Population Data Sheet,* Population Reference Bureau Inc., 1983. Percent Adult Illiterate M/F *World's Children Data Sheet,* Population Reference Bureau Inc., 1982.

adequate diet."[8] A comparative sample of five African countries, five Latin American countries, Indonesia, and the
United States with respect to some key health and education indicators, is shown in Table 4.2. It indicates the degree
to which the people of these African countries have fallen
below the global average with respect to life expectancy,
literacy rates, and such.

It is little wonder that since 1975, 15 African countries
have had to reschedule their debt 47 times. However, the
problems is complicated by the fact that about 40 percent
of such debts are not eligible for rescheduling because the
debts are owed to what are termed "preferred creditors,"
such as the World Bank and the IMF. The need for special

---

[8] A. W. Clausen in a speech on "Poverty in the Developing Countries—1985," *Bank's World,* (January 1985), p. 11.

treatment is thus glaringly apparent. So far the response has fallen far short of even minimal requirements, even taking into account the World Bank's initiative to establish the Special Facility for Subsaharan Africa for which a little more than $1.4 billion was pledged.[9]

Sources: Where Are the Funds to Come From?

There are several sources of funds, none of which looks promising. The prospects for a substantial increase in voluntary commercial bank lending are rather bleak despite the Baker initiative, which is really a plea to "do as I ask, don't do as I do." The levels attained during the 1970s were clearly extraordinary and, *ex post*, are seen to have been exceptional and excessive.[10] The efforts of the U.S. adminis-

---

[9] The 17th member of this new agency, the United States made its contribution, $71.8 million, in early 1986, well over six months from the time the facility went into operation. This contribution was engineered by several Congressmen (led by Democrats S. Lundine, New York; M. McHugh, New York; and D. Obey, Wisconsin) over the opposition of the Reagan administration, which argued, when it decided not to join that facility, that the United States was doing enough for Africa through bilateral channels. Representative Lundine, the chairman of the House Banking Subcommittee on International Development Institutions and Finance, is reported to have observed: "To the best of my knowledge this represents the first time the Congress has mandated U.S. participation in a multilateral development bank when such participation has not been negotiated by the administration." This membership opened up the possibility for the United States to participate in the decision making on the board when loans financed by the facility are under consideration and for U.S. companies to compete for contracts on loans financed by the new facility.

The administration, in its budget document, has since taken credit for this appropriation in describing the contribution as a move that "complements and supports the administration's proposal for a comprehensive IMF-IBRD policy framework approach in the poorest countries."

[10] Bergsten, Cline and Williamson put it succinctly: "In retrospect, it seems clear that in the 1970s the private sector as a whole—and the commercial banks in particular—assumed an excessive responsibility for lending to developing countries. . . . Whether the banks 'overlent' or the countries 'overborrowed' is now a moot point; the operative conclu-

tration to increase bank lending by $20 billion over the next three years will test this judgment as to its achievability—though not its desirability. But, in any case, the amounts aimed for are clearly inadequate. Presumably, the $20 billion target was chosen because it was deemed to be attainable, rather than on the basis of what would be required to meet minimal growth targets.

Clearly, this places the major burden for providing development financing on official development assistance (ODA), whether from bilateral aid programs (which normally provide about three quarters of ODA's $35 billion per year) or from multilateral financial institutions. Bilateral aid prospects are not very promising except for a major surge in Japanese aid and investment. As can be seen in Table 4–3 and Chart 4–1, ODA has remained at roughly half of what had been pledged at the beginning of the Development Decade of the 1960s, namely, 0.7 percent of GDP.[11]

In the case of the United States, the amount of aid, at $8.7 billion was only slightly in excess of 0.2 percent of the GNP, half of the level it was 20 years ago and less than one-tenth what it was in the days of the Marshall Plan. When comparison is made with the other OECD coun-

---

sion is that excessive reliance was placed on this channel in the past," *Bank Lending to Developing Countries: The Policy Alternatives,* (Washington, D.C.: Institute for International Economics, April 1985), p. 14.

[11] Several countries have pledged to attain this target by a certain date (France by 1988, Austria, Canada, Italy, and Finland at the end of the decade with Canada setting an intermediate target of 0.5 percent of GNP by the middle of the decade); others have pledged without specifying a date (Australia, Belgium, Germany, Japan, New Zealand, United Kingdom). Two countries have set a higher target of about 1 percent, (Denmark, Netherlands, Norway, and Sweden). In September 1985, Japan drew up a ODA-doubling plan (its third), which called for a minimum of $40 billion over a seven-year period from 1986 to 1992 and a doubling of the 1985 level by that year.

The numbers over the years can be found in the OECD publication, *Development Cooperation,* and the *World Bank Atlas* issued yearly. On the recipient side, see the OECD publication, *Geographical Distribution of Financial Flows to Developing Countries,* (yearly).

TABLE 4–3   Comparison of Official Development Assistance
By DAC Member Countries

	Total Value ($ million) (1984)	Ratio to GNP (%) (1984)	Grant Element of Total ODA (%) (1983)
Netherlands	**1,268**	**1.02**	**95.2**
Norway	526	0.99	98.6
Denmark	**449**	**0.85**	**96.4**
Sweden	737	0.80	99.8
France	**3,790**	**0.77**	**88.8**
Belgium	480	0.59	97.7
Canada	**1,535**	**0.47**	**99.3**
Australia	773	0.45	100.0
W. Germany	**2,766**	**0.44**	**88.9**
Finland	178	0.36	99.7
Japan	**4,319**	**0.35**	**79.5**
Britain	1,432	0.33	98.4
Italy	**1,105**	**0.32**	**89.5**
Switzerland	286	0.30	98.5
Austria	**181**	**0.28**	**61.1**
New Zealand	59	0.27	100.0
United States	**8,698**	**0.24**	**94.4**
DAC total	28,553	0.36	91.2

NOTES: Totals and GNP ratios for W. Germany, Australia, and DAC (the Development Assistance Committee) are estimates.

Belgian figures are for 1983. Other figures are preliminary.

SOURCE: *Geographical Distribution of Financial Flows to Developing Countries,* OECD, 1984.

tries, the United States brings up the rear, even though in absolute nominal terms the $8.7 billion is the highest of any country and the highest ever achieved by the United States. However, according to the estimate of former World Bank President Robert McNamara, when allowance is made for the military component of this aid and the special geopolitical considerations that influence its allocation, the level of purely developmental aid is less than $3 billion.

This stance has been accentuated in the past few years as the U.S. administration has argued for reduced aid contributions to multilateral aid agencies and multilateral de-

Chart 4–1 Net Flows to Developing Countries in Selected Years, (1970–83)

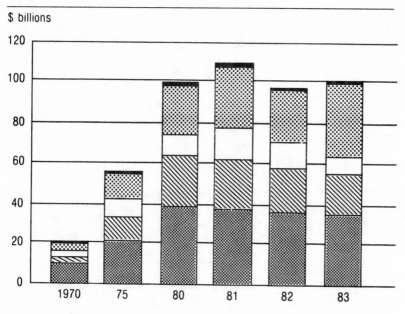

$ billions

Bond markets

Commercial bank lending

Direct foreign investment

Official nonconcessional flows

Official development assistance and grants

SOURCE: OECD 1984.

velopment banks in particular. The ostensible grounds for this policy position has been that such aid is not needed and/or that congressional (popular) support is not likely. This negativism manifested itself most dramatically on two recent occasions:

Chart 4–2   Net Capital Flows (1970–84) (Net flows to developing countries)

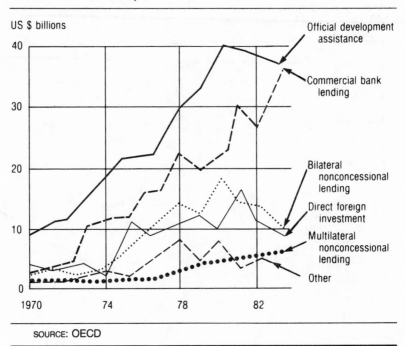

US $ billions

Official development assistance

Commercial bank lending

Bilateral nonconcessional lending

Direct foreign investment

Multilateral nonconcessional lending

Other

40

30

20

10

0

1970   74   78   82

SOURCE: OECD

- In 1982–83, during the seventh round of pledging for the "soft window" or concessional lending arm of the World Bank Group, called the International Development Association (IDA), the United States stood alone as the only country arguing for reducing the level of its contribution. It sought to reduce the amount of IDA funding by 25 percent from the level of IDA 6, a reduction of 40 percent in real terms.
- In 1985 the United States refused to endorse or support the special agency of the World Bank, the Special Facility for Subsahara Africa, which was set

up for meeting an emergency situation in that part of the world. (This facility was conceived in part to make up for the shortfall in the IDA 7 pledges below "minimal" levels.) This policy posture is reflected in Charts 4–3 and 4–4, which show the rapid growth of official aid flows over the 1970s (from $11 billion to $42 billion in multilateral aid and from $6 billion to $18 billion in bilateral aid), characterized by an increase in multilateral aid share from about 15 percent to more than 30 percent and the entry of OPEC and the European Community as significant donors. The trend over the first half of this decade reveals both a drop in official aid flows to about $40 billion in nominal terms (which is a substantial drop in real terms) and a proportionately greater fall in multilateral aid.

Over the next three years the expectation is that roughly $40 billion is the likely maximum contribution from the IMF. Increases in the IMF quota and the General Agreement to Borrow (GAB) would contribute about $15 billion to $20 billion in usable currencies through the quota increase and about $12 billion through expanding the GAB, which, for the first time, has declared developing countries eligible. With regard to the World Bank, on the basis of its present capital base and its "gearing ratio," its rate of disbursements could increase by the $3 billion stipulated in the Baker proposal, but only *if* there was a dramatic shift toward quick-disbursing nonproject lending. This could be a dubious achievement if won at high cost—as discussed later in Chapter 7. Some other concessional sources will need to be found that will not be subject to the vagaries of bilateral aid, foreign investment, and commercial bank flows.

In this connection, many proposals have been put forward for the consideration of the donor community. The

Chart 4–3 Commitments and Disbursements of IMF and World Bank (1976–85)

International institutional lending (fiscal years)

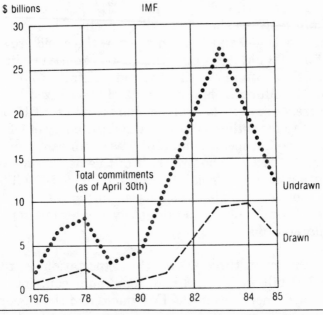

IMF

$ billions

Total commitments
(as of April 30th)

Undrawn

Drawn

1976   78   80   82   84   85

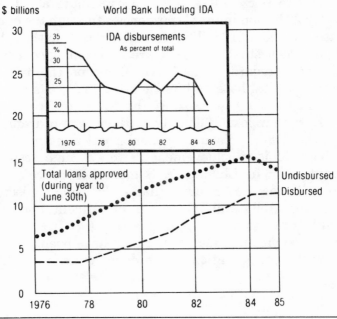

World Bank Including IDA

$ billions

IDA disbursements
As percent of total

Total loans approved
(during year to
June 30th)

Undisbursed

Disbursed

1976   78   80   82   84   85

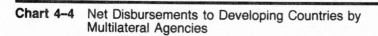

Chart 4–4 Net Disbursements to Developing Countries by Multilateral Agencies

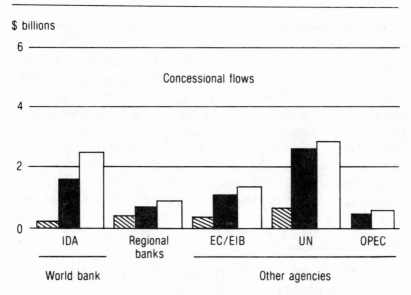

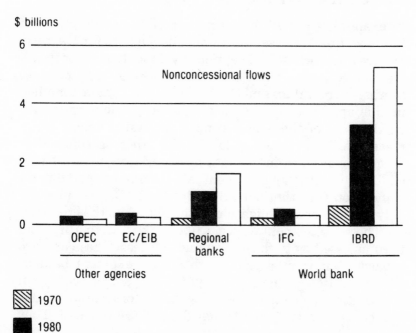

NOTE: Data for regional banks comprise disbursements by the African Development Bank, the Asian Development Bank, and the Inter-American Development Bank. EC/EIB indicates the European Investment Bank of the European Communities.

SOURCE: OECD 1984.

levying of taxes on the use of the common property resources of the globe, the oceans, and space is a perennial.
More than ever, these proposals merit serious consideration. At the same time, special efforts are needed to assure
more effective utilization of such financial resources. The
renewed focus on aid coordination among multilateral and
bilateral aid agencies is a welcome sign that the present
institutional arrangements need to be improved. But none
of this can be expected to yield significant returns in the
near term, which is all important for easing pressure during
the present phase of the debt crisis. The relevance for the
longer-term resolution of the debt crisis (broadly defined)
is, however, very great.

THE IMPACT OF BURDEN-SHARING AND ADJUSTMENT: THE LDC SIDE

In examining the empirical nature of the assumptions of
the modeling exercises that underlie support for the case-
by-case approach, it is exceptionally difficult, if not impossible, to incorporate those other real-world assumptions pertaining to the values and the sociopolitical dynamic implied
in this approach. On one side, the adjustment called for
on the part of the debtor countries entails, among other
measures, import strangulation and other sacrifices that
severely constrain immediate hopes of growth as a trade-
off for debt servicing and eventual attainment of creditworthiness; on the other side, the adjustment process presumably calls for some obligations to be placed on the creditors.

These adjustments need to be looked at in turn and
then assessed as to feasibility and fairness. These are two
separate but related criteria that are important because
the perception of hope and equity are part of reality. In
this context, collective psychological factors cannot be dis-
missed as merely the stuff that dreams are made of. They

are intangible factors, but no less real in their impact—as any politician can attest.

Under the best-case scenario, the case-by-case approach envisages all of the heavily indebted countries (except possibly South Korea) attaining very low rates of growth—if they grow at all in absolute or in per capita terms—until possibly the early 1990s, when their growth rates return to the levels of the 1960s and 1970s. For low-income Subsaharan countries, even this modest per capita growth rate would not be conceivable before the next century—if then.

A recent U.N. Economic Commission for Latin America (ECLA) document notes, perhaps with a little exaggeration but a large kernel of truth, "the spectacular turnaround of about U.S. $33 billion in the merchandise trade balance between 1981 and 1983 was due entirely to the no less dramatic fall of imports."[12] The process is described as a policy of "import strangulation." In some Latin American countries the import cutting process was extreme: Argentina and Chile reduced the volume of their imports by 50 percent between 1980 and 1982, Brazil by 20 percent, Mexico by almost 66 percent since 1981, and Venezuela by more than 60 percent in 1983 alone. Per capita incomes at the end of this "successful" year were almost 10 percent lower than in 1980 and roughly comparable to the level of 1976. The decline in per capita income in 1982 and 1983 occurred in one of every two Latin American countries, a phenomenon that occurred before 1979 in only 1 in 10 Latin American countries. The improvement in the trade balance of the indebted countries was bought at a very high price. How does one measure the social and political tensions and other costs in terms of human welfare? There have been flare-ups of civil unrest, such as the mass demon-

---

[12] *Adjustment Policies and Renegotiation of the External Debt,* E/CEPAL/G.1299, Santiago, April 1984, p. 21 and Tables 4 & 5.

strations and food riots in the Dominican Republic, Morocco, Brazil, and elsewhere, immediately after it was announced that austerity measures included in the recently negotiated debt rescheduling packages called for drastic reductions or elimination of food and other subsidies.[13] The situation in many of the debtor countries has been described as a powder keg waiting for a match.

A World Bank vice president estimated in mid-July 1983 that, in order to meet debt repayment requirements, the import bill of the developing countries would have to be reduced by a further $50 billion per year.[14] The devastating impact this would have on the lives of ordinary people in heavily indebted countries, particularly in Latin America and Africa, makes this prospect unthinkable. Because the cost in social and political terms can be clearly seen only *after* the fact, the breaking point may be uncertain, but the signs of stress are all too evident now. The situation is likely to get worse before it gets better. The current price paid in economic terms may also prove to have been very steep in terms of its effects on essential investment and maintenance, constraining future growth—including export growth.

Without lessening the responsibility and blame of the heavily indebted countries themselves for misguided policies, incompetence and corruption, it bears remembering that the debtor countries have already paid dearly in a material sense and in terms of the traumatic effects of sudden changes of circumstance, much of which lay outside their control. Consider the 1970s with its exceptional vola-

---

[13] The implications of this process are elaborated in profusion. Perhaps the most comprehensive is the document issued by the U.N. Economic Commission for Latin America, (ECLA), *Adjustment Policies and Renegotiation of the External Debt*, E/CEPAL/G.1299, Santiago, April 1984.

[14] Anne Kreuger, in a speech reprinted in *Finance & Development* (July 1983).

tility of exchange rates and the sudden skyrocketing of interest rates and the value of the dollar, the fall in commodity prices, and the related adverse movements in the terms of trade, the oil price hikes with prices denominated in appreciating dollars. Almost all of these conditions were the consequence of policy decisions taken by the major industrial nations and by the United States in particular, given its strategically important role on the global economic and financial stage. When the industrialized nations had a cold, almost all of the developing countries were destined to have pneumonia, unless, like India and China, they were deliberately cautious and decided for political or other reasons to resist the blandishments of bankers flouting the credit that was abundantly available, often at negative real interest rates.

It is difficult to measure the effects of the recession and of other related changes in the terms of trade, interest rates, and exchange rates on the various players on the world stage. But the impact on the developing world was devastating and, as such, severely conditions what they can do to remedy the situation. It is therefore relevant to have a sense of the asymmetrical impact in so far as it affected both developed and developing countries.

For the developed industrialized countries, the effect was appreciable as reflected in increased unemployment and reduced real incomes. With regard to the employment effect, Japan and the United States appear to have suffered least, with unemployment never rising to double-digit percentage levels as happened in Europe. The United States bears responsibility for the sudden and dramatic imposition of an extremely contractionary monetary policy that precipitated the recession as a deliberate price the United States *chose* to pay for curbing inflation and rescuing the dollar. This policy, in attracting capital through high interest rates and in thereby also appreciating the value of the dollar, exacerbated the adverse trade balance with atten-

dant adverse implications for employment and incomes—
and pressure for protection against imports through quotas
and tariffs. A $36 billion trade deficit in 1980 increased
to $123 billion by 1984 and is now in the $200 billion
range.

To turn to the human dimension of the cold statistical
record, this adverse income effect is reflected in several
indicators:

1. The median American family's income in real dollars
   fell by 5 percent from 1981 to 1983, leaving the average wage in real terms of the American worker at
   a level where it had been 20 years before.
2. The level of wages relative to the price of capital
   fell by 37 percent between 1972 and 1983, which
   helped ease the adverse employment impact that
   would have followed.
3. The increase in employment in the United States
   was almost completely in the low-paying service sectors, a sector where a higher percentage of the work
   force receives the legal minimum wage, which is 40
   percent of average hourly wages (with almost 10 percent of them working at less than that legal minimum).
4. The percentage of the U.S. population listed as having too little income to meet minimal needs began
   to rise after 1973, but rose dramatically in the 1981–
   82 recession to reach 14 percent.[15]

There is a price to be paid by even the rich and powerful
countries (but usually borne most heavily by the poor and
weak within such countries) for the slow growth and profound structural changes that have been especially pro-

---

[15] For a broad-brush sketch of the impact, see Professor Robert B.
Reich, "Towards a New Public Philosophy," *Atlantic Monthly.* (May
1985), p. 74. See also Lester Thurow, "America, Europe and Japan,"
Economist (November 9, 1985).

nounced during the past dozen years and particularly the past four. But this pales in comparison to the impact on the developing countries, especially the very poor ones that lack the resistance to shock and the resilience to bounce back.

With respect to the impact on the developing countries, William Cline has estimated that about $250 billion of the external debt of the oil-importing developing countries can be attributed to the increased cost of oil imports from 1973 to 1982. On average an additional $25 billion of foreign exchange had to be spent per year by these countries for this one item and related costs. At the same time, they had to adjust to a reduction in the foreign exchange available to pay for other imports and to service their debts. These items have been estimated by Cline to amount to about $200 billion during the 1981–82 recession, broken down as follows:[16]

1. The annual export earnings of the nonoil-producing developing countries dropped by about $100 billion as a result of the reduction in the volume of exports and the adverse terms of trade (which takes account of the fall in commodity prices to their lowest level in 40 years).
2. The debt servicing costs rose by about $40 billion because of the rise in interest rates above their historic averages and the appreciation of the dollar in which currency most of their loans were denominated.

To this should be added,

3. The reduction in foreign exchange because of the drop in the level of net private lending and private

---

[16] William Cline, "International Debt: From Crisis to Recovery?" *American Economic Association, Papers and Proceedings* (May 1985), p. 186.

investment flows, which declined about $60 billion over the both years (from $50 billion in 1979 to minus $15 billion by 1983).

The estimated impact of these exogenous shocks on the external debt of the oil-importing developing countries

---

TABLE 4–4   Impact of External Shocks on External Debt of Nonoil Developing Countries (billion dollars)

Effect	Amount
Oil price increase in excess of US inflation, 1974–82 cumulative*	260
Real interest rate in excess of 1961–80 average: 1981 and 1982	41
Terms-of-trade loss, 1981–82	79
Export volume loss caused by world recession, 1981–82	21
Total	401
Memorandum items	
Total debt: 1973	130
1982	612
Increase: 1972–82	482

SOURCE: © 1984 Institute for International Economics. Reproduced by permission from William R. Cline, *International Debt: Systemic Risk and Policy Response* (Washington: Institute for International Economics, 1984), p. 13.
    * Net oil importers only.

TABLE 4–5   Impact of External Shock to the Brazilian Economy

Item	1978	1979	1980	1981	1982
LIBOR	8.9	12.1	14.2	16.8	13.2
Terms of trade (1977 = 100)	76	79	65	55	54
Oil price (U.S. dollars, 1977 = 100)	101	127	238	275	260
Actual debt increase (cumulative, billions of U.S. dollars)		7.4	16.7	27.1	35.2
Oil and interest effect[a] (cumulative, billions of U.S. dollars)		3.6	11.7	23.5	34.8

    [a] For method see text.
    SOURCES: IMF.

TABLE 4-6   Impact of External Shocks on the Balance of Payments of Selected Developing Countries (average annual percentage of GNP)

Country	1974-75	1979-80	1981-82
Reschedulers[a]			
Argentina	−0.6	−1.9	−6.4
Brazil	−3.7	−2.8	−8.6
Chile	−4.7	−1.2	−13.3
India	−2.6	−1.6	−4.2
Ivory Coast	0.5	−5.6	−18.9
Jamaica	−9.6	−13.3	−29.4
Mexico	−1.0	−0.2	1.0
Peru	−4.5	−1.5	−5.6
Nigeria	16.7	5.8	3.8
Morocco	0.2	−4.0	−9.7
Philippines	−6.2	−2.4	−10.1
Yugoslavia	−6.7	−2.0	−10.0
Nonreschedulers			
Colombia	−1.4	−3.6	−8.3
Kenya	−8.1	−8.7	−19.0
Egypt	−8.7	−0.8	−1.2
Tunisia	−2.1	2.7	1.9
Korea	−9.5	−8.1	−21.7
Indonesia	12.0	5.6	5.4
Tanzania	−9.3	−6.0	−14.3
Thailand	−3.7	−2.3	−10.1

NOTE: External shocks are defined as the impact on the balance of payments of: (a) changes in the terms of trade; (b) a decline in the growth rate of world demand for a country's exports; and (c) increases in interest rates. Data for 1974–75 show the change from 1971–73; data for 1979–80 and 1981–82 show the change from 1976–78.

[a] Countries that had rescheduled as of the end of 1984.

SOURCE: Balassa 1981; Balassa and McCarthy 1984.

is set out schematically in Table 4–4, on Brazil in Table 4–5, and on several other developing countries in Table 4–6.

Other estimates indicate the impact on the non-oil-producing developing countries is roughly of the same magnitude.[17] The combined effect of the recession and interest rate changes between 1982 and 1984 in terms of foreign exchange losses has on the average amounted to 10 percent of the GDP of the oil-importing developing countries. (Countries such as Jamaica have lost as much as 33 percent and Sri Lanka, 50 percent). For all developing countries, the *Economist* has estimated these losses have amounted to $65 billion in 1985 alone.[18] Even under the most favorable of the scenarios underlying the case-by-case approach there is certainly very little hope of making up for this "loss" of income suffered by the developing countries as a result of the recession.

The Impact of Burden-Sharing and Adjustment: the Banking Side

On the other side of the debt equation are the commercial banks. At the time the debt crisis broke in August 1982, U.S. banks had about $350 billion, or 520 percent of their

---

[17] Dragoslav Avramovic, *South* (April 1983), p. 14, estimates the gap resulting from the recession effects to be $180 billion, of which oil-importing developing countries accounted for $100 billion. Albert Fishlow, "The Debt Crisis: Round Two Ahead," *Adjustment Crisis in the Third World*, ed. R. Feinberg and V. Kallab, (Washington, D.C.: Overseas Development Council, 1984), pp. 36–43, calculates different estimates and would seem to be in line with Cline's estimates in its aggregate.

[18] "Poor Man's Gift," Economist (November 30, 1985), totals the boost to the OECD countries from the last year's drop in prices of commodities (by 10 percent), of metals (by 15 percent), and of oil (by about 6 percent) that have been imported from developing countries during the last year. [With oil prices having gone down by about 50 percent since then, the calculated amount of this involuntary "gift" has increased substantially.] "That means that consumers (in OECD countries) are now paying about $65 billion a year less for the same amount of raw materials than they did 12 months ago . . . (which amounts to) a bonus of 0.7 percent of their GDP." This, it is noted, is more than twice the amount that the biggest debtors have paid to their banker creditors in the past year.

capital (equity, subordinated debentures, and reserves for loan losses), loaned outside the United States.[19] By 1985 this international exposure had been slightly reduced to about $330 billion, but this represented only 340 percent of capital because there had been time to increase equity and loan-loss reserves. Commercial banks' exposure with regard to developing countries went up slightly in those years to about $140 billion but clearly declined as a percentage of their capital and underwent a slight sectoral shift to reduce the relative exposure to the developing countries in greatest difficulty.

As Table 4–7 indicates, the assets represented by these loans to developing countries still amounted in 1984 to more than twice the capital assets of some of the major U.S. banks and much more than 100 percent of the nine major banks in the United States and the six major ones in Canada. The situation with respect to the major European banks was not too different. Notwithstanding these circumstances, the posture of the global banking community has been, at least on the surface, one of calm assurance. But, in the words of Lord Harold Lever, the banking system has "built a structure of debt that must surely be the largest and most remarkable financial house of cards ever created."

The structure has so far proven to be sturdier than the metaphor suggests, but it would be foolhardy to make light of the dangers inherent in this situation should a metaphoric wind begin to blow with some force. The vulnerability to which the private commercial banks, and by implication the entire banking system, are exposed can be discerned from the frequency and frenzy of the emergency rescheduling process, which has been aptly called crisis

---

[19] About $135 billion of this total of international assets, or almost 200 percent of their capital, was owed by developing countries. Developing countries, which subsequently have sought rescheduling, accounted for about 130 percent of their capital.

TABLE 4-7 Exposure of Major U.S. and Canadian Banks to Selected Developing Countries, 1984 (billions of dollars and percent)

U.S. Banks (1984)	Exposure[a] U.S. $	% of Bank Capital			Int. Nonperforming Loans ($mm)	Int'l Loan Losses ($mm)
Manufacturers Hanover	7.8	268.5%				
Chase Manhattan	7.4	212.7				
Citicorp	12.5	206.7				
Chemical	4.6	196.7				
Bankers Trust	3.3	177.6				
Total 9 money center banks	53.2	179.2				
Canadian banks (1985)	Exposure[b] Can. $	% of Bank Capital			Int. Nonperforming Loans ($mm)	Int'l Loan Losses ($mm)
Royal Bank of Canada	5.5	167%			1223	340
Canadian Imperial Bank of Commerce	3.2	130			262	225
Bank of Montreal	5.2	186			606	166
Bank of Nova Scotia	3.9	175			318	278
Toronto Dominion Bank	2.6	105			221	131
National Bank of Canada	1.8	199			37	150
Total of 6 major banks	22.2	160				

SOURCE: (for U.S. banks) Anatole Kaletsky, *The Costs of Default,* (New York: Priority Press Publications, 1985). (for Canadian banks) *Financial Post* (February 15, 1986).

[a] Includes six debtor countries: Mexico, Brazil, Venezuela, Argentina, Philippines, Chile.
[b] Includes all Latin American borrowers.

management.[20] Banking officials have been frantically adhering to a schedule that averages more than one bargaining session every other week somewhere in the world, most often within the framework of the so-called Paris Club."[21]

The present magnitude and intensity of this process can be illustrated by the fact that in the quarter century up to mid-1982 only 24 countries had been involved in renegotiating their debts, an average of one a year. The total for these renegotiations amounted to about $20 billion. In contrast, one year after the crisis broke into the open in mid-1982, 15 countries came to the table to renegotiate almost $6 billion. The process has since been gathering considerable momentum as is shown in Chart 4–5. In all, from 1982 to 1984, 35 countries were involved in debt renegotiations totaling about $170 billion, many rescheduling several times. In 1985 the total rescheduled was $120 billion.[22]

---

[20] Henry A. Kissinger. "International Trade: It's Time to Change the Rules of the Game," *Washington Post* (November 22, 1984).

[21] The Paris Club (and to a lesser extent the London Club) are the labels attached to a process or institutional arrangements for debt relief. The name derives from the locale of the first meeting in 1956 when government-guaranteed debt was rescheduled. The Paris Club concerns itself with debts to governments or debts guaranteed by governments. There are also ad hoc consortia or advisory committees that represent commercial bankers who meet to consider uninsured debts to financial institutions, sometimes called the London Club. They negotiate refinancing of maturing debts and the restructuring of other debts as well as arrangements for new loans if the need arises, a form of lending that is known as "concerted lending." The Paris Club efforts have proven most effective in the case of bunching of loan payments due but much less helpful where structural problems underlie the need for rescheduling.

[22] In the last two years six countries engaged in rescheduling previously rescheduled debt on a total of eight occasions, a pattern that also testifies to the pressure under which these meetings have to operate and the great difficulties the Paris Club has in handling deep-seated debt problems.

Chart 4–5   Multilateral Debt Reschedulings (1975–84)

Number of reschedulings

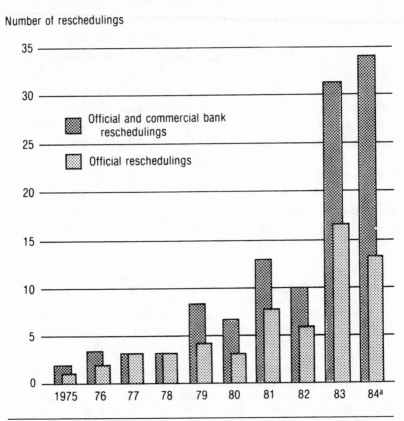

[a] Data include commercial bank reschedulings agreed to in principle but not signed as of the end of 1984.

SOURCE: World Bank data

The era of voluntary lending has given way to the age of involuntary lending or forced marriages. By 1983 about half of the lending by private commercial banks to developing countries was arranged as part of the debt rescheduling packages for 10 of the large debtors, arrangements that incorporated more favorable terms for the lenders, thereby providing incentives for the reluctant smaller banks to stay in the club.

The advantage to the major banks in keeping the smaller ones in the rescheduling arrangements goes beyond the question of limiting what the major banks might otherwise be called upon to add to their existing commitments. The syndication technique is a form of collective action that diversifies risk among a greater number of lenders but, by the same token, can also raise the cost of default to borrowers by giving greater credibility to sanctions when they are collective and, at the same time, reduce the problems of "moral hazard" and the "free rider."[23] As a result of this process, the financial community has been able to reschedule the debts outstanding by a process of concerted lending, the euphemism for forcing reluctant members of the syndicate to stay aboard, so as to avoid the so-called free rider problem. Part of the interest due has been melded into the new loan or capitalized, usually at rates of interest higher than the original loans in terms of the spread above the London Inter-Bank Rate (LIBOR). Only a few have had to write down part of their outstanding loans, some quietly through discounting them on a secondary market.[24]

Thus, the pain inflicted on the private banks has been more of a psychic nature, as they sweat out the rescheduling exercises and are pressured to get in ever deeper. Occasionally they face the question as to whether some loans have to be written down or some proposal for debt relief consid-

---

[23] See Alexander Swoboda, "Debt and the Efficiency and Stability of the International Financial System," *International Debt and the Developing Countries: A World Bank Symposium,* (Washington, D.C.: World Bank, 1985), pp. 158–59; also Jeffrey D. Sach, "LDC Debt in the 1980s: Risk and Reforms," *Crises in the Economic and Financial Structure,* ed. Paul Wechtel (Lexington, Mass.: D.C. Heath, 1982).

[24] Nicholas D. Kristof, "The Marketing of Latin Debt: the Quiet Growth of a Specialty," *New York Times* (July 17, 1985).

ered. This stands in sharp contrast to the sacrifices expected of the debtors.

The case-by-case approach is accepted, albeit reluctantly for now, as "the least bad option," to use Professor Fishlow's phrase. This acceptance, however, is being questioned with ever-increasing skepticism and bitterness, leading many participants and analysts to look to other options, some of which involve only marginal changes: we consider this in the next chapter. The more general proposals, are considered in the sixth chapter.

CHAPTER FIVE

Proposals: Case-by-Case Plus: Going Beyond Damage Control

So far the major Western governments have insisted that the problem be addressed strictly on a case-by-case basis among the IMF, the commercial banks and the debtor countries. This is ludicrous. The debt problem is no longer simply an economic problem but a political one—and it cannot be "solved" until the governments of the developed countries get involved in the negotiations.

A. Roy Megarry[1]

The fundamental problem of many debtors: their debt is growing faster than their new export proceeds; they will simply never catch up. . . . For these countries, the banks and industrial governments should consider writing off part of the debt . . . provided that countries benefiting from such a "radical" treatment do not present a risk to the system.

Christine A. Bogdanowicz-Bindert[2]

---

[1] Publisher of the *Globe & Mail* (Toronto), in an article titled, "Third World Crisis: Trade is the Only Panacea," *Globe and Mail* (May 21, 1985). "Managing the debt problem by stumbling from crisis to crisis is no solution. (Nor is) suggesting that Third World countries simply tighten their belts by introducing austerity programs and reducing government spending which is like telling a starving man to go on a diet for the sake of his health."

[2] Christine A. Bogdanowicz-Bindert, "World Debt: The United States Reconsiders," *Foreign Affairs*, (December 1985), pp. 272–73.

WHY NOT LEAVE IT TO THE MARKET PROCESS?

Realism counsels preparing for the worst while hoping for the best. When the worst-case scenario has a reasonably high probability, voices of prudence arise to warn that no one can know whether—and if so, when—a crisis sequence might arise, triggered by one or more of the so-called problem debtor countries declaring an inability or an unwillingness to service even the interest payments on debts that seem to grow ever larger and carry ever-higher spreads. The same voices of prudence, emboldened by an amalgam of motives from hard-headed self-interest to conciliatory compassion, have moved from issuing warnings to launching appeals for action that goes beyond the ad hoc case-by-case approach.

There is now a long catalogue of proposals meant to transcend the limitations perceived to be embodied in the case-by-case approach. The Bank of England is said to have listed more than 150 of them. Varied as they are, all of them share one common feature, namely, they question the wisdom and/or the efficacy of the present approach—even when it is modified through multiyear rescheduling, which overcomes the serious disadvantages of "short-leash financing."

Before reviewing these proposals, we might consider the approach of those who advocate what might be considered a nonapproach to the debt crisis. These critics would prefer nonintervention by governmental agencies, whether national or international, on the grounds that such intervention, no matter how well intentioned, obscures or distorts the market signals. This assumes it is the so-called market forces that ought to guide the adjustment process and allocate between the debtors and creditors both the costs of mistaken imprudent decisions and the benefits of wise or lucky decisions. Thus, the banks would be forced to acknowledge the loss in value of their loans-receivable assets and the debtors would, presumably, be under much greater pressure from the banks to service their debts.

This is the remedy without illusions. Bankers would have to face the reality squarely that the sovereign debts are not worth their value and would have to do what they could—on their own—to lessen the write-down of the market value of the debts. For the debtors, this process holds a greater likelihood of a reduction of debt and of payments due through a so-called secondary market and loan sales.[3] The serious downside of this *laissez-faire* approach is twofold. First, there is a considerable risk of paralysis and panic in the capital markets and there are associated upfront contingent costs for both the creditors and the debtors. The creditors, especially the major banks, might face immediate book losses that would have to be absorbed. Under certain conditions, such losses could threaten their solvency. Second, public confidence in the banking system might be shaken, which could snowball into a systemwide collapse.

As for the debtors, they might find their loans in an unregulated market falling in value much faster than if there were a referee or organizer involved, such as the IMF. It has been estimated that at the end of 1983, most Latin American loans in an unregulated secondary market were trading between 75 percent and 85 percent of their book value. The most extreme case is that of a Nicaraguan loan traded at 10 percent of its book value.[4] This discount

---

[3] A loan sale involves a bank unloading all or part of a loan on its books to other banks or to pension funds, insurance companies, and so on. Such loan sales are common within the U.S. banking system. No banks were selling loans three years ago and now it is reported that all or most of the leading U.S. banks are doing so. One financial analyst commented that "loan sales (are) one of the most significant structural changes in banking in my 18 years as an analyst."

[4] Peter Brimelow, "Why the U.S. Shouldn't Fill the IMF's Till," *Fortune* (November 14, 1983).

marketing could be very disruptive and exacerbate the problem for those countries that have, or believe they have, a significant enough stake in a process that can keep funds flowing from the private commercial banking sector. Even if that flow has slowed to a trickle for almost all of them, whether creditworthy or not, every drop counts under desert conditions. But all the developing countries would probably unite on an issue of principle. If a risk is to be taken and a price is to be paid in the form of a severe reduction or cutoff of such commercial bank lending, the borrowing countries would want to have that decision made as a matter of deliberate and calculated policy rather than at the whims and fancies of impersonal market forces with its metaphoric invisible hand.

A variant of this market approach has been put forward as a means of easing the debt burden. This proposal would establish, by agreement between the creditors and debtors, some means by which the debts could be converted into negotiable bonds or into shares of some parastatal firms that would give the creditors some claim on the productive assets of the debtor country.[5] The market would determine the value of these assets.

This approach has also received a very cool reception. There are troublesome nuts and bolts questions about some critical aspects of the process of converting the debt assets into equity, such as how the market could be organized without government involvement and how the parties con-

---

[5] The proponents of these ideas include Allan H. Meltzer, "A Way to Defuse the World Debt Bomb," *Fortune* (November 28, 1983), and Norman Bailey, *Exchange Participation Notes: An Approach to the International Financial Crisis*, Washington, D.C.: (Georgetown University Center for Strategic and International Studies, 1983). Professor Milton Friedman, in testifying before a congressional committee, opposed any intervention by the IMF and opposed the increase in the IMF quota on that ground.

cerned can arrive at a mutually acceptable correct price.[6] A more immediate question pertains to how, in the interim, to avoid an imminent threat of panic in capital markets, major bank failures, and a serious breakdown in the global financial system. In any case, neither creditors nor debtors can be assured they would gain any advantage for themselves in this approach. This alone dooms the idea to a marginal role at best.

Without fanfare and proclamations, there has been a slow but steady introduction of ad hoc market developments in the world financial system.[7] The banking community remains hesitant about publicizing this spontaneous development, but it has been looked upon favorably by many, including senior officials of the World Bank who wrote the statement placed before the April 1985 meeting of the Development Committee that stated:

> Wider application of new financing techniques requires broader and deeper secondary markets. (But) secondary markets—especially for loans to developing countries—are distrusted by some bankers who do not want to publicize the fluctuating value of their assets.

This observation touches a raw nerve in the current debt crisis management, namely, the interests of and the receptivity of the financial community to the proposals be-

---

[6] We can count a market-oriented proposal as a form of intervention because the market in this case has to be organized and supported by government even if only to assure a regulatory framework for reasons of safety and fairness.

[7] Nicolas D. Kristof, "The Market for Latin Debt: A Quiet Specialty,—*New York Times* (July 17, 1985) "Sales of Latin debt are believed to have begun (with Argentine loans) in the spring of 1982 during the Falkland War (and) resumed that autumn after Mexico announced it would be unable to meet its obligations. Volume picked up enough in late 1983 (for it) to be called a market." He cites World Bank support for the secondary market as "a means of widening the range of lenders and thus increasing the stability of the global financial system."

ing put forward. Unsponsored and largely unacknowledged, this secondary market for sovereign developing country loans has been insidiously growing in size and scope over the past few years, indicating the power of the market forces to adapt the debtor-creditor relationship to the changing realities of international economic relations. However, there is good reason to fear that this manner of adaptation or adjusting to reality, if it continues to be left unregulated, will exact too high a social, economic, and political price from both the debtors and creditors. Its outcome would inflict greater costs on the weaker or more vulnerable players in this debt rescheduling process. The "law of the jungle" is clearly not acceptable as a generalized solution to this problem.

This points to the Achilles' heel of the free market approach—there is a need for collective action to promote a valuable "public good."[8] That public good is simply the maintaining or creating conditions necessary for growth and other desirable objectives. This, after all, is the basic rationale for governmental intervention directly and through the IMF, the World Bank, and other institutions or instruments. The nature and magnitude of the debt problem, and related issues, makes it one where its costs and benefits are in large part not counted by the players immediately and directly involved. A global frame or reference is needed so as to take account of the costs of widespread breakdown that might follow from a major default and the benefits of avoiding this disastrous outcome. Thus, there is widespread skepticism about

---

[8] On the application of this key concept in welfare economics to the debt problem, see Martine Guerguil, "The International Financial Crisis: Diagnoses and Prescriptions," *CEPAL Review*, no. 24, December 1984, p. 161; and Robert Devlin, "The Burden of Debt and the Crisis: Is It Time for a Unilateral Solution?" *CEPAL Review*, no. 22, Santiago, April 1984. See also, Charles Kindleberger, "International Public Goods Without International Government," *The American Economic Review*, March 1986.

the desirability and feasibility of that market arrangement consensus and strong support for an interventionist approach at least as great as that called for in the case-by-case process, which involves intervention or intermediation by nonmarket participants, such as the IMF, and collusion of the creditors led by a lead syndicate bank.

The case-by-case procedure is, however, ad hoc and eschews the need for a more generalized framework and for instruments or policies to contend with the debt problems of scores of countries. The fact that many have common features and would seem to call for common treatment is considered irrelevant. Dozens of academics, bankers, and others have come forward with proposals that go beyond the case-by-case approach to overcome the limitations of this approach. These proposals could be categorized as case-by-case plus, a sort of halfway house between the present mode of debt crisis management and proposals that could be labeled "the Bretton Woods approach," which would go even further.

A CATALOGUE OF PROPOSALS: DEBT RELIEF BY MANY NAMES

The advocates of the set of proposals we call case-by-case plus share the basic assumption of the simple ad hoc case-by-case approach, that each individual debtor country must have its treatment tailored to its distinctive characteristics with respect to the size and nature of the debt and the ability of the debtor country's economy to cope with servicing it. But, having accepted this assumption, that extra plus is a shorthand for embellishments that go beyond the normal case-by-case rescheduling process to address the thorny issue of how to ease the adjustment costs for both creditors and debtors. The first modification was multiyear rescheduling, which has helped ease the disadvantages of short-leash financing and slow the pace of the process from frenetic to hectic. This was quickly perceived to be inadequate in light of the danger signals that the rescheduling arrangements were pushing against the limits of the debtors' tolerance. Some form of debt relief was called for, but the act needed various guises. The principal features of most of these proposals incorporate such relief. They can be described under the following categories:[9]

i) Canceling all or part of the debt and/or declaring a moratorium for a stipulated adjustment period.

ii) Subsidizing interest rates or in some manner reducing real rates;

iii) Capping interest rates on variable rate loans or issuing variable maturity loans (VML) that become operative when the interest rate exceeds some predetermined limit set in relationship to measurable indicators such as the debt service/exports ratio or the interest component of the debt service/exports ratio.

iv) Capping the percentage of export earnings to be devoted to servicing foreign debt.

---

[9] The most comprehensive compilation of these proposals is provided in *The Debt Crisis and the World Economy,* Report of the Expert Group (chaired by Lord Lever), Commonwealth Secretariat, London, Appendix 2.2, July 1984.

See also Bergsten, Cline and Williamson, *Bank Lending to Developing Countries: The Policy Alternatives,* (Washington, D.C.: Institute for International Economics, 1985), passim, and Wm. Cline, *International Debt and the Stability of the World Economy,* (Washington, D.C.: Institute for International Economics, 1983), passim.

See also an excellent exposition of the various proposals in Martine Guerguil, "The International Financial Crisis: Diagnoses and Prescriptions," *CEPAL Review,* no. 24, December 1984, pp. 147–69. The categories used are (1) enlargement and improvement of existing mechanisms, (2) conversion of the outstanding debt by market mechanisms, (3) conversion by collective action, and (4) conversion by unilateral action.

v) Enabling eligible developing countries to convert some part of their short- and medium-term debts into longer-term obligations.

Each of these merit critical appraisal, particularly in terms of what they imply with respect to the role of the various institutions involved in the debt crisis. If these proposals won't fly for whatever reasons—be they theoretical or practical—then the search must go on even to the degree of considering more comprehensive approaches.

Canceling All or Part of Debt or Declaring a Moratorium

No debtor developing country has found it advantageous to go the complete moratorium or default route alone. The idea has been floated as a trial balloon by several officials of Latin American countries that belong to the Cartegena Group. There are some, such as Celso Furtado, an eminent Brazilian economist and former minister of planning, who have suggested the moratorium route. But this idea has been quickly disowned to remain an idle threat, a bargaining ploy too dangerous to use. Even President Fidel Castro of Cuba, who convened a debtors conference in Havana in August 1985 and called on debtor countries to consider repudiating their debt obligations has remained scrupulously respectful of his own country's debt obligations.

The interests and circumstances of the various debtor countries have been, up to the present, too varied to take a united stand on what is conceived to be so potentially damaging a position. A respected commentator on financial issues, Anatole Kaletsky, has made a thoughtful case for some variants of default as a way out of the debt crisis without necessarily inviting calamity either for the defaulter, the creditor banks, or the global financial system. However, perceptions of the risk have been sufficient deterrent—so far.[10] Conditions have to become more extreme before the glue that holds the system together ceases to hold. A catalytic factor, such as the dramatic drop in the price of oil, might trigger a country such as Mexico to take a lead in the Cartegena Group for a unified position on concrete steps or proposals and not merely on general principles.

Proposals involving some degree or form of forgiveness by lenders of the interest and principal payments from borrowers come up against the moral hazard problem. That abstract concept, however, is bound to be secondary in the case of countries that are, for all intents and purposes, insolvent. There is the thorny problem of determining which debtors are to be favored, what proportion of the outstanding debt is to be forgiven or possibly subsidized, and in what manner and timing. The suggestion that these questions be answered on the basis of the debtor country's ability to pay does not provide a helpful answer as to how and when this is to be done—and under what circumstances, except to suggest, as does Christine Bogdanowicz-Bindert, that there be no "risk to the system."[11] In effect, this constraint would limit its application to smaller debtors that have little or no leverage. In any case, it is being put forward with greater and greater frequency.

Subsidizing Interest Rates

This second group of proposals takes many forms, all of which involve part payment and part capitalization of interest with the conversion of all or part of the debt into public

---

[10] *The Costs of Default,* (New York: Twentieth Century Fund, 1985).

[11] Christine Bogdanowicz-Bindert, "World Debt," suggests consideration of this approach. Scott Thomas of Data Resources Inc. also favors this idea. See "Insolvency and LDC Debt," *Challenge* (January-February 1985), p. 55.

bonds with low real rates of interest, generous grace periods, and long maturities. Dragoslav Avramovic, former director of the Brandt Commission secretariat, has suggested this may be the best solution and has listed in support of this type of proposal such persons as Aldo Ferrer, Mario Henrique Simonsen, Paulo Nogueira Batista, and Celso Furtado, all of whom have held high positions in the economic planning and financial portfolios of their respective governments.[12] To this list could be added others, including Pedro-Pablo Kuczynski, president of First Boston International and former World Bank official; Professor Rudiger Dornbusch of Harvard University; Fred Bergsten, former assistant undersecretary for economic affairs and now director of the Washington-based Institute of International Economics; and Lawrence Klein, Nobel Prize-winning economist.[13]

---

[12] Dragoslav Avramovic, "Interest Rates, Debts and International Policy," *Trade and Development: An UNCTAD Review*, no. 5, 1984, p. 350.

In another article, *Debts in Early 1985: An Institutional Impasse* (February 1985), he lists issues or proportions, interest rates, and payment in local currencies as calling for "further discussion (but) some proposals have already been made." In this connection he cites his own writing: (*Foreign Debt and the Financial System*, International Congress on Economic Policies, Rio de Janeiro, August 1984, and *Debts: Salient Features 1984*, North-South Roundtable, Vienna, September 1984).

[13] Pedro Pablo Kuczynski, "Latin American Debt: Act Two," *Foreign Affairs* 62, no. 1, (Fall 1983); he suggests the IMF play a role in assuring more favorable terms, which might be limited to a spread of 1 percent above LIBOR and reduced rates for at least two years.

R. Dornbusch, *A Stabilization Program for Brazil*, September 1983 (mimeo), proposes that Brazil convert part of its debt into public bonds at a real interest rate of 2 percent, a 5-year grace period and a 15-year maturity.

C. Fred Bergsten and Lawrence Klein, "The Need for a Global Strategy," *Economist* (April 25, 1985), consider "the most important policy step is to reduce interest rates by at least two percentage points in the U.S."

A variant on the interest subsidy idea relates to the provision of some form of guarantee from multilateral agencies that could reduce the interest rates and special charges by reducing risk. Minos Zombanakis, a London banker, and Lord Harold Lever have advanced proposals to achieve this effect through some guarantee arrangement provided by the IMF or the World Bank.[14] This was one of the main rationales for establishing the World Bank, but for various reasons, this function was never made operational. The World Bank has evolved along other lines and at this stage there is little likelihood—because the disadvantages outweigh any conceivable advantage—that some form of guarantee feature could be introduced that, under prevailing conditions, would make a significant difference. As an example, the World Bank under its cofinancing policy already offers a guarantee to commercial banks that it will assume the later years of long-term loans in order to lengthen maturities and lower the interest charged by reducing the risk, but this program has so far had a lukewarm reception from the commercial banking community.

Capping Interest Rates

The third category of proposals is closely related to the previous one, differing insofar as no subsidization is called for. What is advocated is the capping of interest rates on variable rate loans or the issuance of variable maturity loans (VML) that become operative when the interest rate exceeds some predetermined limit, the unpaid portion of interest due then being added to the total debt or, in the case of the VML, to the life of the loan.

The determination of the appropriate level at which

---

[14] Both proposals are presented in the *Economist*. Zombanakis' proposal is in "The International Debt Threat: A Way to Avoid A Crash," (April 30, 1983) and Lever's, "The International Debt Threat: a Concerted Way Out," (July 9, 1983).

to cap the rate puts the focus on what is deemed to be the tolerable limit of debt burden. There are several variants to choose from: the debt service/exports ratio, the interest/exports ratio, the debt/GDP ratio, and so on. These conventional yardsticks could be used as early indicators of trouble, the most directly relevant in the short term being the interest/export ratio and, over the longer term, the debt/GDP or the debt/wealth ratio (wealth being an indicator of the present value of the future stream of national income). While the ability and willingness to meet debt servicing costs (both interest and amortization) directly influences that elusive concept called creditworthiness, the stress in the final analysis is on the interest servicing capability of the borrowers.[15]

The proposal to cap interest rates has many variants, all designed to limit the pressure on the debtor countries so as to enable them to continue servicing their debts with a lessened probability that the process will break down, or with a reduction in the temptation of debtors to contemplate default. Among its advocates are Anthony Solomon, a former president of the Federal Reserve Bank of New York Federal Reserve Board, and Preston Martin, vice-chairman of the Federal Reserve Board.[16]

---

[15] The remarks of Eugene Rotberg, World Bank treasurer, are relevant: "The principal is not going to be repaid . . . By pretending that developing countries will eventually repay the billions of dollars they now owe, commercial bankers are merely drawing attention to the world debt crisis and making it look worse than it actually is. If the money isn't due, then it isn't owed, and if it isn't owed, you take no losses."
Reported in "LDC Loan Principal 'Won't be repaid' Says Banker," the *New York Post* (November 13, 1984).

[16] Paul A. Volcker, chairman of the Federal Reserve Board, recently suggested it was an idea worth considering, but he appears to have changed his views if we are to judge by his sharp disavowal and disagreement with Preston Martin, who had expressed support for such an approach. "I find his (Martin's) reported comments incomprehensible . . . (in) unrealistically *suggesting unorthodox approaches* to the international debt problem." (Emphasis added.)

Henry Kissinger seems to have joined the ranks of the advocates of this proposal in linking it to a Western Hemisphere Development Plan, which he describes as "the modern philosophical equivalent of the Marshall Plan." His variant would be funded in much the same way as the World Bank—through borrowing in the world's capital markets with the lending fixed "at a low rate of interest (with) any difference between the plan's cost of borrowing and this rate added to the principal to be repaid after other scheduled payments." A key feature would be an agreement by the commercial banks to a ceiling on interest charges with the cap on interest rates set at "the historical real interest rate, around 3 percent (with) the debtor paying the difference between that figure and current interest rates in local currency into the Western Hemisphere Development Plan for relending, or it could be added to the principal outstanding."[17]

In September 1984, on a state visit to Washington, former Peruvian President Fernando Belaunde proposed another variant of the same idea. He suggested issuing "a multinational bond issue guaranteed by each debtor country and the large states and perhaps a trustee, (which) could be used, at least partially, for amortization (of the Third World debt)."

Dr. Avramovic has been in the forefront in advocating "concerted international measures to introduce ceilings on interest rates and restore the regulation of capital markets" as a necessary condition to bring down interest rates. He has put forward some specific steps to achieve the desired reduction, namely, having:

> The key governments, in particular those of developed countries, agree on a proportionate reduction of the interest rates

---

[17] "Building a Bridge of Hope to our Latin Neighbors," *Washington Post* (June 24, 1985).

they offer for their borrowing and that of their agencies (which should cause) market rates to fall under the pressure of this collective monopsony of the buyers of funds . . . *It is difficult to see how without such or a similar international effort the present unsatisfactory situation will be reversed.*[18] (Emphasis added.)

The preconditions for such a collective monopsony policy and its implementation is an agreement that such coordination and/or cooperation is both necessary and feasible. This aspect leads to consideration of what we call the new Bretton Woods approach, which puts the focus on what types of economic and financial measures need to be coordinated or handled in a cooperative fashion between nations and how that is to be achieved. (We take this up in Chapter six.)

Capping the Percentage of Export Earnings to Be Allocated to Service the Debt

The fourth group of proposals follows the idea of capping with the very same rationale, but in this case the cap is to be applied to the percentage of export earnings devoted to servicing foreign debt. The proposal received a dramatic emphasis in July 1985 from President Alan Garcia Perez of Peru when, in his inaugural address, he declared he intended to implement, not merely talk about, this idea. At the same time, he assigned a definite number to the percentage of export earnings to be devoted to debt servicing, 10 percent in the initial stage (or $320 million), and added that the IMF would be bypassed. Since then Nigeria's military leader, Major General Ibrahim Babangida, has opted for a similar approach both with regard to bypassing

---

[18] Dragoslav Avramovic, "Interest Rates, Debts and International Policy," p. 350.

the IMF and specifying a fixed percentage ceiling of export earnings (30 percent) to be allocated to servicing Nigeria's $22 billion foreign debt.[19] This action would effectively reduce Nigeria's annual payments to about half of the $5 billion owed.

The idea and the trade-off are by no means new. A year before President Garcia made this declaration, Brazil's ambassador to the U.S., Sergio Correa da Costa, posed the question: "What is to be done?" and answered, "No more than a reasonable percentage of export revenues should be committed to debt service so that adequate levels of internal production can be maintained."[20] In September 1984, in studies prepared for its ministerial conference in Mar del Plata and for the commonwealth finance ministers meeting, the Latin American Economic System (SELA) proposed Latin American countries "pay no more than they can afford and never more than a quarter of export revenues as debt service."

At the time, such ideas were still in the realm of fanciful suggestions and evoked little reaction. When, however, political leaders proclaim the idea as an operational directive, the story becomes newsworthy and can receive a strong reaction such as that of *New York Times* columnist Tom Wicker, who described the message from Garcia as

> "the most imaginative idea yet offered by the leader of a debt-ridden Latin American nation, a possible way out of

---

[19] Because about 94 percent of Nigeria's export earnings are derived from oil, this would make payments fluctuate with the prices of oil. If Nigeria were able to obtain $16 a barrel and sell at its capacity of 1.5 million barrels per day, it is estimated it would barely be able to pay for the $6.7 billion "austerity import bill." Since the price has dropped well below that and Nigeria's realistic export sales are closer to 1 million barrels, the option is further import reduction or a smaller debt servicing payment. The rejection of an IMF loan was based on a referendum.

[20] *New York Times* (April 12, 1984).

the region's dangerous debt crisis that avoids both extremes—default or years of extreme austerity threatening political upheaval."[21]

On the same date in the normally staid and politically conservative *Globe and Mail* of Toronto, the editorial declared:

> The decision of the new President of Peru to flout the IMF is not the act of an angry young man. *How does an impoverished nation with a crumbling economy justify interest payments to foreign bankers while its own people decline into misery and social chaos?* . . . Though it seems provocative, (the Peruvian decision) contains an obvious element of common sense. The question is whether the international financial community can accommodate such candour (especially as), in this circumstance, *the moral, practical and political logic of the present international debt management system seems clearly inadequate, deserving of challenge, requiring innovation."* (Emphasis added.)

The Garcia challenge seems to have struck a responsive chord, reflecting mounting concern, frustration, and fear about the hard line being taken by the banking community and the IMF.[22] There seems to be a chorus seconding the

---

[21] Two other stories appeared in the *New York Times* (July 30, 1985): Alan Riding wrote a quasi-reportorial account from Lima, Peru, under the title "Latin Debt Crisis Seen Intensifying," saw the issue as Peru "throwing down the gauntlet, challenging its creditors (but) important mostly as a symbol and a precedent."

On the front page of the business section, Nicolas D. Kristof ran another interpretative feature, "Peru Debt-Payment Cap is An Important Symbol."

[22] On this point, Michael L. Smith reported from Lima, *Washington Post* (September 15, 1985): "Garcia wants the international financial community to give Peru a chance to put its economy on the road to recovery before the country resumes regular payments on its foreign debt. . . . I believe it would be a grave mistake for the banks to try to force an impossible payment by using coercive measures because they wouldn't collect anything (in such a case)." Subsequent reports indicate

essence (if not the particulars) of this message from Garcia. But in circles where decisions are made, there is hardly any echo—yet.

Converting Part of the Debt into Long-Term Obligations

The fifth set of proposals suggest that eligible developing countries be enabled to convert some part of their short- and medium-term debts into longer-term obligations through:

a) Cooperating with the co-financing program of the World Bank (by means of which longer maturity loans can be arranged with the World Bank taking on the obligation to assume the later years, if need be).

b) Establishing some entity that could be empowered and financially capable of buying the debts from the banks at a discount (giving bonds in return) and then stretch out the repayment period to 10 years or longer at a lower interest rate. This would be tantamount to some forgiveness if the banks did not receive full conversion value, or principal plus interest.

In the chorus putting this proposal forward one can find such academics and bankers as Felix Rohatyn of the investment banking firm Lazard Freres Inc., Professor Peter Kenen of Princeton University, Professors John Guttentag and Richard Herring of the University of Pennsylvania's Wharton School of Business, George Soros, a New

---

the appeal and the threat are being heard, but there is no indication whether it might be heeded, especially with respect to the nonrole Garcia envisaged for the IMF. At Seoul, the Peruvian message was repeated— but to a virtually empty hall (though the line for the speech transcript was second only to that of Treasury Secretary Baker's speech).

York money fund manager, and Mahbub ul Haq, the minister of finance and planning of Pakistan and former World Bank Official. Haq's variant would have the IMF establish a Debt Refinancing Facility, Rohatyn's would be modeled on New York City's Municipal Assistance Corporation or "an international institution such as an expanded World Bank"; Kenen's an International Debt Discount Corporation, and Soros's an International Lending Agency.[23]

These proposals call for the IMF, the World Bank, or some new agency buying the commercial banks' sovereign loans receivables for which the banks would receive long-term, low-interest bonds, effectively making the agency the creditor for a reconstituted debt. In the Rohatyn proposal the model suggested is essentially similar to the one used to save New York City from bankruptcy, the Municipal Assistance Corporation (MAC), or a federal agency akin to the Reconstruction Finance Corporation (RFC) of the early New Deal era of President Roosevelt. Rohatyn's proposal has, in fact, been dubbed by one analyst as a global version of MAC or "Big MAC."[24]

The reluctance of the financial community to consider any such innovative proposals, especially those involving institutional changes, is reflected in the reception given to these suggestions. None seems to have been given serious study or taken up in forums where there might be some follow-up.

---

[23] Mahbub ul Haq, *Proposal for an IMF Debt Refinancing Facility*, Address to U.N. ECOSOC, Geneva, July 6, 1984; Felix Rohatyn, "A Plan for Stretching out Global Debt," *Business Week* (February 28, 1983) and "Build a New Economic Stability," *The Wall Street Journal* (August 9, 1985); Peter B. Kenen, "Third World Debt: Sharing the Burden, a Bailout Plan for the Banks," *New York Times* (March 6, 1983); George Soros, "The International Debt Problem: A Prescription," *Morgan Stanley Investment Research Memorandum*, New York, May, 1984; Professors John Guttentag and Richard Herring, "The Current Crisis in International Banking," *Brookings Institution Paper*, 1983.

[24] *Business Week* (February 28, 1983).

Converting Debt into Equity

The sixth category of proposals takes the previous set of ideas a step further in suggesting that debt be converted into equity in a debtor's state-owned or parastatal corporation. The examples cited have been Pemex in the case of Mexico and Petrobas in the case of Brazil. This arrangement would call for acquiring a quasi-equity asset, which could be achieved through a contractual arrangement whereby the creditors would agree to accept exchange-participation notes that would entitle them to some agreed-upon proportion of a country's export earnings during the life of the loan. This entitlement would be given in exchange for forgoing the payments of principal due on the loan, a device designed to have payments on the loans fluctuate with export earnings.[25]

In the 1985 monograph *Financial Intermediation beyond the Debt Crisis,* Donald Lessard and John Williamson, senior fellow of the Institute for International Economics, suggest consideration of quasi-equities, which would give the investor a share of the income of an enterprise but not a share of its ownership. They estimate an investment flow of about $10 billion per year might be achieved through encouraging international investment in LDC equities by lifting regulatory constraints on such investment by institutional investors, providing incentives for such institutional investors to hold a certain proportion of portfolio in LDC foreign equities, and/or by issuing commodity-linked bonds and indexed bonds jointly guaranteed by groups of borrowers.

---

[25] This variant is proposed by Norman Bailey, formerly of the U.S. National Security Council, in *Exchange Participation Notes: An Approach to the International Financial Crisis,* Georgetown University Center for Strategic and International Studies, Washington, D.C. (mimeo), and in *Economist* (February 18, 1983). Close variants are set forth by Allan H. Meltzer, "A Way to Defuse the World Debt Bomb," *Fortune* (November 28, 1983), and Christine Bogdanowicz-Bindert, "Debt Beyond the Quick Fix," *Third World Quarterly* (October 1983).

The general thrust of these ideas is to place greater reliance on a more market-oriented approach to the debt overhang problem, which is impeding the flow of new capital to the developing countries. It is not clear how this proposal would work to give the creditors an equity *quid pro quo*, or how the assets would be priced and placed. A very heavy discount would probably be involved so the candidate companies would have some takers. Many countries have been prepared to announce ambitious divestiture programs and to declare a range of nonstrategic industries, such as hotels, breweries, and the like, open to foreign investors. Some, like Argentina, which had resisted privatizing its steel industry, have removed the barriers. The invitations have been issued, but it seems few are coming to the party.

Brazil has declared a willingness to sell state-owned enterprises to foreign investors in the form of participation in joint ventures whereby "foreign bank creditors could utilize part of the several billion dollars which has accumulated in the Central Bank as a result of the debt rollovers." Besides uncertainty of a general nature with respect to the investment climate in the debtor nation economies, there remains the problem of determining the terms and conditions for foreign investors to participate in ownership of such enterprises. Not withstanding operational questions, a *Financial Times* report goes on to note, "This move has been described by Mrs. Thatcher and Mr. George Shultz as 'the best solution to the debt crisis.' "[26]

RESISTANCE OR THE OSTRICH SYNDROME

However varied these proposals may be in detail, they contain one important common element—the debt servicing burden must be reduced both for the existing debt and for

---

[26] Andrew Whitley, *Financial Times* (U.K.) (August 28, 1985).

future borrowings. All these proposals advocate an agreement to reduce the present value of the debt service obligations on outstanding debt owed by the developing countries. This implies the private commercial banks will have to eventually settle for less than the terms of their initial and their renegotiated loans, and their role in the international lending process would have to be very much reduced from the exceptionally active level of the 1970s.

Private bankers, central bankers, and finance or treasury officials of many governments have displayed a brittle, unyielding resistance to any of these proposals. As John Williamson observed in a paper given in late 1985:

> So far debt relief has been conspicuous by its absence since the debt crisis erupted in August 1982. Debt has been renegotiated, reconstructed, rolled over and stretched out, but it has not been forgiven, nor have interest rates been reduced by more than modest cuts in spreads.[27]

An amalgam of financial, political, and psychological and cultural factors has created an environment in which the banking community takes a hard-nosed, short-term view of the situation. So long as there is no breakdown in the rescheduling process there appears to be no incentive to entertain even a conceptual foot in the door for debt relief. The power of shortsighted self-interest goes a long way to explain why there is such resistance by the financial community to the reforms suggested by advocates of an

---

[27] *Notes on the Provision of Debt Relief,* a paper prepared for the North South Roundtable, New York, December 13, 1985. The author states, "My own view is that policy of categorically denying the possibility of debt relief is inadmissible on humanitarian grounds, unjust inasmuch as the banks have on occasion contributed to the problem of excessive indebtedness, and unrealistic since in extremis countries will be unable to service their debts however hard they try . . . Moreover, it seems paradoxical in the extreme to deny to sovereign debtors a possibility that creditors with stronger enforcement mechanisms often find it in their own interest to extend to corporate debtors."

enhanced case-by-case approach. "Moral rectitude" is the reason also advanced. Thus, for example, we find protagonists in this real-life global drama, such as the chairman of the Federal Reserve Board, Paul Volcker, in testimony before a congressional panel, saying debtors should not expect creditor banks to ease the debtors' burden by writing down in any way the outstanding loans because: "The debt burden is the result of poorly thought out economic policies in many Third World countries and the proper solution is fundamental policy adjustments (on their part)." The Reuters news agency dispatch that reported this testimony notes Volcker has repeatedly counseled against any official suggestion that loans might be written off for fear that such a move would encourage the debtor governments to weaken in their efforts to pursue the austerity policies which he and the U.S. administration believe are necessary.[28]

A second factor stiffening the resistance of the banking community is the fact that as Professor Paul Klugman has astutely noted: "For creditors as a group, *the current debt strategy has been a pretty good bargain* even in the short run, while preserving the possibility of a return to normal servicing of the debt in the longer run.[29] (Emphasis added.) Bankers seem to be reasoning that the strains built into the case-by-case rescheduling process are on the debtors' side, so why take a risk of conceding something that may not have to be conceded.

One can count politics as a third factor. There is a fear that any move that helps debtors also helps the embattled

---

[28] Mr. Volcker's testimony followed the announcement of Peruvian President Garcia which capped debt servicing payments and rejected IMF intermediation.

[29] Paul Klugman, "Proposals for International Debt Reform," *International Debt and the Developing Countries, a World Bank Symposium,* (Washington, D.C.: World Bank), p. 92.

creditor banks so a "rescue" may be interpreted not as a compassionate action but as an operation supporting *private* institutions with *public* funds. Perceptions count for a great deal in the world of politics. Thus, many political leaders have been able to win broad support from seemingly compassionate constituents for seemingly heartless policies that stonewall measures to ease the strain and pain on the desperately poor people of heavily indebted developing countries.

The more perceptive seem to realize it is self-deluding to imagine the present process can go on without incurring unacceptable risks, and they are therefore prepared to consider various approaches to ease the debt burden. Even some members of the financial community are aware of historical precedents that make the idea of concessions appear more appealing than the worst alternative of outright and overt default. They recall the 1930s when the list of defaulters included not only some developing countries but also several European countries, such as Britain, France, and Germany. They also recall the interesting precedent of a time—only a few decades ago—when a more generous-minded administration and Congress handled the German debt by reducing it by two-thirds and stretching repayment over 35 years at the concessional rate of 3 percent.[30]

A fourth factor in the reluctance to consider debt relief is the difficulty of setting out acceptable criteria and procedures for making any debtor eligible for some form of debt relief. It is a challenge to devise a formula that would not discourage lending and not incur the "moral hazard" of aiding the less worthy. In "Notes on the Provision of Debt Relief," John Williamson has put forward two criteria as

---

[30] Cited by Chandra S. Hardy, *Rescheduling Developing Country Debts, 1956–1981: Lessons and Recommendations*, Monograph 15, (Washington, D.C.: Oversea Development Council, June 1982), p. 41.

necessary conditions for a debtor country to qualify for such assistance—the occurrence of exogenous shock that increased the burden of debt service and low per capita income. He lists five more as worthy of consideration (to be applied in combination):[31]

- Lack of a threat to international financial stability (which accords with Christine Bogdanowicz-Bindert's proposal quoted at the start of this chapter).
- Little prospect of the debtor country being able to service debt with an acceptable cost to human welfare.
- Poor use made by the debtor country of the proceeds of the loans.
- Irresponsible lending by the creditor banks.
- Doubtful legitimacy of the government that contracted the loan.

Williamson has suggested an entity be established with restrospective authority to consider the application of such criteria before events impel some form of relief at great social cost—and likely much greater financial cost to the banking community.

Meanwhile, the banking community has taken steps to defend its interests, beginning with the establishment in 1983 of the Institute of International Finance (IIF) and the appointment as director of the institution of Andre de Lattre, a former banker with extensive experience in

---

[31] The author states: "My own view is that policy of categorically denying the possibility of debt relief is inadmissible on humanitarian grounds, unjust inasmuch as the banks have on occasion contributed to the problem of excessive indebtedness, and unrealistic since, in extremis, countries will be unable to service their debts however hard they try. . . . Moreover, it seems paradoxical in the extreme to deny to sovereign debtors a possibility that creditors with stronger enforcement mechanisms often find it in their own interest to extend to corporate debtors."

the development finance field. Through the IIF, the major banks hoped to be able to collect more up-to-date and comprehensive information on the most heavily indebted developing countries; in this way the banks' present and future lending could be guided by a statistical and analytical base that would be stronger than they could provide through their own efforts.

The IIF is, at best, a very partial and inadequate response to the challenge facing the banking community. The agency is an instrument of the banks and, therefore, unlikely to be given the mandate to let the analytic chips fall where they may. The IIF has already been marshaled to lend support to the Baker initiative through the preparation of policy papers for several well-publicized meetings of its members. There is little likelihood the IIF would do the same for proposals of the "hard" options involving consideration of a significant measure of debt relief, which appears still to be unthinkable for the executives of the major sponsoring banks.

LOOKING AHEAD

Pressures and opportunities are forcing a number of the ideas contained in the case-by-case plus proposals to become reality. Laudable and imaginative as many of the debt relief proposals undoubtedly are, when introduced separately, slowly, and erratically, they fall far short of providing a meaningful framework for effective and concerted implementation. To avoid tensions, frustrations, inequities, and breakdowns, the measures taken must go beyond that to mesh within a larger policy framework in order to attain the intended objectives. Thus, there has emerged a call for a new Bretton Woods.

The most explicit articulation of support for this approach is provided in the Commonwealth Secretariat Report, *Towards a New Bretton Woods: Challenges for the*

World Financial and Trading System.[32] This study was prepared by an appointed group of eminent persons headed by Professor Gerald Helleiner of the University of Toronto. They have argued that if the necessary conditions for the resumption of global growth are to be realized there must be steps taken that go beyond the case-by-case approach—and also beyond the case-by-case plus proposals. While supporting some of the latter proposals, the report takes the position that not enough of the proposals are likely to be implemented in time, in the appropriate manner, or on the appropriate scale.

The recommended approach calls for reconsidering the rules of the international financial game in light of today's altered circumstances and has come to be labeled a Bretton Woods approach. The next chapter considers this third path of dealing with the debt crisis.

---

[32] Commonwealth Secretariat, *Towards a New Bretton Woods: Challenges for the World Financial and Trading System,* Report by a Commonwealth Study Group, London, July 1983. (Known as the Helleiner Report after its chairman and principal author.)

The subsequent report prepared in July 1984 by the Commonwealth Secretariat, *The Debt Crisis and the World Economy,* (known as the Lever Report after its chairman Lord Harold Lever of Manchester) focused more particularly on the debt crisis endorsing "collective determination to take action" and urging that "the aggregate impact of the measures taken should be on a scale which matches the size of the problem."

CHAPTER SIX _____

"The New Bretton Woods"
Proposal: Rhetoric
and Reality

The central elements of the system outlined at Bretton Woods were the establishment of convertibility of currencies and of fixed but adjustable exchange rates, the encouragement of international flows of capital for productive purposes . . . (and) the creation of the Bretton Woods twins—the IMF and the IBRD or World Bank. . . . The participants were determined to design an international economic system where "beggar thy neighbor" policies, which characterized the international economic community when World War II began, did not recur.

World Development Report, 1985[1]

The biggest politico-economic challenge to statesmen is to integrate national policies into a global perspective, to resolve the discordance between the international economy and the political system based on the nation state . . . The spirit that produced Bretton Woods reflected the realization that in the long run the national welfare can only be safeguarded within the framework of the general welfare. . . . In (today's) circumstances the international economic system operates—if at all—as crisis management. The risk is, of course, that some day crisis management may be inadequate. The world

_____
[1] World Bank, Washington, D.C., p. 15, Box 2.1.

*will then face a disaster its lack of foresight has made inevitable
. . . My major point is that the world needs new arrangements.*

Henry A. Kissinger[2]

THE CONCEPTUAL RATIONALE FOR A BRETTON WOODS II APPROACH

There are many voices putting forward proposals that fall within the rubric of what has come to be called a "new Bretton Woods approach." At first blush this chorus has one common refrain—that the *ad hoc* short-term framework of the case-by-case approach in both its simple and modified versions is not sufficient, meaning we will lurch from one emergency situation to another if we only apply bandages. The advocates go further to suggest that a long-term and holistic perspective is necessary because the crisis will be resolved only when the preconditions for long-term health are created; unless and until there is also action on the broader framework, the palliative short-term treatment will be to little or no avail.[3]

There is also agreement on a time dimension, that the need for a new approach is urgent. At best, a little time will have been bought by the present approach, but the position is that too little is being done to ease the festering conditions. The pressure for action arises from both sides: the banking community is under extreme pressure to "get in deeper" and the debtor countries are sinking deeper into debt and also suffering from increasing social and political

---

[2] *International Economic and World Order*, the Motta Lecture, Washington, Sept. 24, 1984. Reprinted in op-ed page of the *Washington Post*, "International Trade: It's Time to Change the Rules of the Game," (Nov. 22, 1984).

[3] Setting out the sufficient conditions to achieve this objective goes well beyond those elements directly germane to the debt crisis and its resolution. The Bretton Woods focus is therefore more limited in scope as to objectives and modalities.

tensions and erosion of sovereignty, a condition that has been aptly called "debt trap peonage."[4]

The underlying premise is that if there had been an appropriate system in place during the 1970s, it would not have been possible to pile up the troubling mountain of debt because the global financial system would have had an adequate *control* mechanism. Under a properly functioning global economic and financial system, the countries on a borrowing and lending binge—it takes two to tango—would have been brought up short by the Bretton Woods reins. The United States found out about this constraint when, in the mid-1960s, it pursued domestic policies that brought on inflation at a rate exceeding that of the other major industrialized nations. Pressure was exerted on the dollar and a gold rush was set in motion reflecting waning confidence in the dollar.[5] U.S. policy makers had to choose between reining in the inflationary forces by tough fiscal and monetary policy measures, thus adhering to the obligations the country had assumed under the Bretton Woods agreement, or breaking out of the agreement. The United States selected the latter course and thereby permitted—if not abetted—the process leading to the present debt crisis, which is, at bottom, a crisis of the global financial system.

The contention is that the demise of the Bretton Woods system in the late 1960s and early 1970s enabled the creation of a debtor's paradise in which inflationary expectations (with concomitant negative interest rates and devaluation of the U.S. dollar) induced excessive borrowing.

---

[4] This term is used by Chinweizu, editor of the *Guardian* (Lagos, Nigeria), in a paper presented at the conference on "Foreign Debt and Nigerian Economic Development," which was held in early March 1984 at the Nigerian Institute of International Affairs. Reprinted in *Monthly Review*, November 1985 (New York).

[5] This was dramatically reflected in events that can be dated almost precisely: on March 1, 1968, the upward spiral of gold prices commenced, ending only after the price had risen past $800 per troy ounce.

On the lending side, the conditions were extraordinarily attractive since there were plentiful petrodollars to recycle and control was virtually nonexistent with the weakening of the Bretton Woods system and of one of its institutions, the IMF. This condition enabled—perhaps made necessary—both the rise of the Eurodollar market phenomenon and the concomitant spectacular increase of commercial bank lending in the international arena as the main conduits for handling the challenge of petrodollar recycling.

The rationale for the calls for monetary reform is rooted in the failures or weaknesses of the prevailing system that have evolved after the abandonment of the Bretton Woods system. These failings or weaknesses could be listed as follows:

- The absence of policy coordination that followed with the weakening of U.S. leadership. A very powerful economy can impose coordination; when that economic might is overwhelming, every country has no option but to follow. The follow-the-leader regime is sustainable if the players find the outcome is either tolerable and/or the costs (and risks) of opting out are intolerably high.
- The absence of a sufficiently early early warning system and an adequate response mechanism. "Adequate" is a relative concept; what was acceptable yesterday may be wholly unacceptable today when:
   1.) Changes in the speed and direction of exchange rates and capital transfers are much too rapid and massive to be adequately handled in the conventional manner through negotiated aid agreements and traditional investment channels.
   2.) When current account balances move with a speed, amplitude, and volatility that puts correc-

tive steps beyond the response capability of any governments or multilateral institution.

* The absence of any form of control (braking and/ or steering) mechanism on the mobility of capital. The ability to control is inversely correlated to the speed and mass of the object to be controlled. It is, thus, an increasingly more difficult and dangerous a situation:

    1.) When the Eurodollar market and other foreign exchange transactions have doubled between 1979 and 1984 to attain a global volume of $150 billion per day or $35 trillion per year.

    2.) When cross-border investment and trade in goods have increased by about 20 percent a year to attain a volume of almost $2 trillion.[6]

    There are important implications not only in the sheer magnitude of the absolute amounts involved but also in their dynamic and particularly in the shift of their relative volumes.

While the destabilizing potential of these changes is very worrisome—and we already have a foretaste of the enormous potential for such damage in the current debt crisis—the worry is compounded by the fact that control by any one nation or small number of nations (such as the G-5) is becoming much more difficult with each passing business day. There is, of course, the further worry as to whether such control would be exercised in the interests of the global community of nations. But, everything being equal, an expanded control group is to be preferred.

Bretton Woods I seems to have been an appropriate enough response to the challenging problem faced by the world community *at that time.* At least there appears to

---

[6] These statistics are taken from *The Foreign Exchange Market in the 1980s,* (New York: The Group of Thirty, 1985).

have been some mutually supportive relationship between the global economic and financial system that was in place and the increase of international trade of about 250 percent and of GNP of about 150 percent over the two decades when it was operative. There were, of course, other factors that might have played a causal role, so the historical correlation is put forward without claiming more for the Bretton Woods agreement than can be rigorously supported. But it would seem safe to regard this as more than coincidence. This being so, the question being asked is: what should be the appropriate response *at this time?*

DISTINGUISHING BETWEEN THE SUBSTANTIVE AND THE PROCEDURAL

It has long been recognized that if the concept of *coordination* and its counterpart, *constraint,* are to be more than pious hopes, leadership is needed to provide this international public good.[7] This would call for a significant change in the behavior of the leaders of the major industrialized nations who could provide such leadership. Professor

---

[7] "Public goods" or "collective goods" are defined as "that class of goods (or services) like public works where exclusion of consumers may be impossible, but in any event consumption of the good by one consuming unit—short of some level approaching congestion—does not exhaust its availability for others."

Professor C. P. Kindleberger of M.I.T. provided this succinct definition in his presidential address to the American Economic Association annual meeting on December 29, 1985 (reprinted in "International Public Goods without International Government," *The American Economic Review,* (March 1986). He points out that public goods are typically underproduced since its voluntary provision "is plagued by the free rider." In the international sphere the primary public good is the restoration and maintenance of peace. In the economic sphere the list would include: "an open trading system, well-defined property rights, standards of weights and measures that may include international money, or fixed exchange rates, and the like."

Charles Kindleberger described the current situation succinctly:

> After about 1971, the United States, like Britain from about 1890, has shrunk in economic might relative to the rest of the world as a whole, and more importantly, has lost the appetite for providing international economic public goods—open markets in times of glut, supplies in times of acute shortages, steady flows of capital to developing countries, international money, coordination of macroeconomic policy and last-resort lending.[8]

Formal coordinating meetings between countries to discuss economic and financial issues have been going on all the time on a regular basis within the framework of the IMF, the World Bank, and the United Nations and its agencies and on an ad hoc basis through global and regional conferences such as those on environment, new sources of energy, food, and so on. In addition there are the OECD meetings on aid, trade, and a range of economic and financial issues; and there are the most publicized of all such conclaves, the so-called summit meetings. But these have had—and undoubtedly will continue to have—negligible effect so long as the major players on the economic and financial stage pursue highly divergent policies and regard the outcome with a quotient of indifference when the outcomes are far from benign.

---

[8] Charles P. Kindleberger's comments on this matter are also apropos: "What I worry about mostly is exchange policy and macroeconomic coordination. The U.S. Treasury under Donald Regan was committed to the policy of neglect, presumably benign, but in any event ideological. And the commitment to consultative macroeconomic policies in annual summit meetings of seven heads of state has become a shadow play, a dog-and-pony show, a series of photo opportunities—whatever you choose to call them—with ceremony substituted for substance. The 1950s and 1960s, when serious discussions were held at the lowly level of Working Party No. 3 of the O.E.C.D., were superior because the United States and other countries took them seriously," *ibid*, p. 10.

The first signs of change in this regard was evidenced in September 1985 when U.S. Treasury Secretary Baker requested a meeting of the finance ministers of the five leading industrialized nations, the G-5, in New York at the Plaza Hotel (to keep it informal). This was a first step and heralded as a change in U.S. policy from indifference to concern. It started the series of such meetings that have been followed by coordinated action on interest rates as well as exchange rates. This development is welcome for all that, but should be recognized as but the beginning, hesitant steps along the path that the advocates of a Bretton Woods approach seem to have in mind. This process also requires an explicitly declared dedication to problem solving of the debt-related issues through the initiation of a process defined by its scope (the interrelated issues of trade and investment flows, commodity prices, exchange and interest rates, and so on) and by its objectives (ensuring adequate and continuing global growth with diminishing income disparities, and so forth).

Talk of a Bretton Woods approach as a way of resolving or easing the debt crisis conjures up images of a replica of a Bretton Woods-type gathering at which there would be proposals for sweeping or radical proposals involving structural or systemic change. This approach would be characterized more accurately by reversing the causality. The structural or systemic changes that have already occurred call for commensurate ways of coping with the consequences of such changes, one of which is the present debt crisis. The world has long lived with indecision, inefficiency, and inequity. Few of the advocates of a new Bretton Woods would be moved to urge changes on that account, but they make common cause in feeling that—as a matter of pragmatism, not morality—the present arrangements are unsustainable. The key question then becomes will policy and institutional changes be made by volitional decisions in a controlled and orderly way to take advantage of the greater

integration of the global economies or will policies and institutional arrangements be changed by *force majeure,* that
is, in an uncontrolled and precipitous manner? Should the
changes come about in the second manner, the solution
or outcome is likely to be a retreat from the 40-year-old
trend toward interdependence to autarkic policies as each
of the industrialized countries endeavors to minimize the
damage to itself by adopting "beggar-thy-neighbor" policies.
This set of options gives the problem and the solution or,
rather, the approach to finding a solution, an element of
urgency.

Many voices are now calling for a new Bretton Woods
approach to the debt problem. However different may be
the vantage from which they speak, they share the concept
of Bretton Woods as containing the following two compo-
nents:

- First, there is the aspect of *scope* that is wide enough
  to include consideration of a broad range of policies
  and changes in the existing institutional arrangements to achieve a greater measure of coordination
  and cooperation in the economic and financial
  sphere, which is generally recognized to be an essential condition for contending with the formidable
  present and looming problems of the global economy.
- The second aspect relates to the *modalities,* the ways
  to go reach meaningful agreement for such coordination and cooperation and for assuring the agreement
  is respected. In this regard, one of the range of options to consider would be the preparations for and
  the convening of a conference along the lines of the
  Bretton Woods Conference of 1944. Though the concept of Bretton Woods is indelibly associated with
  that historic event, there are other organizational
  or procedural options that might embody the spirit
  of that occasion without the literal emulation of a

staged conclave at a secluded resort with an all-star
cast and an all-encompassing ambitious agenda.

While these two strands run through the statements that
have been made in support of a Bretton Woods approach,
there is a great deal of ambiguity. Some advocates put the
accent on the substance and others on the process.

THE CHORUS CALLING

The list of advocates for consideration of a Bretton Woods
approach is long and, in terms of the political spectrum,
wide. That list includes eminent persons from both developed and developing countries and from the two solitudes,
the business and financial world and the academic.[9] Under
the circumstances, there is great danger that, as in the
case of the conservation movement—to cite President

---

[9] The following list is illustrative: Leonard Silk "Seeking a New
Bretton Woods," *New York Times* (March 25, 1983) cites support for
the idea by Professor Robert Mundell of Columbia University and William McChesney Martin, former chairman of the Federal Reserve Board,
and his colleagues of the Atlantic Council. William D. Rogers, former
under secretary for international economic affairs, has added his voice
("Reform World Finance," *New York Times*, April 4, 1983) as have Congressman Jack Kemp ("A Floating Dollar Costs Us Jobs," *Washington
Post*, May 15, 1983).

From the Third World, Justinian F. Rweyemanu: "The establishment of a new system must be an overriding political aim. A reform
package is no substitute. A U.N. Conference on International Money
and Finance remains a fundamental need—Restructuring the International Monetary System," *Development Dialogue*, 1980:2. This reiterated
what has been called "the Arusha Initiative," proposed at a June 1980
South/North Conference on the International Monetary System and
the New International Order held in Arusha, Tanzania.

A Canadian voice (apart from that of Professor Gerald Helleiner):
"The creation of a better system for international contracyclical macro-
economic policy coordination is urgently needed": Professors A. R. M.
Ritter and D. H. Pollock, "Better Economic Policies Required to Combat
Debt Crisis," *Ottawa Citizen*, (April 17, 1984).

Theordore Roosevelt's famous lament—"everyone is for it, no matter what it means."

Some examples of support might illustrate the range of meanings and of views. We can start with President Reagan's proposal in his February 1985 State of the Union message to Congress wherein he directed that the secretary of the treasury undertake a study on the international monetary system to consider whether an international conference on the issue should be convened. This position was applauded by the Democratic majority of the U.S. Congress' Joint Economic Committee in its annual report issued in mid-March 1986. The report went on to urge "speedy action on a new conference patterned after the Bretton Woods meeting of 1944."[10]

From Japan there have been similar signals. A November 1985 news item on the subject in the Japanese daily *Mainichi* revealed:

> One of the proposals to emerge from a ministerial consultative committee set up by Prime Minister Nakasone was a call for a "new Bretton Woods" to reform the international monetary system and to aim for the creation of a world fund to harmonize the interventions of central banks on exchange markets.

From Europe, the French have sent the same basic message. On a state visit to Brazil in mid-October 1985, French President Francois Mitterrand observed, "There is no durable solution to the foreign debt problem without . . . reforms in the international monetary system."[11] This state-

---

[10] Reported in *Washington Post*, (March 12, 1986). The committee report characterized the prevailing system governing exchange rates as a "nonsystem" and "broke" and recommended an international monetary conference, one objective of which would be to consider fixing it with an agreement to establish a target zone approach.

[11] Reported in a Reuters report from Brasilia, "Mitterrand Backs Brazil on Debt Issue," *International Herald Tribune* (October 18, 1985).

ment reaffirmed his comment on the subject two years before when he called for "a carefully organized international monetary conference at the highest level (to establish) common rules of the game and clear perspectives without which we will not emerge from the (present debt crisis) situation."[12]

There is a strong measure of support from those who would reform the international monetary system. This group includes individuals from the New York investment financial community, such as Felix Rohatyn ("a successor conference to the Bretton Woods agreement should study a more orderly international monetary system").[13] It also includes the G-24 group of Third World ministers who have been calling for:

The convening of an international monetary conference (as) . . . an important and essential step . . . in moving towards a thorough-going reform of the international monetary system which would secure the objective of exchange and monetary stability on the one hand, and address itself to the special concerns of the developing countries on the other.[14]

There are some advocates who focus on the process, as, for example, Sir Robert Muldoon, former New Zealand

---

President Mitterand is also quoted as stating that "developing country debtors should not have to repay at the cost of unemployment and recession; it is indefensible that developing countries be left with no other options than recession and stagnation over the next 15 to 20 years."

[12] Reported in *New York Times* (May 10, 1983). He added that "the work of overcoming the crisis is not that of a single conference or of a single year, but an immense task on the scale of a generation."

[13] "Build a New Economic Stability," *The Wall Street Journal* (August 9, 1985). See also, "A New Chance for the Economy," *New York Review of Books* (April 24, 1986).

[14] *The Reform of the International Monetary and Financial System: Revised Program of Action,* Intergovernmental Group of Twenty-four on International Monetary Affairs, Task Force on Reform of the International Monetary and Financial System, September 2, 1983.

prime minister and minister of finance and sponsor of the resolution to have the Commonwealth Secretariat prepare a study focusing on the desirability and feasibility of a new Bretton Woods. It is his view that:

> (We must commit ourselves to) start a systematic process which looks to significant changes in the structure of trade, payments, development efforts and exchange rates. . . . Basic preparatory work would be undertaken first by a small group of 20 to 25 experts—who have the political backing of their governments—with the IMF, GATT and maybe UNCTAD sitting in. To have real influence requires a body of the highest political profile which is what's lacking now at the IMF. . . . *A second Bretton Woods conference (would) come at the end of this process rather than at the beginning.*[15] (Emphasis added.)

There would seem to be general agreement that something more must be done and that defining what constitutes "more" calls for considering a process to lead to significant changes in the way we do things. There is, however, a great deal of divergence with regard to procedural specifics except for the general point that the concept of Bretton Woods serves as a shorthand way of referring to the formalization of the process of coordination that would both guide and constrain the conduct of economic and financial affairs

---

[15] "Muldoon Outlines Priorities of a Second Bretton Woods: Wants Global Monetary Structure Revamped," the *Washington Post* (February 26, 1984). Mr. Muldoon sketched out his conception of the process, which would culminate in a big conference that would try to agree on a statement of principles creating a new world economic governing body, an "economic security council," whose findings would influence, but not bind, sovereign governments.

A more-than-usual elaboration of the new Bretton Woods concept in both procedural and substantive terms has been set forth in an article by Professor Gerald Helleiner, "An Agenda for a New Bretton Woods," *Foreign Policy Journal,* (winter 1984), which summarizes and sharpens ideas contained in the 1983 Helleiner Report, which was written for the Commonwealth Secretariat.

among nations. However, this does not imply one big meeting along the lines of the 1944 affair. That meeting was historic and probably will never be replicated in terms of what was accomplished in so short a time. To attempt to do so would be foolhardy and counterproductive. The conditions that made it possible were unique. Thus, as interpreted and used here in this context, the procedural aspect is secondary. What is important is finding a way to encourage policy coordination that would provide the basis for trade and capital flows expansion that would ease the debt crisis and promote global growth with equity.

THE CASE AGAINST A NEW BRETTON WOODS APPROACH

It is very fashionable in some quarters to dismiss advocacy for a Bretton Woods approach to the debt crisis as premature, naive, unrealistic, and, above all, unnecessary and possbily harmful. The argument has several strands, the main one being that nothing is likely to be achieved by this process except the raising of expectations that are likely to be dashed when the spotlights are turned off and bland communiques are all that is left to show for the circus.

Perhaps the most articulate concise statement of the skeptics' position is the one presented by Edward Bernstein, who, as assistant director of monetary research at the U.S. Treasury in 1944, participated at Bretton Woods as a member of the U.S. delegation. In a retrospective article, he addresses the question head-on: "Do we need a new Bretton Woods?"[16] He concludes quite categorically: "There is no need for a conference to deal with international monetary

---

[16] Edward M. Berstein, "Do We Need a New Bretton Woods?" *Finance and Development*, (Washington, D.C.: World Bank/IMF, September 1984). Mr. Bernstein is now a guest scholar at the Brookings Institution.

problems." Leaving aside the reference to *a* conference as
a nonrelevant issue, we can focus on the substantive argu-
ments put forward.

Three main reasons are generally advanced in opposition to the concept of a new Bretton Woods, and Edward
Bernstein presents two of them. Each should be considered.

- The first reason is that the IMF is already available
  and is both mandated and adequate for bringing
  countries together for meaningful, well-focused discussion, and follow-through action:

  > Because the Bretton Woods Agreement established
  > the Fund as a permanent institution for consultation
  > and collaboration on international monetary prob-
  > lems, there are no problems that could come before
  > an international conference that the Fund is not al-
  > ready empowered to deal with. *As a practical matter,
  > the Annual Meeting of the Board of Governors of the
  > Fund is in every respect an international monetary con-
  > ference.* . . . An international monetary conference,
  > called to consider a wide range of questions, some of
  > which would be irrelevant and on none of which is
  > there a consensus, would inevitably cause confusion
  > and interfere with the *orderly* evolution of the interna-
  > tional monetary system. (Emphasis added.)

- The second reason is that the root cause for the present problems of volatility of exchange rates and,
  what is euphemistically called, "the imbalance in
  international payments" is to be found in *"the dis-
  ruptions in the world economy,* (which), although
  matters of urgent international concern, *have to be
  dealt with initially through national policies."* (Emphasis added.) The prescription Dr. Bernstein outlines as perhaps the only way:

  > A well-balanced pattern of international payments
  > with stable and orderly exchange rates can be restored

by the U.S. putting an end to their inflation through appropriate fiscal and monetary policies which would lead to a decline in interest rates, to higher rates of growth of output and of world trade and to remunerative prices for basic commodities.[17]

• A third argument advanced against the concept of a new Bretton Woods is enunciated by a breed of critic (or cynic) who might be labeled "the no-nonsense realist." These critics contend there is not now—or is there likely to be in the foreseeable future—a willingness or capability on the part of the U.S. administration and/or any powerful and/or influential congressional bloc to enter into any such agreement because it would constrain U.S. sovereignty. Accordingly, there is no point in pushing for it to happen. Most of those belonging to this school of thought would brush aside the argument that this stance is inconsistent with the United States continuing to respect constraining obligations under the IMF and World Bank's Articles of Agreement and other such agreements that underlie U.S. participation in multilateral institutions. The response would be either that this inconsistency is more apparent than real because the IMF's management is expected to talk with the master's voice, that of the largest shareholder, notwithstanding views to the contrary that might be expressed in meetings of the executive board of these institutions.

Each of these points merits attention before one can turn to the agenda items of the new Bretton Woods and (in the final chapter) consider what might be done to forge

---

[17] *Ibid,* p. 14. No elaboration is provided as to how one can recognize what is appropriate or how commodity prices could be raised to remunerative levels and the export markets assured.

our future, rather than standing by in a responsive mood waiting for our future to happen.

Is the IMF the Appropriate Instrument?

The fact that the IMF has the mandate and could, in theory, do the job is not being questioned. The strongest advocates for a new Bretton Woods, the deputies of the Group of 24, are in agreement on that point. In the final draft of their presentation prepared for the Interim Committee meeting scheduled for early October at the time of the annual IMF/World Bank meeting in Seoul, they concede that "a framework for policy coordination exists under the IMF Articles."[18]

However, the practical aspect is the governors have polarized into the G-10 and G-24 and the forums for the verbal jousting provide scarcely any opportunity for interaction and discussion, meaningful or otherwise.[19] In the Interim

---

[18] Intergovernmental Group of Twenty-four on International Monetary Affairs, *The Functioning and Improvement of the International Monetary System: Report of the Deputies of the Group of 24*, Washington, D.C., August 21, 1985, p. 3 (mimeo). The report is, however, critical of how the IMF exercises this responsibility and urges that "issues of a systemic character" and "the needs of developing countries" be given greater consideration.

[19] The Interim Committee was once known as the Committee of 20. Its official name is Committee of the Board of Governors on Reform of the International Monetary System and Related Issues. It meets at Annual Meetings and on an ad hoc basis when decisions have to be made.

The Development Committee's formal name is the Joint Ministerial Committee of the Board of Governors of the Bank and the Fund on the Transfer of Real Resources to Developing Countries. It also meets at the time of the Annual Meetings and often in between. The pattern of the committee's meetings changed at Seoul in as much as its duration was for two days and this provided opportunity for less formal afternoon sessions for some interaction on agenda items. The committee at present has no analytic/writing staff resources of its own but must draw on bank and fund staff. It has a potential usefulness in providing an opportu-

Committee, amendments to the IMF's structure (programs) and resources have been introduced but are not hammered out through a give-and-take discussion in the committee meeting. Anyone attending these meetings and familiar with the ways and mores of this institutional arrangement is bound to be impressed by the formalism and dismayed by the limitation of these ritualistic procedures. But that is, of course, the way those who favor the status quo would have it. So the ritual dance goes on from year to year.

One has only to look closely at the nature of the reforms already incorporated into amendments to the IMF's Articles of Agreement to see the recommendations, which were later incorporated as amendments, are hardly more than accommodation *ex post*. It suffices to quote one excerpt from a commentary by Joseph Gold, former general counsel and director of the fund's Legal Department, with regard to the reform on exchange arrangements incorporated in the Second Amendment of the Articles of Agreement. This amendment became effective in April 1978, almost five years after the *de facto* end of the par value system set up under the Bretton Woods Agreement. The Interim Committee approved an amendment that "represents *a complete departure* from the central feature of the original Articles, the par value system. . . . The emphasis in these provisions shifts from stable exchange rates to the orderly economic and financial conditions that will promote a stable system."[20] (Emphasis added.)

The IMF was henceforth to be relied on to ensure the

---

nity for governors to put some items on the global agenda (which can assume a life of their own in other forums), but its capacity for decision making is extremely limited by virtue of its ambiguous mandate and the way it is presently operated.

[20] Joseph Gold, "Some First Effects of the Second Amendment," *Finance & Development*, (September 1978). Reprinted in *Bretton Woods at Forty, 1944–84*. pp. 16–17.

effective operation of the international monetary system operating under the newly formalized rules. However, the record of performance of the IMF in the discharge of this surveillance responsibility has prompted the G-24, in its report prepared for presentation at the Interim Committee meeting in October, to comment about and deplore the IMF's asymmetrical, biased, and imbalanced application of this function. The complaint is that the surveillance "has so far been largely ineffective on major industrial countries (but has) fallen disproportionately on developing countries."[21] The asymmetry is especially significant with respect to the IMF's impact on the industrialized nations and particularly on the United States as the country that has a special responsibility when "the dollar standard" is the prevailing one. It is clear that responsible policies from an international perspective would call for the United States to constrain its level of consumption and investment, thereby reducing the unprecedented inflow of savings from the rest of the world, and for Germany and Japan to expand their levels of consumption. The IMF in its reports makes these points but has no leverage on the industrialized countries.

It is difficult to assess the damage this imbalance and impotence does to the IMF's reputation as a neutral agent in helping manage global monetary conditions and, within that framework, the debt crisis. The weakening of this role "impresario" diminishes the potential contribution the IMF can make to the resolution of the debt crisis. This adverse effect is compounded by the critical views surfacing with regard to its role in relation to those developing countries facing formidable debt problems. The emerging image is reflected not only in the speeches of Peruvian political figures but also in the commentaries of responsible columnists

---

[21] *The Reform of the International Monetary and Financial System*, p. 3.

writing for responsible journals—as, for example, Don McGillivray of the staid *Financial Times* (Toronto), who observed, "The IMF, in its attempts to clamp austerity on nations, is the present day equivalent of debtor's prison," and Peter Montagnon, Euromarkets correspondent of the *Financial Times* (U.K.), who noted that there are "increasing doubts over the IMF's actual competence and its ability to prescribe the right medicine."[22]

A question arises as to whether this image of the IMF can be overcome so as to enable it to exercise a role that is more evenhanded and more effective, two attributes that are very closely related. An assessment on this matter now is not encouraging because there seems to have been a serious weakening of the IMF management's position regarding its largest shareholder, the United States. This has eroded the IMF's reputation as honest broker, which underlies its surveillance function, and of its good offices in playing a mediating role between the policy positions of the ministers of the G-24 and the G-10.

The submissive posture of the IMF regarding the United States is well illustrated by the record of the IMF's role in the run-up to the debt crisis when the institution's ability to meet the global liquidity requirements were severely constrained. This was largely because of U.S. resistance to the IMF playing a more active role. The First Amendment, which enabled creation of Special Drawing Rights

---

[22] Don McGillivray, "Peru Takes New Approach to Paying Debt," *Financial Times* (Canada) (August 5, 1985). The column was sympathetic to President Garcia's decision to bypass the IMF in negotiating Peru's external debt problem.

On this point it might be pertinent to cite a comment by Peter Montagnon, "The Warning Lights Flash Again," *Financial Times* (U.K.) August 27, 1985: "Throughout Latin America a third year of crisis has provoked increasing doubts over the IMF's actual competence and its ability to prescribe the right medicine. Austerity is all well and good, the argument goes, so long as it produces results. . . . (As things are working out) it is hard even for Sr. Jesus Silva Herzog, Mexico's finance minister, to argue the case in favor of traditional IMF prescriptions."

(SDRs), was agreed upon only after great delays occasioned by U.S. opposition. SDRs were finally approved when the global financial situation had become very strained and, when finally issued, were grossly inadequate, so much so that the global liquidity requirements had to be met by default through the growing Eurocurrency market, with all that that type of strucutural change in the world's financial markets implied.[23]

The IMF has a very important role to play in helping ease the debt crisis and implement the necessary global conditions for a better world. But as a practical matter, the IMF as it exists today is seen to be too partisan and unimaginative in responding to the debt crisis, as it had been during the 1970s when the crisis conditions were being set in place. Thus, it is hardly surprising that there is a search for other avenues on how to achieve the necessary policy cooperation and coordination in the sphere of trade and finance, which are essential conditions for the longer-term resolution of the present crisis.

Can We Expect National Policies— Particularly that of the United States— to Be Devised with Due Regard to Broader Global Responsibilities?

The IMF Articles of Agreement, in Article IV, obliges each country to have "due regard for the circumstances of each

---

[23] For a concise summary, see "The Institutional Evolution of the IMF," *Finance & Development*, (September 1984). This is not meant to imply that the IMF could have been able to meet the challenge *alone* through a much expanded issuance of Special Drawing Rights and policies of linkage with liquidity requirements. But it seems clear there was resistance by the United States (and sometimes others) to even attempt to have the IMF play a more important role in the 1970s. The commercial banks were left to do their thing.

member." It is relevant to ask about the probability of this happening, particularly with respect to the United States and Japan and other industrialized nations. The Bernstein thesis (and the rationale for the recent amendments to the IMF Articles of Agreement) is that in a world of flexible exchange rates there would be stability and balanced international accounts over the long run *if:*

i) The underlying factors influencing these rates and balances were themselves stable.

ii) The volume and direction of the flow of resources through trade and capital movements were to adhere to the logic of the debt cycle hypothesis.

In order to attain those desired conditions the major trading countries must discharge certain obligations with regard to the formulation of their national policies that have to do with being sensitive to the impact of their policies on other countries.

This applies with special relevance to the United States, not because it is the most delinquent in this regard, but simply because, as Dr. Bernstein implies, the most powerful economy and reserve currency country has to lead the way for these two conditions to be met. Yet, as the history of the post-war decades reveals, the United States in the past four decades has rarely played the role expected of it within the framework of the Bretton Woods agreement when circumstances forced a choice between short-term parochial interests and longer-term global interests. The United States has abandoned the obligations whenever it became the hard way to go, whenever immediate politically unappealing measures with respect to monetary and fiscal policy were called for to maintain the value of the dollar and provide other international public goods that would help assure global growth.

There was even little regard shown for both the logic and civility of cooperation and coordination. Some of the

most drastic policy decisions, which affected most severely
other countries, were taken without consultation or even
warning. Commentators, as far apart in the vantage from
which they have viewed the world scene as Drs. Raul Prebisch and Henry Kissinger, speak with one voice on this
issue:

Dr. Prebisch:

The use of the dollar as an international as well as a national
currency has given the United States the privilege of creating
international money and obtaining free of charge part of the
product of the rest of the world in exchange for this money.
At the same time, it has imparted to the United States the
responsibility of following principles inspired by the needs
of the world economy. Full use has been made of the privilege,
but the way in which the responsibility has been carried out
can hardly be the subject of admiration.[24]

Dr. Kissinger:

We live with the paradox of a global economy which lacks
a system for setting agreed long-range goals, . . . (a system
characterized by) incongruity between the internationaliza-
tion of the world economy and the dogged strengthening of
national autonomy in economic decision-making . . . A case
in point (is) the unilateral decision by the United States in
1971 to suspend the convertibility of the dollar and to impose
a 10 percent surcharge, the effect (of which) was to overthrow

---

[24] "International Monetary Indiscipline and the Debt Problem," p.
173. He added, "The creation of international currency has thus been
governed by domestic consideration—namely, the monetary policy de-
sires of the main dynamic center of capitalism. An inflationary situation
had been developing in the United States even before the first oil crisis."
   Professor Kindleberger, in his paper on international public good,
addresses the question of whether, as the provider of the reserve currency
or international money, the United States is extracting seignorage: "The
dollar is not a monopoly currency and foreign holdings earn modest
rates of interest," *ibid,* p. 10.

the Bretton Woods arrangement affecting all countries—without prior consultation or notice to anyone.[25]

With these questions about discordance becoming rampant, with the capacity for leadership of the dominant economic and financial nation significantly weakened, and with severe strains in the prevailing system breaking out in the form of debt crises, it is to be expected that a new institutional framework would have to adapt either gradually or dramatically. National policies of economies as dominant as that of the United States need to be devised on the basis of the perception of its *global* responsibilities and not merely on the basis of its narrow national interests or there will be a heavy price to pay for both the United States and the whole global community. The experience of the breakdown of the Bretton Woods agreement illustrates this point dramatically. The historical record indicates what happens, when, in this highly integrated economic and financial global village, the United States tries to go it alone. One episode from the recent past can dramatically illustrate this point, though the train of events that unfolded had deep roots in past U.S. fiscal and monetary policy, particularly during the Vietnam War period, and in global structural changes that, since World War II, had brought about a diminution of the overwhelming preeminence of the U.S. economy.

March 1, 1968, marks a symbolic turning point. On that day the London gold market was besieged by buyers. Its normal level of sales, 3 or 4 tons per day, suddenly shot up to 40. Within two weeks, it was 10 times as high, forcing the U.S. Treasury to sell a million dollars worth of gold from its inventory every two or three minutes, a drain that would have exhausted its stock within weeks. The gold binge was on, with a spectacular rise in gold prices to levels

---

[25] *International Economic and World Order.*

in excess of $800 per troy ounce. Meanwhile, in mid March, Treasury Secretary Connally opted to restrict the sale of gold to exclude private buyers on the London gold market and asked governments not to convert their dollar holdings into gold, lest it further undermine the value of their own reserves, which were largely in dollars.

This was a desperate measure to meet the collapse of the public's confidence in the willingness of the U.S. administration to maintain the dollar at the parity postulated in the Bretton Woods agreement. During the Vietnam War, the United States had embarked on an inflationary course in its monetary and fiscal policies, a choice that was made in response to domestic political considerations. Over the next three years, no effective steps were taken to reassure foreign holders of U.S. dollars that the value would not erode further. Thus, this 1968 decision was the inexorable prelude to the 1971 decision to formally announce the closing of the gold window, which, in effect, precluded even central banks from converting their dollar holdings into gold. This was the action that formally broke what Professor Richard Cooper called "the Bretton Woods bargain."[26]

The subsequent history—leading up through the recession and shocks of the 1970s to its culmination in the present global debt crisis—attests to the high price paid by all for breaking an agreement of this kind, which sets forth the rules of the game and is in the nature of an international public good or service.[27] There is obviously a compel-

---

[26] "A Monetary System for the Future," *Foreign Affairs* (fall 1984). Professor Cooper, former under secretary of state for economic affairs, writes that Bretton Woods was an understanding or a bargain wherein the United States was to play a pivotal role as stabilizer, exercising an overwhelming measure of control over key features of the international financial system such as the global money supply and exchange rates.

[27] To cite but two aspects of this cost in the case of the United States alone: it is estimated by a congressional committee that since 1981, as a direct result of the reduction in Latin America's imports

ling need in a highly integrated economic world for an international economic and financial modus operandi based on collectively acceptable and collectively enforceable behavioral rules that would temper the pursuit of short-term parochial interests, or constrain the formulation of national policies by factoring in broader obligations. Leadership is called for to provide those international public goods necessary for global growth. The question is: Can it be expected even under pressure of a threatened breakdown of the global economic system?

Will the United States Have to Acquiesce to a New Bretton Woods?

As unfolding events continue to demonstrate that the present case-by-case approach will not suffice, more favorable consideration likely will be given to a policy of global policy coordination on trade and capital issues that lay at the heart of the original Bretton Woods agreement. This time, the participation will not likely be done in the spirit that characterized the U.S. role at Bretton Woods in 1944. The exceptional circumstances of that period enabled the U.S. policy makers to formally assume global economic obligations despite the opposition of vociferous isolationist members of the Senate. The overwhelming dominance of the United States assured a coincidence of interest between what was in the U.S. interest and what was ostensibly in the global interest, but there was also a measure of compassion in this international policy position. The United States had emerged from World War II as the recognized leading economic power whose industrial might topped that of the

---

(which is directly related to their debt situation and the related global recession, i) the U.S. trade deficit has increased by about one-fifth; ii) between 800,000 and 1.4 million jobs in the United States have been eliminated.

rest of the world combined, a world exhausted from the ravages of war. While both mood and circumstances have changed over the intervening decades, the background provides a perspective on the current pressures and the limited choices now open to the U.S. leadership.

The preparatory work leading up to the Bretton Woods conference was begun soon after the decisive victories at Stalingrad and El Alamein, when thoughts began to turn from exclusive concern with survival to the more mundane, yet vital, issues of the kind of world that would, or could be made to, emerge from the carnage. These very special circumstances made it both imperative and feasible to contemplate imaginative institutional initiatives. It was believed that in the aftermath of the war there would be a clean slate on which to write the framework or guiding principles for future economic and financial arrangements. Thus, international currency proposals were being put forward and ideas for new institutional agencies were being forged before the war had even ended.[28] There was a widely held view that out of the crucible of breakdown would emerge innovative arrangements to facilitate trade and thus growth with financial institutional arrangements in the service of trade. The arrangements were guided by an

---

[28] M. Kalecki and E. F. Schumacher, "International Clearing and Long-term Lending" and other articles in "New Plans for International Trade," *Bulletin of the Oxford Institute of Statistics*, supplement, (August 1943).

See Robert Asher and Edward Mason's, *The World Bank Since Bretton Woods*, (Washington, D.C.: Brookings Institution, 1973) and Robert W. Oliver, *International Economic Cooperation and the World Bank* (London: Macmillan Press, 1975), which provide excellent background indicating the spirit of that era and the key roles of J. M. Keynes and William White. Michael Moffitt in his book *The World's Money (op. cit.)* has an interesting chapter on this titled, "From Bretton Woods to Camp David." On the occasion of the 40th anniversary there have been some interesting recollections printed in various journals including *Finance and Development* issues of March, June, September, and December 1984.

attitude that one observer identified as "a conscious political and moral reaction against prewar conditions."[29]

While the Bretton Woods conference had a very exceptional mandate and there is little literal resemblance between the years predating Bretton Woods and today's conditions, one common feature is an awareness that a crisis has occurred that portends major change, whether willed or not. It thus seems safe to say that a breakthrough action will occur soon. The pressures are building too fast and too awesomely for even the cynics to be complacent. They, too, must answer to the consequences of continuing on a business-as-usual course or trying to manage the debt problem as if the old rules apply and pretend that a few dollops of extra cash are all that is necessary to sweeten the bitter pill of adjustment.

It matters whether the movement toward a new Bretton Woods is made by design or forced by events. The preferred method is to be guided by forethought and design, but even the second-best route to the destination may suffice—if we don't fall off the figurative cliff in the meantime. Once the current debt crisis is seen as an integral part of a deep-seated transformation of the global economic and financial system, the door is open to considering policy approaches that have the breadth and depth commensurate to the problem.

There is a growing recognition that a turning point requiring a series of hard choices is imminent. There is, however, less recognition that the profound changes wrought over the past four decades are of a structural nature both

---

[29] Josef Steindl, "Stagnation Theory and Stagnation Policy," *Cambridge Journal of Economics* (October 1979), p. 8. He identifies this psychological factor as one of two major driving forces for the postwar growth decades of the 1950s and 1960s. The other one he lists is "tension between the two superpowers which led to large armament spending and technological competition as well as to the economic cooperation of the western industrialized countries under the leadership of the U.S."

in terms of 1) how trade and finance are handled and the size and direction of these flows, and 2) the ability of the United States to take on the type of leadership responsibilities that were assumed at Bretton Woods and the necessity of sharing such leadership with Japan and other nations.

These changes are basic to any resolution of the debt crisis. The need is for systemic measures to overcome the larger problem of which the debt crisis forms a part. The exact features of any eventual agreement will not resemble the 1944 version anymore than the circumstances of the two periods resemble each other, but the underlying principles of institutional arrangements of policy coordination and policy discipline will bear very close resemblance.

THE BRETTON WOODS II AGENDA ITEMS

The agenda would include the full range of issues that directly and indirectly affect the debt burden, such as volatile exchange rate movements, high real interest rate levels, low commodity prices compounded by increasingly unfavorable terms of trade, growing protectionism, stagnant official aid, declining private capital flows, and so on. It would be a full agenda but the core ideas are limited to a few:

1. How to make operational the policy discipline and the policy coordination so as to stabilize or dampen fluctuations in exchange rates, make trade and capital flows more conducive to healthy growth and so forth.
2. How to bring interest rates down to their historic levels and keep them steady.
3. How to get aid flows up toward the 0.7 percent of GNP target and beyond.

These three agenda items merit amplification and will be discussed in Chapter Eight.

The drafters of the guidelines for a new Bretton Woods

agreement will have two advantages—the perspective that comes with experience and the existence of two seasoned institutions, the World Bank and the International Monetary Fund and a panoply of related regional development banks and agencies within the U.N. system. New paths will have to be charted in the fulfillment of their present and future mandates. Recognizing the nature of the present reality and the formidable challenges ahead implies a central role for these institutions. One of the governors of the IMF at the 1985 meeting posed the question:

> Can we select for (the annual meeting of) 1986 the theme of a fundamental restructuring of the Bretton Woods institutions? Instead of slogans of a second Bretton Woods, can we analyze the past 40 years' experience dispassionately . . . and offer some constructive solutions?

The next chapter explores some salient aspects of past and current policies and actions and the potential these international financial institutions might exercise in relation to the global debt crisis both to ease the adjustment and help assure longer-term growth objectives.

CHAPTER SEVEN

The World Bank and the International Monetary Fund: Possible Roles in and beyond the Debt Crisis

It has to be accepted that LDC debt problems would not have reached such troubling dimensions had the major industrial powers and official institutions played a more assertive role in the initial period following the second oil shock. Of course, the IMF and the World Bank are limited by the wishes of their member governments. But passivity was an unfortunate response.

Rimmer de Vries[1]

This is certainly not the finest hour for multilateralism. But the fault is not that of the Bretton Woods institutions. They would have liked to do more, much more. They have often acted with rare courage. The fault is really ours—the member governments and we, the governors—for we have failed these institutions and betrayed our own heritage.

Mahbub ul Haq[2]

---

[1] Senior vice-president, Morgan Guaranty Trust Company, in a talk on "International Balance of Payments Financing and Adjustment," *IMF Conference on International Money, Credit and the SDR*, March 24, 1983. (mimeo, p. 9).

He goes on to say, "If the fund and bank were not going to provide credit to the graduate borrowers, a closer working relationship with the commercial banks, who were assuming the financing burden, should have been developed well before the present debt difficulties."

[2] Pakistan minister for finance, planning, and economic affairs and governor of the Fund for Pakistan, formerly director, policy planning, World Bank. Statement made at Annual Meeting of World Bank/IMF, Seoul, October 10, 1985, (Press Release no. 7).

THE RESPONSE TO MEET THE SHORT-TERM ASPECTS OF THE DEBT CRISIS

When the debt crisis was triggered in the summer of 1982, the International Monetary Fund and the World Bank were the principal institutions to which the world turned for a response. The Bretton Woods institutions were approaching their 40th birthday and the warning signals had been flashing for many years, but the response, when it came, had to be improvised and strongly bolstered by fashioning ad hoc rescue packages that called also for the involvement of other institutions such as the Bank for International Settlement (BIS) and of several governments, particularly the United States, whose banking system had a great deal at stake.

While the IMF was quick to engage in a rescue role, the World Bank—given its longer-term mandate—was rather sluggish in reacting to the emergency of mid-1982. One commentator, Pedro-Pablo Kuczynski, voiced a widely held view: "The World Bank has the image of having slept soundly through the (first phase) of the debt crisis." Federal Reserve Board Chairman Paul Volcker was moved to ask World Bank officials, "Where have you been?"

The announcement of Barber B. Conable's selection as the U.S. nominee for president of the World Bank to succeed A. W. (Tom) Clausen provided an occasion for the U.S. administration to reaffirm its position on this issue when President Reagan indicated he will look to Conable to "remake the bank into the lead agency coping with the Third World's debt crisis." The implication is clear. In the eyes of the Reagan administration, *if* it is to play that leading role, the World Bank is in need of reform.

This issue of reform of the World Bank and the IMF is not a new theme, but placed in this context there are two related questions that need to be posed: What is meant or implied by the phrase "leading agency coping with the debt crises"? If the World Bank were to assume this role, what are the implications with respect to its relations to the IMF, which has the short-term fire-fighting role, and to its main mandate for long-term development?

The issue becomes complicated because of profoundly divergent assumptions about the appropriate roles of these two institutions. This is not an academic issue. Some of the recommended changes could destroy or seriously damage these institutions, particularly, the World Bank if, in being bent to meet the exigencies of the moment, it is severely crippled in meeting the development mandate that has been its main focus and unique responsibility.[3]

A sketch of how the IMF and the World Bank have each responded to the emergency phase of the debt crisis provides the basis for consideration of what role they each should play and could play, separately or together, in the short term. The long-term aspect, which relates to the future beyond the immediate crisis period, needs to be considered separately. From this emerge some ideas as to what constitutional and policy changes in these institutions are both desirable and feasible.[4]

---

[3] For a succint recent review of this issue, see Khadija Haq, ed., *Crisis of the '80s: World Monetary, Financial and Human Resource Development Issues,* (Washington, D.C.: North-South Roundtable (SID), 1983), especially, Chapter 22 by Khadija Haq on "The Need for Institutional Reform," which summarized the discussion of the Instabul meeting in August 1983 sponsored by SID and the U.N.D.P. See also chapters by Sidney Dell and by Michael Sakbani on that theme. See also Gerald Helleiner, "The Rise and Decline of the IMF," and R. Cranford Pratt, "International Bankers and the Crisis of Debt," in *Banking on Poverty: The Global Impact of the IMF & World Bank,* ed. R. Cranford Pratt, (Toronto: University of Toronto Press, 1984).

[4] Changes that call for such constitutional amendments to the Articles of Agreement in theory can be made by the governors who hold the shares for their respective countries. The weighted voting arrangement gives the governors of the powerful and richer nations an overwhelming influence on such constitutional issues. Indeed, on such matters the United States has a veto power by virtue of the number of

THE IMF's RESPONSE: FIRE FIGHTING WITHOUT MUCH WATER PRESSURE

After the initial oil price increases in 1973 and 1974, there were early tremors of an incipient debt crisis. The fear of such an eventuality was real enough to prompt the governors of the central banks of the major industrialized countries, acting as the Group of 10 (or G-10), to announce in a short communique issued in the spring of 1974 that "means are available for the provision of temporary liquidity and will be used if and when necessary." The words were probably meant to reassure the financial community, which was expected to undertake the petrodollar recycling process on an unprecedented scale.

Meanwhile, it was decided to open up two new windows of concessional aid: 1) an oil facility that, between 1975 and 1977, lent $8.2 billion to more than 100 countries at lower rates and longer maturies, and 2) a gold trust fund that lent $1.3 billion over four years.[5] Over each of these years, on average, the IMF lent slightly more than $3 billion, a sum that takes on significance when measured against the $40 billion deficit of the oil-importing developing countries in 1974 and compared with the annual $6 billion in aid during that period from the OPEC nations alone.

---

shares and the minimum percentage required to make such changes. This does not, however, apply to normal policy issues of an operational nature relating to the criteria and procedures for lending and borrowing.

Policy changes can be made relatively easily from a procedural standpoint, while constitutional changes call for amendments to the Articles of Agreement of these institutions. No issue related to managing the debt crisis need require changes of a constitutional nature, which would be much too difficult to achieve. This is not to say that such changes ought to be ignored if, from a broader and longer perspective, they are considered desirable. The difficult ought not to preclude the desirable.

[5] The funds were secured from the sale of part of the IMF's gold reserves. The reflow from the loans made from this fund is included in Treasury Secretary Baker's proposal.

Over the first three decades of its existence, the IMF had established a financial safety net comprised of the following:

1. The Compensatory Financing Facility, which provides immediate liquidity to countries temporarily suffering a deterioration in their balance of payments.
2. Standby Credit, which provides support for a jointly negotiated economic adjustment program for one or two years.
3. The Extended Fund Facility, which can be used in support of structural adjustment program for three years.

This is in addition to the resources available under:

4. The Quota Entitlement, which is tantamount to a membership share that is held on deposit with the IMF, available in tranches (or slices), the first of which is provided automatically. Each member's quota is based on its gold and dollar reserves, its average imports and exports, and their ratio to its national income. The first quota tranche of 25 percent can be drawn without conditions imposed while the others are available with severe conditions incorporated in standby agreements, which set out the policy proposals. The agreements specify monetary and other targets meant to correct the balance-of-payments imbalance that occasioned the need for the standby agreement. These funds are not paid out at once and can be stopped in the all-too-frequent event of noncompliance.[6]

---

[6] On joining each country pays in 25 percent of its quota in gold or dollar equivalent and the remainder becomes callable in its own currency. The quota determines its voting strength, and on that basis, the United States has 126,000 votes or almost 20 percent of the total, while 40 African countries have an aggregate vote of less than 35,000. The quota determines the total credits it can draw upon.

5. The General Agreement to Borrow (GAB), which was established in the early 1960s by the large quota members and, until 1983 available only to them. (In that year the access under GAB was broadened.) The GAB set special constraints on access to limit claims on the regular funds of the IMF in the event that several of the countries with large quotas applied at the same time.

These resources were never meant to meet a challenge of the nature and scale of the debt crisis that erupted in mid-1982 and were, therefore, insufficient.

The IMF has always been constrained by the major shareholders, particularly the United States, from playing a major role either as a source of liquidity or as a regulatory force in the international financial system. Before 1982, frequent requests were made by the developing country governors and executive directors (as well as IMF management) for enlarged access to Quota Entitlements, increases in General Agreement to Borrow (GAB), and the creation of more Special Drawing Rights (SDRs).[7] The United States (sometimes joined by Japan, the United Kingdom, and West Germany) opposed granting these requests. Thus, during the 1970s, while the private banking community forged new modes of operation, the IMF was being reined in. Mean-

---

[7] SDRs are the IMF's official unit of account. They are also known as paper gold and valued on the basis of a basket of currencies. The SDR as a reserve asset has a value determined by that of the five currencies to which it is linked. SDRs were introduced in 1970 to provide a source of liquidity other than the U.S. dollar.

After four years of negotiation in the late 1960s the United States was prevailed on to agree to the creation of SDRs as an addition to but not a replacement for the dollar and gold basis of the monetary system then in place. Even after agreeing, the United States then sought to severely limit the increases to the very modest amount of $9.5 billion over the years 1970–72 on the grounds that the new SDRs would augment global liquidity, which might, in turn, rekindle inflation. Almost 10 billion SDRs were distributed over three years in the initial period and 12 billion over the three years after 1979 on the basis of the quotas of each country. Developing countries thus received only about one-third.

while, the volume of operations of the Euromarket expanded from $60 billion to $600 billion with the IMF authorizing about $30 billion ($25 billion SDRs) to contribute less than half of 1 percent to the expansion in total global liquidity. The IMF suffered a relative setback in other important respects: from 1974 to 1981, the IMF financed only about 3 percent of the $427 billion total cumulative current account deficits of oil-importing developing countries and provided about 4 percent of the total gross capital flows. By 1982 the percentage of the IMF quota allocations to the volume of world trade fell to less than 4 percent, a dramatic decline when contrasted with the 1945 level of about 16 percent. In effect, the IMF was consigned to play a role of a spectator and commentator, able and willing to reveal some disquietude about developments but impotent to do much about it.

When, in the summer of 1982, the problem took on the dimensions of a crisis, the major powers turned to the IMF to play a central role in providing capital to the debtor countries so as to prevent threatening defaults. The IMF was unable to provide the financial resources commensurate with the need. Thus, the financial contribution of the IMF was to forestall or slow the withdrawal of funds by nervous creditors and, at the same time, to assure the injection of additional funds both from the banks already committed to a limited extent and from its own resources. However, the IMF's main role was organizational.

The IMF focused on convening and servicing consortia for public debt renegotiation under the Paris Club and for commercial bank debt rescheduling under ad hoc arrangements. Despite the rash of reschedulings, the IMF was able to intervene in all cases so as to enable the creditors and debtors to reach some understanding to prevent default. In terms of this limited objective, the IMF response was quick and eminently successful.

The infusion of adequate new funds proved to be difficult, particularly as bankers were eager to reduce their exposure and the IMF had little financial clout. The weakness dates back many years. In September 1982 when the IMF governors at the meeting of the Interim Committee gave the IMF management encouragement to act, they did not provide the requisite financial resources with which to do so. The existing weak financial safety net had to be buttressed by contributions from various sources, such as key central banks and other institutions and governmental agencies as well as from the Bank for International Settlements (BIS), which contributed $4 billion.

In the spring of 1983 the task was made easier when the Interim Committee approved a 50 percent quota increase amounting to about $30 billion over three years and a $12.5 billion expansion of GAB (from $6.5 billion to $19 billion). Thus, when the debtor countries of Latin America came to the rescheduling table, the IMF was able to contribute more than $16 billion. By the end of 1984 the IMF had disbursed more than $22 billion to more than 60 countries and made commitments for another $8 billion. The fact that the IMF was able to put together a rescue package of this magnitude was impressive in light of the hurdles it had to overcome.

At first the United States opposed the requested increases for additional financial resources on the grounds that the IMF in its role as convener or organizer of the debt would be welcomed by both creditors and debtors rescheduling exercises. This position was modified only when it became clear that the imposition of severe terms on its loans to balking debtors called for backup financial clout.[8] The IMF was then provided with only enough deemed to be sufficient to ensure its debt policing function. This policy of keeping a tight financial rein on the IMF was maintained

---

[8] Even then, the U.S. administration requested a cutback of the proposed quota access to a limit of 115 percent in any one year and 450 percent on a cumulative basis, a request to which the other major powers acquiesced.

even at the annual meeting in Seoul in October 1985. There, despite the bleak prospects for commodity prices, the governors decided to slightly reduce Quota Entitlement limits and to reduce the limits for assistance under the Compensatory Finance Facility (CFF), actions that had the effect of reducing yearly and cumulative access to IMF funds. This decision was taken despite the fact that the 15 countries identified in the Baker initiative would be obliged to make net repayments to the IMF in 1987 and 1988 amounting to about $3 billion on the basis of financial resources available under current IMF programs.[9]

At first glance, the policy of reducing financial aid at a time of greater need seems incomprehensible. However, there appears to be a logical explanation: since member states have an "entitlement" merely by virtue of membership, the effect of such decisions is to reduce the amount of financing the IMF can make available unconditionally that thereby making IMF conditionality apply to a greater proportion of its remaining available funds. The donor countries thus can gain greater clout through the IMF at a time when the IMF is relied on to apply tough measures. The advice that is backed by money can be tough. It can also extend in scope to issues well beyond the balance-of-payments aspects of macro-policy that have been the traditional and designated domain of the IMF. Sidney Dell, a former U.N. official, has characterized this role as grandmotherly.[10]

---

[9] Eleven of these countries will be making net repayments. This negative flow is due in some measure to the fact that since the debt crisis of '82, the IMF provided about $15 billion to a dozen of the 15 countries. However, their obligations to the IMF over the same period will amount to about $10 billion.

[10] Sidney Dell, in his essay "The International Monetary System: Some Reflections on Institutional Reform," *Crisis of the '80s*, pp. 264–65, is critical of this "grandmotherly" role:

"The fund cannot and should not supervise the running of national

THE WORLD BANK's RESPONSE: FLEXIBILITY AT WHAT PRICE?

The World Bank is the major channel through which the developing countries can tap the international financial markets, an access that traditionally has been almost exclusively related to specific development projects or programs. The project cycle process of identifying, preparing, and appraising these projects takes considerable time and staff resources since the bank works closely with the borrowing country.[11] Once approved, the disbursements are made against performance on a prearranged schedule that usually requires a further number of years before the loans are fully disbursed. Thus, in mid-1982, by virtue of its mode of operation and its orientation toward longer-term development, the World Bank was severely constrained from actively participating in the immediate debt rescue operation.

Nevertheless, the World Bank did manage to increase lending to the debt-strapped developing countries by shifting a greater proportion of its loans into quicker-disbursing modes. In the late 1970s, the Bank's Executive Board made a policy decision to devote about 10 percent of its lending for nonproject purposes. When the challenge of the debt crisis arose, this type of lending was conceived as a means of gaining greater policy clout over borrowing countries

---

economies which involves political and social as well as economic accountability. The fund's evaluations of its own programs indicate a failure rate sufficiently high to warrant considerable caution regarding the capacity of an international organization to prescribe workable and acceptable domestic policies for countries. The fund should address itself much more to balance-of-payments than to domestic policies, and the performance of borrowers should be judged much more in terms of balance-of-payments results than in terms of the domestic policies pursued."

[11] The median *elapsed* time from departure of appraisal mission to board presentation is 43 weeks with the range as low as 11 weeks and as high as 226. The median *applied* time is 66 staff weeks. "World Bank Lending Approaches," *World Bank News* (April 1986), p. 9.

while speeding up the lending process and the rate of disbursement against loan commitments.

By 1980 the first structural adjustment loan (SAL) had been added to the bank's repertoire. Another type of loan quickly followed, the special assistance program, that was designed to provide foreign exchange to meet emergency needs for spare parts and maintenance to keep existing projects operational.[12] Today the classification of the bank's lending operations is more finely shaded, eliminating the sharp distinction between project and program lending and between slow and rapid disbursing loans. Ranked in order of speed of disbursement, apart from the SALs, which have a disbursement period of from one to three years, and the special assistance program loans, the list of loan types is as follows:

- Sector adjustment loan, one to four years.
- Emergency reconstruction loan, two to five years.
- Technical assistance loan, two to six years.
- Financial intermediary loan, three to seven years.
- Sector investment and maintenance loan, three to seven years.
- Specific investment loan, the traditional project loan, four to nine years.

Despite very strong support by the U.S. administration for lending under the quicker-disbursing types of loans, particularly the SALs, the rate and geographic scope of

---

[12] The "special action program" was conceived to be experimental to help break bottlenecks on ongoing projects caused by shortage of foreign exchange and was limited in total amount to only $500 million during a trial two-year period. It played a critically important role in breaking bottlenecks in more than 250 projects that were threatened by foreign exchange shortages and enabled additional disbursements to be made, amounting to almost $5 billion on projects in process.

such loans has been limited by circumstance and mandate.[13] After five years in operation total SAL lending had amounted to less than $5 billion for 30 projects in fewer than 20 countries, of which five countries absorbed more than 40 percent.

The SAL type lending had initially been rationalized by the desirability to diversify the World Bank's product mix with a variety of lending approaches. In response to the special circumstances of the period, program lending justification changed qualitatively from a process that was discretionary in its timing and volume to one that was urgent and imperative. Quick disbursement was required by hard-pressed debtor countries. Thus, in fiscal year 1983–84, Brazil was accorded special treatment: it was permitted to double the amount borrowed in that year as compared with the $2.3 billion level of the years before the crisis. At the same time, the total lending to the other Latin American countries went from $6.4 billion to $5.7 billion.[14] In the spring of 1986, again under extraordinary circumstances, Mexico received similar treatment: at one board meeting about $1 billion in loans were approved, a $465 million loan for reconstruction pertaining to the September 1985 earthquake and a $500 million SAL.

---

[13] Hobart Rowen reported that U.S. Treasury Secretary James Baker III, in testimony before a Senate Appropriations subcommittee on March 12, 1986, stated, "Under the new policy that the U.S. is encouraging at the World Bank, there will be more structural and sectoral loans, and less project lending": "Senate Wary on Funds for Multilaterals: Baker Told Development Banks May Feel Gramm-Rudman Lash." *Washington Post* (March 13, 1986).

[14] In doing so the bank exceeded the 10 percent guideline on limiting exposure to any single borrower. The rule set by the board was applied flexibly by management. In reporting on this, it is envisaged that the percentage might rise to 11.5 percent at some point during the next few years. The only other country currently affected by this guideline limit is India.

Significantly, these SALs were characterized by a more pervasive conditionality and were more blatantly articulated. For example, the SAL to Mexico calls for an unprecedented interventionism aimed at encouraging Mexico to implement a program of reduced import barriers and export subsidies and other measures that indicate "a commitment to market-oriented economic reforms."[15]

This emphasis on market-oriented economic reforms as a condition of World Bank assistance raises serious questions about the shift in the role of the World Bank both in relation to the short-term debt problem and the bank's long-term development mandate. There would be no contentious issue if the expedient was also manifestly the desirable course to follow; under circumstances when this is not so clear, we confront a hard choice. On this score there are two related issues that merit consideration.

The first aspect relates to the World Bank's expertise. Having been recruited and promoted on the basis of the project orientation of bank lending, does the management and staff have the competence, both technically and judgmentally, to be advising on macro issues involving social, political, economic, and financial dimensions? Stanley Please, a former World Bank staff member with long years of experience, makes a case for "substantive refocussing of the World Bank's activities towards supporting policy and institutional reform rather than project objectives," and assets that, whatever absolute advantage the World Bank might have as a project lending agency, its compara-

---

[15] In announcing this loan, a World Bank spokesman made reference to the Baker initiative and explained the timing: "This happens to be when the countries' internal policies now qualify them for new loans." He was referring as well to a $350 million loan to Argentina to speed up agricultural reform, a loan that called for revision of subsidy, pricing, and tax policies in the agricultural sector.

tive advantage must certainly be in handling policy issues (of a 'macro' nature)."[16]

One could juxtapose differing judgments as, for example, the opinion of an executive director, Ferdinand van Dam, who holds the view that, "We (in the World Bank) are not made for that debt-financing business. Our capital, our reserves, our staff is not built for debt financing. It simply is not our field of work."[17]

Whether the World Bank structure, policies, staff expertise and experience are readily adaptable to undertake different responsibilities is debatable. What is more important is the recognition of the qualitative difference between structural adjustment lending and project loan conditionality.[18] Macro-policy advice incorporated in SALs touches the very core of the development policy-making process. One might describe this in terms of a medical metaphor as the difference between treating the heart and brain as compared with treating the arms and legs. The rate and manner of growth and other related societal objectives

---

[16] See Stanley Please, *The Hobbled Giant: Essays on the World Bank*, (Boulder and London: Westview Press, 1984), pp. 17–39. He recognizes the political implications of this and accordingly urges "reform of Bretton Woods as it relates to the World Bank . . . to develop voting, management, and staffing patterns that would make the bank more acceptable politically in undertaking its policy responsibilities."

[17] *Institutional Investor* (December 1985), p. 284.

[18] There is a certain degree of fuzziness between conditionality in relation to project financing and program lending in as much as even well-planned and executed projects can fail because of an inappropriate framework of macro-policies relating to pricing, taxes, and so on, which cannot be addressed on a strictly sectoral level. First-rate engineering and socioeconomic analysis applied to a project or program is not helpful in an economic and political environment that is not congenial. However, there is little doubt that a structural adjustment or program loan involves intervention on a massive scale; whereas, the project approach calls for a more modest degree of intervention usually limited to the relevant sector.

of the recipient countries are the very stuff of that elusive but important concept called sovereignty. Thus, this shift of emphasis in the bank's operations calls for an even greater degree of sensitivity to the views of the debtor developing countries. Now, when the major burden of adjustment is being borne by the people of the borrowing countries, when they are already in a very weak financial position and when the global economic conditions are hardly buoyant, the task is particularly awesome.

The second aspect follows from this difficulty. The massive SAL intrudes into key facets of the life of the recipient countries and is likely to arouse resentment. This is particularly so when the failure rate of such interventionism is bound to be very high under prevailing conditions, whether or not the quality of the advice being offered to debtor developing countries by World Bank and IMF staff with regard to macro or structural issues is sound. This is partly attributable to volatile global conditions and partly to a policy of rigid adherence to the "country focus" on a case-by-case basis, which makes the task more difficult. The country-by-country advice currently being offered on macro policy by the World Bank and the IMF has the earmarks of a boiler-plate prescription for easing the debt problem. The standard features of which need to be questioned:

a. Recommending a course of action that calls for restructuring or reorienting the recipient countries' economies so as to increase exports to earn the foreign exchange needed to both service debts and pay for essential imports. This advice comes up against the "fallacy of aggregation": what may be possible and "good advice" for one or a few countries may not be possible or desirable for a large number of countries. This is clearly the case with regard to the policy that urges an export orientation. Fostering greater dependence on foreign markets is a risky course to follow as the history of the movements of commodity prices and terms of trade can attest. The most questionable aspect of this advice is that there are no assurances that, on the other side of the trade equation, the industrialized developed countries are prepared to import the goods the developing countries can export and to do so at reasonable prices.[19]

b. Recommending policies designed to attract foreign investors to dismantle or "privatize" public enterprises, to deregulate, and so forth. It cannot be taken for granted that there is available both the requisite entrepreneurial talent and the infrastructural base that investors need. Nor is there assurance that the terms under which such investment by native and foreign entrepreneurs might occur would necessarily be compatible with the public interest in the broadest sense. Thus, the advocacy of this private enterprise/ market policy as an objective, rather than as means to an end, may in all likelihood be more harmful than helpful especially when it operates on the basis of *a priori* reasoning without special attention to specific cases and circumstances. In some cases, such a policy might exacerbate the debt situation. Should the incoming capital not earn a *financial* rate of return greater than the repayment obligations in-

---

[19] Escott Reid, a former World Bank director, in his perceptive book written in 1973, *Strengthening the World Bank*, (Chicago: The Adlai Stevenson Institute, 1973), p. 200, commented on this asymmetrical aspect of the World Bank's advisory role, as follows: "The World Bank Group has been able to influence the development policies of its poorer member countries; it has had little influence on the development policies of its rich member countries. One of the most important problems facing the bank is what steps can be taken to increase the bank's influence on the policies of the rich countries on issues affecting the development of the poorer countries." The comment applies with even more force today.

curred by foreign loans or investments, the debt hole would be dug even deeper. This would be true even in the event that the loan or investment is socially desirable, or when the *socioeconomic* rate of return is greater than the real cost of invested or borrowed capital.

c. Recommending policies on the basis of the impact on the balance of payments is much too narrow. The criterion for judging the success of a policy must go beyond how well the foreign debt is being serviced. This criterion could be running counter to how well the policies contribute to a renewal of growth in per capita income and other sociopolitical objectives. Most of the successful cases being hailed in 1984 were temporary not only because the "success" was more due to import compression rather than export expansion, but also because the export expansion was almost completely dependent on the accessibility of the U.S. market, which absorbed more than 90 percent of Latin America's exports in that year.

The shift in the World Bank's product mix toward the SAL type of lending raises an issue that is a matter of policy as well as procedure, namely, the nature, degree, and mode of collaboration or cooperation between the World Bank and the IMF. There is bound to be a great deal of overlapping in lending programs when the World Bank engages in quick-disbursing lending to meet short-term balance-of-payment problems of the heavily indebted countries because both agencies are then working the same macro-economic territory. SAL is closely akin to the IMF's standby agreement. Over the past few years the informal off-and-on informational exchanges between the staff of the two institutions have taken on a new formality, intensity, and dimension. This collaboration has now been carried a significant step forward with the recent establishment of the first jointly financed program, the Structural Adjustment Facility, which is a new lending pool of $3.1 billion derived from the reflow of funds to the IMF Trust Account and from untapped IDA money.[20]

Until quite recently the IMF has played the starring role on the debt crisis stage. But the World Bank is now expected to come out of the wings. The ostensible reason is that the focus has shifted from belt-tightening austerity toward growth. However, it is more accurate to see this shift as drawing the World Bank into the main fire-fighting role.

The key question is whether there is compensating advantage: is the World Bank, in the execution of its longer-term development mandate, being strengthened by this accommodating flexibility? This is doubtful. The press-ganging of the World Bank onto the figurative short-term debt-salvage ship poses dangers of diversion that could weaken it for the main task of helping assure a funding level for the developing countries that goes beyond debt servicing to a level adequate for the resumption of growth and hope. The bank is being asked to be flexible, but there is a point where flexibility spells weakness. That point may already have been reached.

---

[20] The facility is available for the least developed countries, principally those in Subsaharan Africa. The eligible debtor countries (the 60 poorest countries meeting IDA eligibility criteria except for India and China, which have agreed not to apply) will receive assistance in restructuring their economies by adopting three-year policy frameworks that will incorporate benchmarks related to specific policies and targets that borrowing countries must meet as a condition for receiving further loans. These would include such issues as reducing the number of parastatal enterprises, revising pricing and tax policies, etc. The loans carry an interest of 0.5 percent with five and a half years of grace. About four fifths of the funds will go to Subsaharan African countries. Each country will be eligible to borrow as much as 47 percent of the IMF quota, 20 percent in the first year and, if the targets are met, 13.5 percent in each of the following years.

This fear is reinforced when considering the thinly veiled calls for the reform and restructuring of the World Bank and when there is extreme pressure being exerted for much more SAL at the expense of project lending. One form that pressure takes is to describe the World Bank as "conservative," "bureaucratic," and "ponderously slow." These derogatory attributes are partly based on the fact that in fiscal year 1985 the bank did not commit all the funds at its disposal under the "sustainable lending level" formula. Bank standards for projects or programs are then deemed to be too rigid or too narrow. Such critics are impatient with the answer that in fulfilling its primary function as a development agency, there are cogent reasons the World Bank project lending process takes so much time in completing the identification, preparation, and appraisal phases of what is called "the project cycle." The critics ignore or minimize the need to spend time working with officials, technicians, professionals, and implementers in the borrowing countries to gain a better understanding by both parties as to what is both desirable and workable. The critics applying strong pressure on the World Bank (and the regional banks) to shift from project lending to the quick-disbursing operations would not object if these institutions became more like cash-dispensing machines rather than development agencies.

The collaboration, in any case, is likely to be rocky given the clash of cultures between those who work in the fire-fighting brigade and handle short-term emergencies and those who work in the fields where the long-term aspects dominate.[21] In Gresham's law we'll likely find a clue to

---

[21] Erik Ipsen, "Can the IMF and the World Bank Ever Work Together?" *Institutional Investor* (September 1985), quotes a view of a member of the banking community that is apparently widely held: "The guys at the World Bank go out on missions, stay six to eight weeks, come back and take a couple of weeks off before they write their report. There is no hurry, because they are trying to improve the situation

the danger: just as bad money drives out good money, the short-term will tends to dominate, especially when crisis and panic are in the air. Therein lies the greatest danger for the development mandate of the World Bank.

THE WORLD BANK's RESPONSE: GIRDING UP TO DO MORE

Former World Bank President Clausen has often spoken of the need for imaginative and bold initiatives that operate with a scope and in a manner commensurate with the magnitude and depth of the debt problem. Besides displaying flexibility in the shift of the lending product mix toward quicker-disbursing loans such as SALs and loans under the Special Action Program, several initiatives were launched in recent years that were designed to increase the flow of financial resources to the developing countries. The list includes:

- A co-financing program introduced to entice more commercial bank lending on longer terms through the World Bank working more closely with other lenders and investors. In 1983–85 this attracted about $2.5 billion from commercial banks, leveraged by about $360 million of World Bank backup.
- A 50 percent guarantee provision in a recent $300 million co-financing loan that was syndicated as part of a larger loan of more than $1 billion to Chile, a move that has brought the bank into the rescheduling process in a more direct way than heretofore.
- A loan sale program (which had been terminated in 1980 after $3 billion worth of loan sales had been made) offering investors and bankers $300 million

---

20 years down the road." Ipsen concludes that the World Bank "must somehow pick up its ponderous pace. It grew up planning 15 and 20 years out while the IMF developed a fire fighter's mentality."

of the early maturities in its portfolio of loans to a selected list of countries that are not in the process of debt rescheduling (this expands the bank's capacity to lend within the same capital base).

- The doubling of the capital base of the World Bank affiliate, the International Finance Corporation (IFC). The IFC is mandated to encourage private investment in developing countries through joint equity participation and other means. Assuming maximum leverage from the IFC's capital increase, the investment stimulated or facilitated by the IFC could amount to more than $6 billion a year over the next five years.

- The establishment of the Multilateral Investment Guarantee Agency (MIGA) to stimulate private investment by offering guarantees against political risks and by offering a range of promotional services.[22] (It is an open question as to how much *additional* investment will likely ensue because of MIGA's guarantee and insurance coverage.)

The contribution from all these sources, even under the best of circumstances, will likely be modest in relation to the need. Nor is there any compensating bright spot on the near horizon given the trends that World Bank analysts expect over the next few years:

- Commercial bank exposure growing at less than half the annual growth rates of the 1970s.

---

[22] The Board of Governors of the World Bank recently approved the draft convention establishing MIGA for transmittal to member governments and Switzerland for signature. It becomes operational upon ratification by 5 capital-exporting and 15 capital-importing countries and the concurrent subscription of at least $360 million. MIGA will be legally and financially separate from the World Bank and will have its own Council of Governors.

- The flow of direct foreign investment to the developing countries remaining at levels less than half those of the early 1980s.
- Capital flight diminishing but continuing at about half the level of the early 1980s.
- Official development assistance (ODA) remaining at or close to its low-level plateau in volume but changing in its composition in ways that are disadvantageous for the poorer developing countries.

Given this situation, the burden falls all the more heavily on the shoulders of the international financial institutions concerned with long-term development—the regional banks and the World Bank Group.

The World Bank's management has sketched a somber picture with regard to its own capacity to meet the need. According to the best estimate prepared by the World Bank on its total volume of lending commitments over the next three years, the optimistic end of the range would be increasing lending to a possible high of $21.5 billion by fiscal year 1990. To achieve this, estimates of capital requirements range from about $30 billion to nearly $90 billion or from 40 percent to more than 100 percent of existing capital.[23] Thus, the main thrust, in terms of responding to the financial requirements beyond the emergency phase of the debt crisis, will be to expand the lending capacity. This requires both a General Capital Increase (GCI), and an expanded IDA replenishment. Each of these faces different problems and calls for different approaches.

---

[23] The key variable with regard to capital requirements is the operational capacity the World Bank *should* have over the rest of the decade. Obviously the appropriateness of any given level of lending capacity is a very judgmental factor. The other variables are the degree of enhanced flexibility the bank should have with regard to repayment terms, particularly speed of disbursement and length of maturities.

A GCI to Expand Lending from the World Bank's "Hard Window"

There is a compelling case for an increase in the bank's capital base if the net disbursements are to be maintained at current levels. We need look no further than at what would happen without such an increase. Based on reasonably realistic assumptions, with the World Bank's present capital base and the retained earnings accumulated over 40 years (which now amount to more than $10 billion), there would have to be a reduction in operational commitments by the bank of about one-quarter (in real terms) over the next five years. This is shown in Chart 7-1. Thereafter there would be more funds flowing to the World Bank than going out. Merely to maintain the level of net disburse-

---

CHART 7-1 Additional World Bank Net Disbursements with Increased Lending (Fiscal 1985-2005)

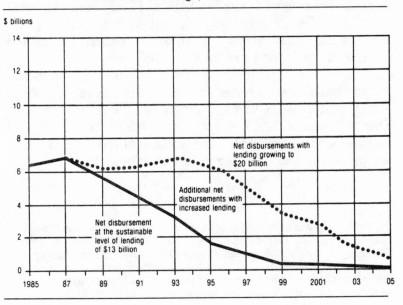

ments at zero, the commitments would have to increase at an annual rate of more than 6 percent. This is a matter of urgency with many countries now paying back more than they are receiving, particularly low-income African countries. Their net transfers from the World Bank have been steadily declining since 1978 and have been negative for the past three years, reaching *minus* $42.6 million in 1982.

Creditworthy countries that have access to the bank's hard window (those with per capita incomes of more than $400 per year) face the prospect of substantial reductions in their borrowing limits in net real terms. Those developing countries with per capita incomes of more than $2,440 per year, many of which are carrying heavy debt burdens, also face the dismal prospect of having the proportion of World Bank lending they receive decline from 12 percent of the fiscal years 1979 to 1983 lending program to 7 percent of the 1984 to 1988 lending program. Clearly, World Bank lending in net terms is falling far short of what is required at a time when so much more is needed.

Despite the ominous prospect, it has been exceptionally difficult to get some of the major shareholders, particularly the United States to agree on a GCI. It should be recognized by responsible legislators that the countries in authorizing a GCI need not pay in any cash, so this reluctance would hardly seem to be inspired by concern about the budgetary implications for the donor countries. The only obligation is to subscribe "callable capital."[24]

---

[24] All that is required is an authorization by the governors of the World Bank to expand its lending. Because the World Bank's Articles of Agreement limit the bank's lending and guarantees to an amount no greater than the sum of the paid-in capital, the callable capital, and the retained earnings or reserves—the famous 1 to 1 gearing ratio— the need is for authorization that de facto is a commitment regarding callable capital that will never be required. Since the callable capital

In testimony before a congressional subcommittee, U.S.
Treasury Secretary Baker explained that the callable capital would only be required on the basis of a doomsday scenario. Should the callable capital ever be required, the bank
would have to be on the point of closing its doors.[25] Thus,
since no cash contribution is called for, the U.S. resistance
to a GCI seems hardly comprehensible. The ostensible budgetary reasons are unlikely to be the real ones. On this
point it is relevant to note the net financial contribution
of the United States over the life of the World Bank. By
the end of fiscal 1985, the paid-in capital from member
governments had amounted to $3.2 billion, which enabled
the bank to make loan commitments of more than $113
billion and disburse about $68 billion.[26] Of this $3.2 billion,
the U.S. paid in total slightly more than $1 billion over

---

will not be required to operate the World Bank, either to pay administrative expenses or to make disbursements on loan commitments already
made or to be made, there is only one eventuality that is relevant,
namely, the winding up or the insolvency of the bank. This issue is
well expounded by the bank's treasurer, Eugene Rotberg, in a speech
made in Seoul in October 1985 at the time of the annual meeting. At
the same time, he argued against the idea of gaining more leverage
through changing the gearing ratio, which would increase the level of
lending sustainable in perpetuity without any additional capital. The
present capital/lending ratio assures the best possible rating for World
Bank borrowing, an advantage that is passed on to the bank's borrowers
through lower interest rates. Changing the ratio is not, therefore, a
promising or costless option.

[25] In testimony before the Senate Appropriations subcommittee on
March 3, 1986, the request of the administration in the spring of 1986
was for $3.8 billion in callable capital and $1.4 billion for other obligations.

[26] From 1965 to 1985, the bank was able to lend more than $100
billion and disburse more than $60 billion on the basis of an increase
of $1.4 billion paid in over that period. During the next three years
the bank plans to make between $40 billion and $45 billion in new
loan commitments financed by borrowings in private capital markets
at market rates of interest of about $140 billion or about $12 billion
to $13 billion each year over the next years, almost all from the sale
of World Bank bonds virtually exclusively from Japanese, OPEC, Swiss,

the last two years, as Table 7-1 reveals. The United States, as the largest shareholder, made an initial cash payment of $635 million in 1947 and over the succeeding four decades has paid in only an additional $479 million—an amount that is less than the misplaced or stolen weaponry the Pentagon reports as being lost each year, or less than the cost of one destroyer. Furthermore, the United States has benefited financially out of all proportion to this payment. Some examples follow:

1. The borrowings and handling of the bank's liquidity, have involved the placing of World Bank bond issues in non-U.S. capital markets and the holding of more than $10 billion in U.S. banks and U.S. Treasury bonds.

2. U.S. firms have won contracts on projects financed by the World Bank, amounting to more than $10 billion.

3. The United States as the major shareholder enjoys an indirect benefit from the fact that, under the financial management of Senior Vice President Moheen Qureshi and Treasurer Eugene Rotberg, the operations of the World Bank showed a profit of more than $1 billion in the last fiscal year and almost $700 million for the first half of fiscal year 1986, a record amount for any six-month period in the bank's his-

---

and German savings. These figures are taken from a speech by World Bank Treasurer Eugene Rotberg at the 1985 annual meeting of the World Bank and IMF. He notes, on this last point, that "of the World Bank's currently outstanding loans of $41.3 billion, only $6.7 billion is denominated in U.S. dollars (which is) an amount less than the U.S. dollars borrowed from sources outside the United States, that is, from central banks or in Euro or Asian markets or from other member governments as part of their capital contribution in dollars. Indeed, the World Bank holds upwards of $10 billion in liquidity in U.S. banks or government bonds. Thus, for the most part, the U.S. dollars borrowed in the United States or elsewhere were reinvested in the United States as part of the bank's liquidity pending disbursements on loans."

TABLE 7-1 World Bank Capital Subscriptions and Loans (1946–85)

(millions of dollars)

	U.S. Capital			Total Capital					
FY	Subs.	Paid-in	Callable	Subs.	Paid-in Avail. for Operations	Total Paid-in	Call-able	Re-serves²	Outstanding Borrowings
85	12,297	1,114	11,183	58,846	3,205	5,143	53,703	5,157	50,242
84	11,452	1,057	10,395	56,011	3,106	4,968	51,043	4,342	45,015
83	10,923	1,025	9,898	52,089	2,923	4,719	47,370	4,179	39,553
82	9,667	934	8,733	43,165	2,680	4,105	39,060	3,721	31,761
81	8,434	843	7,591	36,615	2,576	3,661	32,954	3,469	27,757
80	9,348	935	8,413	39,959	2,877	3,996	35,963	3,481	29,635
79	8,938	894	8,044	37,429	2,754	3,743	33,686	2,905	26,253
78	8,414	841	7,575	33,045	2,484	3,305	29,740	2,483	22,581
77	7,809	781	7,028	30,869	2,300	3,087	27,782	2,235	18,459
76	7,809	781	7,028	30,861	2,405	3,086	27,775	2,136	14,636
75	7,809	781	7,028	30,821	2,553	3,082	27,739	2,177	12,275
74	7,809	781	7,028	30,431	2,486	3,043	27,388	1,908	9,636
73	7,809	781	7,028	30,397	2,349	3,040	27,357	1,936	8,868
72	6,894	689	6,205	26,687	2,169	2,661	23,946	1,779	6,938
71	6,350	635	5,715	23,871	1,929	2,387	21,484	1,656	5,424
70	6,350	635	5,715	23,159	1,884	2,316	20,845	1,542	4,568
69	6,350	635	5,715	23,036	1,845	2,304	20,732	1,426	4,081
68	6,350	635	5,715	22,942	1,816	2,294	20,648	1,329	3,290
67	6,350	635	5,715	22,850	1,786	2,285	20,565	1,193	3,075
66	6,350	635	5,715	22,426	1,737	2,243	20,183	1,096	2,806
65	6,350	635	5,715	21,669	1,703	2,168	19,501	1,031	2,724
64	6,350	635	5,715	21,186	1,683	2,120	19,066	944	2,492
63	6,350	635	5,715	20,730	1,644	2,074	18,656	813	2,519
62	6,350	635	5,715	20,485	1,601	2,050	18,435	699	2,521
61	6,350	635	5,715	20,093	1,545	2,013	18,080	602	2,228
60	6,350	635	5,715	19,308	1,451	2,025	17,283	506	2,073
59	3,175	635	2,540	9,557	1,307	1,911	7,646	420	1,905
58	3,175	635	2,540	9,405	1,150	1,881	7,524	350	1,658
57	3,175	635	2,540	9,268	999	1,854	7,414	289	1,034
56	3,175	635	2,540	9,051	915	1,810	7,241	228	850
55	3,175	635	2,540	9,028	870	1,806	7,222	184	852
54	3,175	635	2,540	9,149	833	1,830	7,319	146	777
53	3,175	635	2,540	9,057	797	1,807	7,230	114	556
52	3,175	635	2,540	8,454	765	1,691	6,763	86	500
51	3,175	635	2,540	8,339	745	1,668	6,671	62	325
50	3,175	635	2,540	8,349	774	1,670	6,679	14	261
49	3,175	635	2,540	8,349	679	1,670	6,679	22	254
48	3,175	635	2,540	8,286	633	1,657	6,629	7	254
47	3,175	635	2,540	8,025	589	1,605	6,420	(1)	—
46	3,175	159 (1)	2,540	7,670	Not avail.	384	7,286	—	—

¹ Partial Payment

² Defined as General Reserve plus Special Reserve plus Accumulated Net Income plus Cumulative Translation Adjustments

³ Includes Loans committed but not yet effective

⁴ Excluding IFC Loans

			Loans[4]				

Gross Disbursements		Repayments		Disb & Outstand	Undisbursed[3]	Loan Commitments	
Annual	Cumulative	Annual	Cumulative	Cumulative		Annual	Cumulative
8,645	68,430	2,932	19,011	41,382	40,201	11,358	113,164
8,580	59,785	2,510	16,079	37,292	38,207	11,949	101,806
6,817	51,205	2,028	13,569	33,246	35,597	11,136	89,857
6,326	44,388	1,682	11,541	28,672	31,598	10,330	78,721
5,063	38,062	1,415	9,859	25,484	28,079	8,809	68,391
4,363	32,999	1,158	8,444	26,277	24,772	7,644	59,582
3,602	28,636	824	7,286	22,459	21,718	6,989	51,938
2,787	25,034	816	6,462	18,937	18,360	6,098	44,949
2,636	22,247	694	5,646	15,321	15,254	5,759	38,851
2,470	19,611	599	4,952	13,205	12,384	4,977	33,092
1,995	17,141	561	4,353	11,920	9,959	4,320	28,115
1,533	15,146	480	3,792	10,316	7,751	3,218	23,795
1,180	13,613	452	3,312	9,569	6,086	2,051	20,577
1,182	12,433	385	2,860	7,700	5,298	1,966	18,526
915	11,251	319	2,475	6,528	4,599	1,896	16,560
754	10,336	329	2,157	5,945	3,725	1,680	14,664
762	9,582	298	1,828	5,614	2,907	1,399	12,984
772	8,820	237	1,530	5,205	2,301	847	11,585
790	8,048	188	1,293	4,741	2,286	877	10,738
668	7,258	166	1,105	4,214	2,316	839	9,861
606	6,590	136	939	3,818	2,153	1,023	9,022
559	5,984	118	803	3,461	1,740	810	7,999
620	5,425	112	685	3,177	1,541	449	7,189
485	4,805	105	573	2,969	1,708	882	6,740
398	4,320	100	468	2,901	1,333	610	5,858
544	3,922	74	368	2,887	1,120	659	5,248
583	3,378	45	294	2,566	1,041	703	4,589
499	2,795	28	249	2,192	905	711	3,886
332	2,296	26	221	1,790	715	388	3,175
284	1,964	24	195	1,536	699	396	2,787
274	1,680	123	171	1,680	594	410	2,391
302	1,406	4	48	1,406	468	324	1,981
227	1,104	2	44	1,103	457	179	1,657
185	877	4	42	877	506	299	1,478
78	692	6	38	686	404	297	1,179
88	614	20 (5)	32	614	185	166	882
56	526	12 (6)	12	526	124	203	716
378	470	0	0	470	27	263	513
92	92	0	0	92	158	250	250
0	0	0	0	0	0	0	0

[5] Includes cancellations and refunds
[6] Sale of securities
SOURCE: Annual Report International Bank for Reconstruction and Development
FILE: USCapital

tory. The bank has been able to show a return in excess of 12.6 percent on its liquid investments of about $20 billion and a return on the original "encashed" investment that is beyond calculation. This performance has enabled the bank for the seventh consecutive time since mid-1982 to reduce its interest rate charge below what it might otherwise have been and to contribute to IDA replenishment and the bank's reserves.

This record has prompted Rotberg to ask:

> What then, considering the cost—which is *de minimus*—the measurable leverage of the paid-in capital contributions, the fragility of the financial system, the political implications of not lending, is the debate all about as we move ahead in our discussions of a capital increase for quality lending supported by quality development advice?

This rhetorical question is prompted by the reluctance shown by the U.S. administration and Congress over the past four years to authorizing a GCI despite the potentially grave consequences of this posture. One plausible rationale is simply that offered by one of the bank's executive directors, Ferdinand van Dam: "They (the U.S. Administration and Congress) have made the capital increase a hostage of the Baker Plan." In holding out on this GCI issue, considerable leverage is gained over bank policies. This leverage has become unabashed with respect to marshaling support for the Baker initiative and is clearly reflected in statements and actions taken on a number of occasions. One glaring example involves the Inter-American Development Bank. As reported in a news story in the *New York Times* headed, "U.S. Seeking Changes in Latin Bank's Policies":

> The Reagan Administration is pressing for sweeping changes in the lending policies of the Inter-American Development Bank and says if these are accepted it is prepared to support a "substantial" increase in capital to increase future lending

by the bank. The plan was worked out in Cabinet-level discussions (in Washington) and presented to the IDB's annual meeting in San Jose, Costa Rica, by James W. Conrow, Deputy Assistant Treasury Secretary . . . The U.S. is calling for restructuring the IDB as part of the negotiations to replenish IDB capital to support lending over the next four years.[27]

This strategy should cause concern about the continued viability of the World Bank, the IDB, and other multilateral development banks as international institutions.

The GCI issue was brought before the governors of the World Bank in 1984 but was put on a back burner because both management and board members believed that the United States was unlikely to change its opposition to such an increase *at this time*. That reasoning hardly suffices as a convincing argument to deter the campaigning that seems necessary to build up pressure and bring the day of a satisfactory resolution on the GCI closer. Furthermore, such a campaign, when pursued vigorously, sends a message that the strategy of placing conditionality for a GCI agreement on the changes in the policy and operations of the World Bank itself is unacceptable.

Replenishing IDA, the World Bank Group's "Soft Window"

The replenishment of IDA is an exceptionally pressing issue. The reduction in IDA pledges between IDA 6 replenish-

---

[27] Clyde H. Farnsworth, *New York Times* (March 26, 1986). The news dispatch goes on to add, "The principal change sought by the U.S. would make the bank's loans conditional on market-oriented policy shifts, such as more divestiture of public enterprises, faster deregulation and greater liberalization of foreign trade policies . . . The U.S. is also seeking an effective veto on all lending by the bank and placement of more North Americans in policymaking positions . . . The U.S. has been pressing for a similar approach in loans made by the World Bank which lends about four times as much as the IDB."

ment (1980–83) and IDA 7 (1984–87) has had a tragic impact: the decrease from $4 billion per year to $3 billion amounted to a reduction in nominal terms of 25 percent, in real terms of more than 40 percent and, when account is taken of China's membership, of 70 percent in real per capita terms. The prospects of the current replenishment efforts for IDA 8, to take effect in 1987, continue to look bleak in relation to the long-term IDA record of an annual increase of 8 percent in real terms from 1961 to 1981 and the maintenance of its highly concessional terms (50-year term, of which 10 years are a grace period, and a nominal administrative charge of less than 1 percent). In IDA 8 negotiations the United States pressed for the introduction of interest rate charges and shorter maturities as well as harder conditionality.

In the negotiated rules pertaining to the IDA replenishment process, the United States, by virtue of the fair share criterion, is obliged to contribute at least 25 percent of the total amount pledged. (Initially in IDA 1, the U.S. percentage was 40.) The size of the U.S. pledge thus determines the total amount of IDA. In IDA 7 negotiations, the U.S. decision to reduce its contribution below $1 billion per year led to a total IDA replenishment of only $9 billion, when $16 billion was targeted as an amount that would have only maintained the level of IDA 6 in *real* terms. In IDA 8 negotiations the U.S. position is once again the "holdout" for a smaller than targeted pledge and for harder terms. Thus, the triennial IDA replenishment ritual has been an excrutiating, long-drawn out process that needs to be reconsidered if its size and other features are to be commensurate with growing need. Temporary expedients to cover IDA pledge shortfalls, such as the Special Facility for Subsaharan Africa and the joint World Bank/IMF Structural Adjustment Facility designed for IDA-eligible countries, excluding China and India, are improvised responses to a desperate situation. This only accentuates the most serious problem of the IDA replenishment process, uncertainty. In large measure, this uncertainty arises because the IDA replenishment process requires annual congressional appropriations, thereby holding IDA hostage to its avowed detractors in Congress.[28]

It would take a concerted stand by other governments to overcome this weakness in the present arrangements. One approach would be to ask other donors to ignore the fair share criterion. Another variant would insist on a fair share ride and proceed with the IDA program at a level agreed to by, say, 75 percent of donors (weighted by contribution size). IDA would then become operational without any U.S. contribution unless it is paid in full in accordance with the fair share criterion. The principle would be: "there are no discounts on membership in the IDA club," or, "no pay, no play." Meanwhile, U.S. firms could be excluded from bidding on contracts financed by IDA funds and would, at that point, very likely become a pressure group for a "full and fair" IDA contribution from the United States. This exclusion from bidding on contracts appeared to be a factor in the congressional action to pressure the administration to join the Special Facility for Subsaharan Africa. In that instance, once the United States paid its full membership contribution of about $70 million, U.S. firms were eligible to bid on the contracts awarded from the $1.3 billion program that is being funded by the Special Facility.

A third option is to abandon IDA, opting for an approach

---

[28] This pressure is blatant in the case of Congressman Jack Kemp and others. They set conditions as to how much more market oriented the bank's lending must become to secure the congressional seal of approval for IDA. The World Bank's borrowing (and therefore, lending) program is not affected in the same immediate way as IDA since, in the case of the World Bank, access to the U.S. capital market does not require congressional approval. The U.S. administration can deny such access—as during a period of the 1970s—but it would be difficult to do so on political grounds.

not encumbered by the inordinately long and cumbersome ritual of the IDA replenishment process. After seven go-arounds it seems there is a need for rethinking old patterns, including well-entrenched ones such as IDA. There is no need to give up on IDA before new programs have been forged that can both augment significantly the flow of capital to the poorest countries and be insulated from reliance on the vagaries of fortune of the U.S. budget process.

An expanded World Bank and IDA lending program would, of course, be helpful. This would not, however, be enough. If the bank is to realize its potential, it is vital that the bank go beyond the country-by-country approach to a regional and international focus. This broader focus and the traditional country focus are reinforcing and can provide a longer-term and global framework for the bank's operations beyond the emergency phase of the debt crisis.

THE RESPONSE BEYOND THE EMERGENCY PHASE: A LEADERSHIP ROLE?

Most of the proposals for escaping or easing the pain of the current debt crisis—as described in Chapter Five—call for the World Bank and/or the IMF to act on behalf of the collectivity of nations, a procedure that has been called collective intermediation. At one level, many of the case-by-case plus proposals for easing the debt problem call for some form of debt relief arrangement that would involve the World Bank and the IMF. These take the form of proposals that these institutions would convert foreign debts of developing countries into international public bonds and offer an official collective guarantee for those making changes with regard to debt maturity, interest, and the value of the debt now owed by developing countries.[29]

---

[29] Thus, for example, proposals by Professor Kenen, Felix Rohatyn, and Richard Weinert would have a multilateral agency (sometimes specified as the World Bank) act as intermediary in swapping the commercial

The World Bank has so far taken a very cautious stance on such international-scale initiatives. Its involvement has been mainly confined to making speeches, sponsoring seminars, and providing reliable and comprehensive statistical and analytic documentation. Serious consideration has not been given to taking specific steps beyond changing the size and composition of the lending program to quicker disbursement. Agnosticism seems to be the posture toward any proposals for debt relief in any form other than assisting individual countries in stretching out the existing debt.

The World Bank's mandate calls for it to be reactive to any short-term remedies that might hurt long-term development prospects of the countries concerned. The World Bank has not as yet taken a proactive position to identify and help remedy underlying structural or systemic weaknesses in the international economic and financial system. Both the World Bank and the IMF management and their governors and executive directors, who are proxy holders for the governors as shareholders, have been subjected to justifiable criticism:[30] Where were their searching questions

---

banks debt securities with their bonds of longer maturities, lower rates of interest, and other features that ease the burden for the debtor countries and necessitate an acknowledgment by the banks of a loss of value of their account receivable assets owed by sovereign debtors. Bernardo Grinspun, former minister of economy in Argentina, proposed that the Inter-American Development Bank be used for a variant of this type of debt-securities/bonds swap. The guarantee variants include proposals by Mahbub ul Haq, Harold Lever, and Minos Zombanakis with the IMF as the agency offering the guarantee to the banks (or establishing a special facility), on the basis of which they would have an incentive to stretch out maturities, lower interest rates, and so forth.

[30] The culprits are not too clearly identified in terms of the decision makers, that is, as to whether the fault lies with management and/or the governors and their proxies, the executive directors, who are in full-time residence as board members. In theory it is, of course, the governors who are ultimately at fault for not exercising their responsibilities either with respect to specific policy issues or with respect to the system or rules by which governors as shareholders related to management. This is the message of Mahbub ul Haq's statement, which is the quotation that heads this chapter.

and interventions as the system built up pressures which erupted in the debt crisis? Why have they not assumed responsibility "to strengthen the international financial system?"[31]

The World Bank has been in the forefront on what might be called the poverty issue, especially as the debt burden affects the Subsaharan countries. Establishment of the Special Facility for Subsaharan Africa and the Structural Adjustment Facility is illustrative of initiative. But this leadership does not seem to have extended to examining program possibilities that go beyond the country focus, which has been the basis for the bank's operations. The rarity of the exceptions, when regional and international frameworks have been adopted, may serve "to prove the rule." The list is short: an office to service a region embracing several small island nations of the East Caribbean and the international consultative groups in the fields of agriculture, nutrition, and specific tropical diseases.

Focusing on a particular case illustrates this passive policy posture. An example is provided by the nature and degree of past involvement of the World Bank in international programs such as the Consultative Group for International Agricultural Research (CGIAR) and similar international-scale arrangements in the fields of health and nutrition. These initiatives were co-sponsored by the then-World Bank President Robert McNamara and by the governors and executive directors of the time who approved the policy decisions and budgetary allocations that enabled the World Bank to play the leading role.

---

[31] Hobart Rowen, "Critics Feel World Bank Could Have Done More in Crisis," *Washington Post* (September 23, 1984). He reported, "There is a certain amount of uncertainty and floundering at the bank's headquarters here as it belatedly seeks to define its role for the years ahead." He has been a friendly critic who has found fault with persons and policies that have not gone far enough "to reach into the structure of the problem itself, into the rules of the road?"

The financial resources devoted to these international programs have been extremely modest—less than 5 percent of the World Bank's administrative budgetary expenditures and less than one-fortieth of the fiscal 1985 net profit.[32] Yet the return on this type of expenditure has proven to be extraordinary, particularly when account is taken of the wide ramifications of the green revolution it helped spawn. The World Bank has not energetically explored the possibilities for replicating this type of program in other important sectors, such as the development of solar, wind, and biomass energy sources, which is of critical importance to the oil-importing developing countries.[33] There has been

---

[32] The bank's pledge for CGIAR has been less than $25 million, yet in 1985 this involvement undoubtedly acted as a lever to attract an additional $150 million for the program, which supports 13 research centers, 2 of which have provided new wheat and rice varieties that form the underpinning for the Green Revolution. The financial resources devoted to these international programs are classified as special programs and placed in the administrative budget though they are not relevant to the other expenditures that have to do with the running of the organization such as salaries and travel. The amounts involved are, however, indicative: these programs account for less than $25 million while the administrative budget is about $600 million. With profits in excess of $1 billion but normally in the $600 million to $700 million range, the minuscule expenditure on these programs is evident.

[33] Bank staff pushed this issue in a paper drafted for the U.N. Conference on New and Renewable Sources of Energy, "A Proposal to Promote the Development of Energy Technologies for Developing Countries," drafted by R. Ridker, April 30, 1981, revised July 13, 1981. While World Bank staff attended the U.N. Conference on New and Renewable Sources of Energy, held in Nairobi in the summer of 1981, it appeared quite clear they had received directives to keep bank involvement to a minimum.

The conventional wisdom has it that the energy crisis is past. Yet for most developing countries dependent on oil, the cost, which is denominated in U.S. dollars, had gone up dramatically. For example, between 1982 and 1984, the price of oil for Senegal rose 123 percent, for Morocco 130 percent, for Kenya 147 percent, for the Philippines 185 percent, and for Jamaica 239 percent. The dramatic fall in the price of oil has eased this problem, but for many the real cost is still very high when

considerable promise of board support for such an initiative. However, the prevailing structure and rules of procedure at the World Bank make it exceptionally difficult for board members to follow through, especially on programs that do not have management's active support and are international in scope.

There are several reasons for this state of affairs, among which one could list the short term of executive directors, which limits the institutional memory of the board. Another critical aspect is the organizational structure and procedure of the World Bank. With a strong centralized operational mode of work, the regional vice presidents are on a very short leash. The opportunity cost of this is that the top echelon of management is too immersed in day-to-day operations, leaving little time or energy for conceptualizing and working on significant departures in policy. There is, so to speak, too little room for thinking "big" or "bold" and too little tolerance for suggestions of this nature.[34]

The increased responsibility that is now and will more and more devolve on the World Bank and the multilateral development banks provides an opportunity of unprecedented scope and a challenge. As the responsible international developmental institution, it would be incumbent on the World Bank to take initiatives on such global and regional issues as the level of real interest rates, trade policies, and other factors that are exceptionally critical to promoting the flow of long-term capital flows at volumes

---

account is taken of changes in the exchange rates and the terms of trade.

In any case, the avoidance of the devastating ecological damage that arises from heavy dependance on fuelwood would, itself, make this search for alternative indigenous energy sources a matter of high priority.

[34] On this issue, see the essay by S. R. Sen, a former World Bank executive director, in the *Annex to the Brandt Commission Report.*

and terms that are sustainable. Not to do so would be tantamount to accepting the status quo with all its fragility and inequities and leaving the way open for a diminution of the World Bank's international role. In that case, the World Bank would clearly not be fulfilling the aspirations of the developmental mandate upon which it was founded at Bretton Woods. Meanwhile, the World Bank must escape being coerced into programming for the short-term emergency phase of the debt crisis to a degree and in a manner that would prejudice its main role as a major conduit for the long-term transfer of capital and technical know-how.

Steps on the Road beyond the Crisis

I am frightened and utterly baffled.
We are getting into totally uncharted waters.

Felix Rohatyn[1]

Perhaps fear of mutual peril will be the forcing mechanism rather
than mere high-minded appeals to concord, reciprocity, and team-
work. A poem by Lewis Carroll is apt:
"The valley grew narrower and narrower still,
And the evening got darker, and colder,
Til merely from nervousness (not from goodwill),
They marched along shoulder to shoulder."

Sylvia Ostry[2]

MOVEMENT TOWARD A NEW BRETTON WOODS: POLICY COORDINATION

Conventional wisdom held that the gap between the need for coordinated international action and the ability to achieve it was too wide to be bridged. Then, over a nine-month period culminating in the Tokyo summit of May

_____

[1] Quoted by Lester Thurow in op-ed column, "Smelling 1928–29 Fever in the Air," *New York Times* (December 28, 1985).

[2] Sylvia Ostry, Canadian ambassador for multilateral trade negotiations, in a talk, "Coping with Global Interdependence," at a December 8, 1985, meeting of the Global Economic Action Institute, New York.

1986, came the succession of meetings in hotels and palaces that moved the value of the dollar and interest rates. "Policy coordination" had become a buzzword. Intervention—at least to a degree—was sanctified.

The concept had been stigmatized as naive and impractical in a world where the leadership of some of the major economic powers placed their faith in the beneficence and efficacy of the market adjustment process. The triple-headed debt crisis was believed to be self-correcting. Instead, the situation has been worsening to a degree that threatens breakdown. A frightening sequence of events could be foreseen: Unless the U.S. dollar was brought down in value relative to the Japanese yen and other key currencies (and interest rates were reduced as well to discourage the capital inflow that has been holding up the value of the dollar), the adverse trade balance with Japan—more than $50 billion in 1985—would continue to deteriorate; protectionist pressures would then be overwhelming: Third World debtors would then find themselves even less able to service their debts; and, with defaults, a dangerous chain reaction would ensue culminating in each nation adopting politically self-protective autarkic measures. The era of Pax Americana, which had lasted 50 years and been characterized by increasing global economic and financial interdependence, would have given way to an era of "beggar-thy-neighbor" policies, a term that to this day remains the indelible hallmark of the Great Depression.

The cold bracing winds of the real world have broken through the sheltered fantasy world of the market-magic ideologues to make it painfully clear that a noninterventionist policy was unacceptably risky. The policy turnaround reached an important milestone in the hyperbolic announcements that a "new" approach had been formalized at the Tokyo summit—the Akasaka accord. It is difficult enough at the best of times for governments to maintain a consistent policy as circumstances change, but there are limits to the permissible gap between changing circumstances and rigid policy positions. The threat that an unacceptably high price would probably have to be paid tomorrow for today's errors of omission and commission seems to have made an impact on policymakers faced by the imminence of disaster.

Other factors have lent support to the idea of policy coordination as both necessary *and* desirable. One is the growing recognition of the underlying theoretical and practical reasons for international economic policy coordination that relate to the benefits that stem from the establishment and maintenance of "order and stability." This is labeled a "public good," the provision of which is the basic rationale for the existence of governments. In the international arena, the provision of this public good takes the form of coordination between governments to establish rules of conduct and institutional arrangements to give them effect.[3]

The most convincing case for such coordination is to imagine its absence. The breakdown of the Bretton Woods Agreement during the late 1960s and early 1970s has provided a real-life laboratory. The tragedy of the events of the past two decades is that much of the costs of the infla-

---

[3] For a succint overview of this issue, see Michael Artis and Sylvia Ostry, *International Economic Policy Coordination,* (London: The Royal Institute of International Affairs, 1985), especially Chapter 1, "Interdependence and the case for coordination," pp. 3–21.

The mongraph concludes that "expectations about summits as forums for coordination should be prudently modest. Yet in those (one hopes) rare cases in which serious imbalances and systemic strain require coordination to manage or avert a crisis, summits remain 'the only game in town.' It is in such instances that the role of leadership in the strategic game theory sense becomes essential. The uniquely decentralized system of policymaking in the United States may present 'structural' problems in this context (since this weakens) the ability to announce a credible commitment to action in either fiscal or trade policy."

tionary booms and the recessions were probably avoidable if a single nation or a group of nations *through coordination* had seen fit to provide the public good of greater stability in the global economic scene.[4]

If, beyond the limited objective of having the international system operate in an orderly way, there is a further objective of having it operate in a "fair" way, there is an additional need for coordination. This equity aspect is especially relevant in the international arena on two grounds: the market process as it operates between nations is skewed heavily in favor of those that are larger and more powerful, and the decision-makers in the international market place, particularly in the case of policy decisions of the political leaders of the industrialized countries, are likely to ignore or minimize both the favorable and the unfavorable impacts of such decisions when their effects are not factored into their benefit/cost calculations. These effects, referred to as "externalities," are exceptionally important in the operation of the global economic system. An example is the widespread and uneven impact of the abrupt anti-inflationary monetary policy decision taken by Paul Volcker in 1979 that brought on the deep recession and precipitated the debt crisis a short time later. While there was an almost universal adverse impact, there is little dispute the adjustment medicine has been and still is much more bitter for the developing countries, particularly for the smallest and poorest.[5]

---

[4] The coordination necessary for securing an "equitable order" might be temporarily put aside. Equity will not be served by instability and breakdown that are conditions under which the poor and powerless usually suffer the most.

[5] Unlike the severe recurrent economic and financial breakdowns as occurred in the 1820s, 1870s, 1890s, and 1930s, that of the early

Those skeptical about the possibilities of such coordination and a systemic approach to global economic and financial problems might well look back to the era of the Bretton Woods Agreement, which provided a framework for such policy cooperation for about a quarter century starting in 1944. The basic rationale for that agreement rested on the perceived benefits for trade and capital movements arising from cooperation between the major governments. Out of the carnage of World War II some semblance of a new order of things would have emerged, but the slowness of this process was likely to inflict further hardship on the populace of the war-ravaged prostrate economies. Some key "rules of the game" had to be set down.

The Bretton Woods Agreement established such a relationship between the dollar and other currencies and gold within the framework of a "pegged rates system." The agreement, however, contained an operational ambiguity because there were no specified adjustment mechanisms,

---

1980s was deliberately brought on by the so-called Volcker shock, which was designed to "break the back" of inflation. The ultimate rationale for this policy in its rapidity and severity is that the high price for achieving this objective was, on balance, justified, at least from the perspective of the United States. This judgment can be disputed, as does Professor David McLain in an op-ed piece titled "The Recessions Weren't Worth It," *New York Times* (December 1, 1985):

"In light of my findings, the case in the late 1970s for engineering a recession to lower inflation was not overwheming—unless one believes that the economy was on the verge of hyperinflation. And I do not share that belief. . . . the past five years have been a time of structural upheaval and bizarre and contrasting combinations of national economic policies . . . Knowing that at least half the disinflation of that period would have occurred even without a recession, it is safe to say that there must have been a better way to treat the patient."

This assessment applies with more force to the developing countries, which felt the impact in an amplified fashion given the fragility of their economies.

or clearly established benchmark signals to indicate when adjustment was to be made and how large that adjustment should be.[6] It was believed that the frequency and amplitude of exchange rate fluctuations would be dampened if some understanding existed that the dollar would play the pivotal role as "stabilizer." Given the overwhelming strength of the U.S. economy, this was a reasonable expectation. There was, as well, a further assurance in the commitment by the leaders of a strong, dominant American economy that they would act responsibly in the sense that externalities would always be factored into decisions on monetary, fiscal, and trade policy, that is, they would be sensitive to the impact of U.S. policy on non-Americans holding the dollar as a reserve currency.

At the time, this constraint was not thought to be a serious problem because it was believed that U.S. policymakers would have no great temptation to depreciate the value of the dollar, and if they did have such a temptation, they would resist it in the interest of maintaining a global monetary system within which they enjoyed the benefits of seignorage. It was believed the dollar would always be "as good as gold." It was, of course, also assumed that the U.S. economy, as the linchpin of the Bretton Woods system, would maintain its dominant role. During the late 1960s

---

[6] Robert Solomon, as senior fellow at the Brookings Institution, has observed that the participants at the Bretton Woods meeting did not set up a system in any meaningful sense of the "system" concept (taking system to mean "organized whole"). The system was incomplete because no mechanism for adjustment was put in place, nor was there provision for determining how and by what criteria global expansion of liquidity could be provided within the framework of the monetary system. In this sense there really was no "Bretton Woods system" as contrasted to a "nonsystem," which some believe characterizes what we have today. "Reforming the Exchange-Rate Regime," *International Economic Letter* (Washington, D.C.: RS Associates Inc., July 18, 1983).

and early 1970s, when the system built on that agreement began to come apart, the lack of "responsible" leadership by the United States exacted a heavy toll in terms of erratic exchange rates, rapid changes from inflationary to deflationary conditions, culminating in the double and triple debt crises we are contending with today.

There has now dawned a recognition of a desperate need for an international monetary agreement to achieve a more controlled system. An indication of the seriousness of the situation can be gleaned from the fact that, at long last, the U.S. President has commissioned a study of the international monetary system and its adequacy and is prepared, as demonstrated at the Tokyo summit to actively contemplate an interventionist role in the operation of the global economic and financial system. While unfavorable economic circumstances on the trade and capital front provided the push, it is clear that the pull factor was the optimism born of the success of Treasury Secretary Baker's multinational initiatives with the G-5 countries. "Improved coordination," he observed, "breeds improved coordination." There is a dynamic at work that was reflected in the final communique of the Akasaka Palace meeting in Tokyo, which pledged that the G-7 nations would, henceforth, "work together more closely and more frequently."

The focus of these meetings in the economic sphere has been principally on exchange rate stabilization measures and on vaguely defined procedures. The accord has endorsed a system that is called "managed floating" backboned by "enhanced surveillance." This calls for each of the seven participating governments to answer to the others in the course of periodic meetings of financial officials who assemble to discuss the state of their economies and the range of policies required to achieve some acceptable measure of convergence or compatibility. Through this process, which may be open to the public, it is envisaged that international political pressure will be brought to bear on each of the participating countries to constrain domestic political interests to meet the interests of a broader global constituency.

The role that the United States should and could assume in all this differs widely from that vested in it at the time of Bretton Woods, as it must by virtue of the changes that have occurred since then. The United States would be *primus inter pares* (first among equals), but within the framework of an agreement involving the curbing of sovereignty with regard to policies affecting interest rates, exchange rates, and so on. It would also involve sharing the seignorage role as the global reserve currency with the SDR, the European Currency Unit (ECU), and the yen. It would, therefore, be a diluted or shared responsibility for leadership in the global economic and financial scene. The Tokyo summit communique thus reflects the changed circumstances from the era of Bretton Woods I four decades ago.

Left unanswered is a host of troublesome questions as to whether it is realistic to expect "peer pressure" and "public pressure" to suffice, and, if the pressure proves ineffectual, what alternative adjustment mechanism would be relied upon to reconcile or harmonize the broad thrust of national policies when they come into conflict. That mechanism would have to contend with the difficulties faced by countries in changing policies even when the politicians and officials promise to do so and make that promise with sincerity.

Then there are the questions related to surveillance and the indicators to be used for guidance. How many are amenable to change through policy decisions on, say, the size and balance of the budget, the money supply, and the exchange rate? The scope of issues to be harmonized is broad enough to provide a field day for widely divergent views. The exchange rate provides a good example. Is the objective of dampening the movement of exchange rates realizable when there is not even a consensus as to what the rates should attempt to achieve: rough purchasing power parity or balanced trade flows? It appears difficult enough, then, to decide on a set of "equilibrium" rates to be targeted.[7]

Even more troublesome is the fact that beneath divergence in policies lie fundamental factors related to differences in culture, social objectives, ways of living, and such. In effect, the "hard core" test this approach must pass is an operational one: how to achieve the desired coordination when its attainment conflicts with either domestic political goals and constraints or with the long-term welfare of the global community.[8]

---

[7] On this point see Michael Artis and Sylvia Ostry, *International Economic Policy Coordination*, (London: The Royal Institute of International Affairs, 1986), p. 18, where reference is made to the lack of consensus among economists who are advising on policy and to differences of perception as to the likely outcomes, both of which create decisive barriers to effective policy coordination.

This is well illustrated by Professor Ronald I. McKinnon, "Getting the Exchange Rate Right," *The Wall Street Journal* (May 12, 1986). Professor McKinnon observes that the balanced trade criterion, which would roughly balance the flows of imports and exports of each country, "shows no explicit concern for the state of inflation or deflation across trading partners . . . could vary continually with world-wide changes in commodity prices . . . and moreover, is logically incomplete in saying nothing about the saving-investment imbalance in the domestic economy. Analysts who wish to push the dollar down further usually have the goal of improving the trade balance in mind." The equilibrium dollar—yen rate would be appreciably different under the two criteria.

[8] On this point, the observation of John Williamson is apropos: "It would be interesting to have a test of whether a country's policies are principally motivated by considerations of national wealth, national power, or an incurable attachment to sovereignty." "International Liquidity," *Survey of Applied Economics, 2,* (London, Macmillan, 1972). This raises another important institutional aspect: even were there to be a consensus on such an issue as the appropriate criterion for determin-

This problem has led advocates from far different ends of the political spectrum in the past few years to call for international economic policy coordination "with teeth." Despite its weakness, the original Bretton Woods Agreement serves as a point of reference or model for most of these proponents in so far as it is understood to have laid down rules that were meant to constrain each nation from adopting destabilizing "beggar-thy-neighbor" policies. It did, indeed, for all but the United States, which, by virtue of its overwhelming economic preponderance, provided the "discipline." The agreement fell apart when reliance was placed on self-discipline and when the hitherto unchallenged dominance of the United States was subjected to the pressure of competition.

Congressman Jack Kemp, a supply-side champion, put the issue clearly in setting forth a case for establishing a pegged rate system tied to gold or to a basket of currencies:[9]

> In 1970 the U.S. faced a critical choice: either cooperate in fixing the Bretton Woods system or abandon gold for paper money. Our decision was not in the spirit of Bretton Woods. Hoping to gain an advantage, we suspended gold convertibility and inflated the currency, expanding the supply of world dollar "reserves" and shattered the system of stable exchange

---

ing the exchange rate equilibrium, given the decision-making structure and process with which they must contend could the U.S. political leaders deliver on a promise to make the appropriate set of decisions? This point is also referred to in footnote 3 where mention is made of "the uniquely decentralized system of policy making in the United States [that] may present 'structural problems.'"

[9] "A System With a Heart of Gold,"*New York Times* (August 12, 1984). Congressman Kemp would set up highly restrictive objectives and methods for any new formalized arrangements of the world financial system. His proposal could be characterized as a "reconditioned Bretton Woods" with the refurbished parts, made of gold, acting as a speed control device.

rates. . . . *(The answer is) to initiate a positive and far-reaching reform of the world economic system as in 1944 . . .* (that is), an international system with a heart of gold." (Emphasis added.)

Another congressman, Representative David Obey, for basically similar reasons, has come out in support of a "target zone approach," a proposal that was put forward some time ago by John Williamson of the Institute for International Economics and now is back on the agenda of official international economic conclaves. In the spring of 1986 at the Interim Committee meeting, the French government formally presented a variant of the target zone proposal for international monetary reform. The French suggestion is built around so-called reference zones for stabilizing exchange rates.[10] The "managed float" put forward at Tokyo is now sharing center stage with this proposal.

The debate has apparently opened up on a wide front and advanced to the point of discussion about how, when, and under what circumstances the various approaches can be translated into action. A significant dimension has been added, however, when officials of one of the G-5 nations asserts:

> We know there is no going back to fixed rates, but we know the mood has changed around the world, and almost everybody—(except possibly some officials in West Germany and

---

[10] Daniel Lebeque, director of the French Treasury Department, has formulated a proposal that is really akin to the "target zone" idea. "We don't like the phrase . . . the word 'target' sounds like something military . . . The prime aim is to restore an approved set of exchange rates to its rightful eminence in economic policy decision making . . . In effect, the IMF would construct a 'grid' of exchange rates (initially unpublished but over time published along with a range of proposed 'restrictive mechanisms.' Governments would be pressured in the process) to relinquish at least some of the autonomy that national monetary authorities enjoy—or think they enjoy." Hobart Rowen, "France Offers New Proposal for Global Monetary Reform," *Washington Post*, (February 13, 1986).

Japan)—now agrees that something has to be done to change
the floating rate system . . . Remember you can't have a
monetary system without the south. You can't have a north
system imposed on the rest of the world.[11]

This touches on a serious bias in the summitry process.
While the leaders of the seven industrial nations can
"pledge afresh to fight against hunger, disease, and poverty,
so that developing nations can also play a full part in building a common, bright future," no attention seems to have
been paid to the Third World debt issue or the involvement
of other nations outside the G-7 that are most acutely affected by this problem.

The G-24 has long been calling for major trading Third
World countries' participation in effective forums so the
debt problem and distributional aspects of growth can be
treated as a major objective of policy at the global level.[12]
These calls have become more strident as the pressure has

---

[11] *Ibid,* p. E3.

[12] In this connection it is relevant to cite the statements of the
G-24 and those in such documents as the *UNCTAD Review on Trade
& Development,* where the complaint has been lodged that the issues
under discussion in international forums have been imbalanced, neglect-
ing the distributional aspects of international liquidity and relying exces-
sively in the past on the U.S. balance of payments deficit for the creation
of international liquidity.

"In practice, the international monetary system established at the
Bretton Woods Conference in 1944 was the preserve of the developed
countries alone . . . During the 1960s, the developed countries' prime
concern with the international monetary system was concentrated on
two related aspects: the inadequacy of global liquidity, rather than the
distributional aspects of liquidity, and the deficiency of an international
monetary system that relied mainly on the existence of a balance-of-
payments deficit in the United States for the creation of international
liquidity. After the effective collapse of the Bretton Woods system in
1971, the developing countries for the first time had the opportunity
to participate fully in the reform of the international monetary system."
Trade and Development: an UNCTAD Review, (November 5, 1984), pp.
22 and 23.

been building, bringing into question the adequacy of the present policy framework within which the debt crisis is being managed. This pressure, in large measure, stems from concern about the basic assumptions of the global economic system within which the debt crisis is being managed. Establishing an international economic environment more congenial to trade, investment, and lending flows is recognized as an essential short-term objective. However, as the case-by-case approach to debt management is increasingly seen as inadequate, there is a reiteration of supportive changes of a general or systemic nature that go beyond exchange rate stabilization measures, welcome as that might be.

If the debt crisis is to be overcome in a equitable and sustainable manner, there are two key sub-objectives of the process of policy coordination:

1. Lowering real interest rates.
2. Increasing resource transfer to the developing world, principally through highly concessional aid to the poorer countries and through greater reliance on the multilateral development institutions as the main channels for such transfers.

In the course of considering how these two necessary conditions are to be achieved, we come face to face with the issue of conflicting policies among the G-7 and what is implied in reconciling these policies. In most cases, one or more parties in the bargaining process would have to agree (with varying degrees of coercion) to sustain some losses or suffer some adjustments that are economically, culturally, or politically painful. We can use the interest rate issue as the litmus test for the "new" coordination process. In contending with the debt crisis it is not sufficient to lower real interest rates; they must be lowered to an "appropriate" level. The questions are: to what level need the rates be brought down? How is it to be achieved?

THE INTEREST RATE FACTOR: BRINGING THEM DOWN TO HISTORIC LEVELS

The real rate of interest developing countries must pay is one of the most important factors in the development process. The need to lower interest rates is a common thread running through almost all current proposals for resolving the debt crisis in a manner that would facilitate Third World development.[13] As early as 1969 the authors of the Pearson Report, *Partners in Development* observed that a debt crisis would loom within a decade. This prognosis was based on trends in the volume and terms of lending in 1968 when rates and maturities were far more favorable and the total international debt outstanding of developing countries was less than $50 billion.[14] Though the numbers have changed, the analysis and its conclusions apply with even more force today.

The critical element is the real rate of interest on loans in relation to the contribution the borrowed capital can make both to the growth of the borrowing country and to the rate of increase in foreign exchange earnings with which to service the debt. The sustainable level of real interest rates is determined by the availability of foreign

---

[13] The significance of the level of interest rates was noted by Dragoslav Avramovic and Ravi Gulhati in the early 1960s in their World Bank study on Third World debt. See Dragoslav Avramovic, Ravi Gulhati, and others, *Economic Growth and External Debt,* Washington, D.C.: Johns Hopkins University Press, 1964).

[14] "The future depends on the course of future lending and whether the relative role of hard and soft lending will change. If the flow of new lending were to remain at the level of 1965–67 with no change in its composition, the projection shows that by 1977 debt service would considerably exceed new lending, except in South Asia—Middle East where they should be about equal. . . . Over-all there would be a large net transfer (after deduction of debt service) arising from lending and going from developing regions to the industrialized countries" *Partners in Development,* chaired by Lester B. Pearson, (Praeger, N.Y.: Commission on International Development, 1969), pp. 74–75, 153 and 164–65.

exchange, which, in turn, is based on the productivity of capital. Whether derived through trade or capital flows, these factors indicate that the level of *real* interest rates needs to be very much lower than the 6.8 percent average level of the past five years. How much lower? Proposal after proposal for resolving or easing the debt crisis refer to or recommend a return to a level of real interst rates close to or only slightly higher than the historic average. Though the "historic rate" seems to vary with different proponents, the mean average is about 2 percent.[15] It does not suffice merely to lower real interest rates, this order of magnitude—less than one third the present level—is the target to be aimed for, having in mind the longer-term resolution of the debt crisis.

Three approaches to achieving this target can be identified:

---

[15] In a recent paper by Dragoslav Avramovic on the debt problem titled, "Interest Rates, Debts and International Policy," he asserts, "The rate to aim at should be perhaps around 2 percent per annum in real terms, (which) in the words of the Council of Economic Advisers of the United States, (is) the historically typical real interest rate." The source cited by Dr. Avramovic is *The Annual Report of the Council of Economic Adviser*, Washington, D.C., (February 2, 1983). He goes on to note that according to the *Annual Report of the Bank for International Settlements*, (June 1983), "the average real rate in the post-war period 1963–1982 in five leading countries—the United States, United Kingdom, Japan, Federal Republic of Germany and Switzerland—was lower, 1.1% per annum." See also his article in *Trade and Development, an UNCTAD Review*, (November 5, 1984), pp. 361 and 363.

Professor Rudiger Dornbusch has calculated that during the period from 1930–80, the real rate of U.S. government bonds was less than 2 percent.

As already noted, the authors of the Pearson Report, *Partners in Development*, suggested as early as 1969 that rates for official development assistance loans be "no more than 2 percent with a maturity of between 25 and 40 years with grace periods of from 7 to 10 years."

For a convenient summary listing on the range of estimates, see M. Guerguil "The International Financial Crisis: Diagnoses and Prescriptions," *CEPAL Review*, December 1984, p. 166.

Congressman Jack Kemp talks of 6 percent as the historic level to be targeted.

- Lowering the real interest rates in the private financial markets.
- Expanding the funds available at concessional rates.
- Expanding the sources for interest-free funds under official development assistance programs (ODA) and granting special taxing and royalty rights on the "global commons."

Reducing the Level of Market Interest Rates

The first and main focus must be on lowering the level of real interest rates in the major private capital markets. The U.S. rate is the most critical by virtue of the importance of the U.S. economy in world trade and capital flows, but the range of concern must be widened to take in other players such as Japan and the European Economic Community, whose policies now have significant impact on trade, capital flows, and exchange rate changes. In any case, the United States could not act on this matter alone or the purpose of the change in interest rate could be offset or nullified by the actions of other countries that chose not to follow suit or cooperate. On the lowering of the level of rates, there is virtually unanimous agreement that:

1. The United States must reduce its budgetary and trade deficits.
2. The Japanese (and Germans and others) need to spend their trade surplus in ways through reflating their own economies as well as providing massive concessional aid and investment flows to the debtor developing countries.[16]

---

[16] The focus on the Japanese is not meant to imply the exclusion of other countries with substantial trade surpluses. What is said about the Japanese case would apply *pari passu* to the others.

As a donor, the Japanese have already overtaken France (with ODA

On this level of discourse, the necessary first steps are clear. Acting in concert can be effective, just as the G-5 meetings succeeded in bringing down the value of the dollar and interest rates. Agreement can be reached without too much pain and delay despite conflicting views as to the timing and speed of change so long as there is no disagreement about the direction and the question of the limits of such change. However, this consultation cum coordination becomes more difficult to resolve when it is a zero-sum situation where what one party gains is matched by what the other party loses. Under such circumstances, gentle but persuasive coercion might do the trick as the powerful lean on the weak. The real difficulty arises when coordination requires applying pressure for policy changes that are so fundamental as to be tantamount to calling for transformations in long-standing cultural patterns related to such seemingly innocuous "economic" activities as "consumption," "savings," and "investment." These activities need to be altered if coordination is to succeed. The Japanese and Americans are in the same boat in this respect because the changes required are sweeping.

It is recognized that the Japanese must recycle the surplus money they derive from trading by spending it at home or spending it abroad. This is more difficult than it appears, as Flora Lewis has pointed out in two perceptive newspaper columns datelined Tokyo. She writes:

---

of $2.8 billion) and West Germany ($2.8 billion) to become the second largest donor after the United States ($8.7 billion). The government has announced an aid program doubling the 1985 level of $4.3 billion by 1992. However, the Japanese position in IDA replenishment negotiations is that it wishes to reduce its percentage share on the grounds that it is already bearing an unduly large burden. The nub of the problem is that it contributed over 18 percent to IDA but holds less than 5 percent of the voting power in the World Bank, whereas the United States contributes 25 percent to IDA and has over 20 percent of the bank's voting power.

Both ideas (related to spending) butt up against deeply in-
grained Japanese tradition which they feel strongly define
their specific identity . . . Those who think beyond method,
such as tax reform aimed at reducing the incentive to save
or increasing government spending, talk of forcing a change
of society (that) could be as great as the change brought by
America's Commodore Perry, who battered open Fortress Japan and led to the 19th century renewal of the Meiji Emper-
or's supremacy, or by General Douglas MacArthur's occupa-
tion regime . . . A cultural, philosophical, even moral
transformation is involved and it won't happen overnight
. . . (As for aid), the obvious answer when riches become a
burden is to give them away . . . But the Christian tradition
of charity is not a part of the Confucian order. Japan will
have to learn about giving, as well as earning.[17]

It would appear that the stimulation of Japanese domestic consumption and investment might most effectively be
achieved through reducing the interest rate. But if this is
done without a concurrent reduction in U.S. interest rates,
funds would continue to flow from Japanese accounts to
the United States and continue to finance more than half
the U.S. budget deficit. The yen would likely once again
depreciate relative to the dollar and continue to exacerbate
the problem of the U.S. trade deficit. While the U.S. budget
deficit remains on its present trajectory and the savings
(and taxes as forced savings) rate of Americans remains
extremely low, it would not be possible to reduce interest
rates so as to enable the Japanese to do so.

But the matter goes deeper than that. It would not be
possible unless the productivity of the U.S. manufacturing
sector also were to greatly improve so the American economy could effectively compete. U.S. manufacturing productivity has been increasing over the past few years at

---

[17] Flora Lewis, "Japan Joining the World?" and "Japan's Moral
Crossroads," *New York Times* (May 7 and May 11, 1986).

a rate that is about one third that of Japan. Tracing the causal factors leads us to the lower rate of investment and the higer cost of capital. This has resulted in a situation where the rate of "tangible capital" formation per worker in the United States (as contrasted with "knowledge-related capital") is one third that of Japan, and the real cost of capital is three times higher.

At the end of the line, the nub of the problem is the low U.S. saving rate and the use of a great part of its savings for current consumption and "unproductive investments" as exemplified by military expenditures.[18]

It is this parlous condition that has been characterized by *Business Week* as "The Casino Society" syndrome and by Professor Robert Reich as "Military Keynesianism." In this connection there are two ominous symptoms that have attracted the most attention:

- The rate and manner of household consumption and of a substantial part of business and government expenditures have resulted in a rate of increase in household and business debt of over 15 percent annually, a rate that takes on significance when contrasted with the 3 percent rate of growth of income.
- The federal budget deficit of the United States doubled between 1980 and 1985, a rate that also takes on significance when it is recognized that the deficit accumulated over 200 years doubled in the span of 5 and that payment of interest on this debt absorbs an amount equivalent to three fourths of net private savings.

The basic problem is that without increased savings and taxes (a form of involuntary saving) and without a

---

[18] This issue is treated in Chapter Two in discussion of the "shrinking of America" and what this implies. For a provocative article on this subject, see George N. Hatsopoulos, "Productivity Lag is Real Trade Barrier," *The Wall Street Journal* (May 14, 1986), p. 30.

diminution of private spending on current consumption and of government expenditure on the military—rather than on income-generating investment for education, research, and infrastructural improvement—the financial well is running dry.

If interest rates are to be lowered *appreciably* and if *sufficient* capital is to be made available for investment, lending, and aid to the Third World, these spending/saving trends must be slowed and soon reversed. If these trends are not correct, Americans face a dilemma:

- To reduce the value of the dollar and the trade deficit, the rate of interest must be lowered;
- This would have the effect of reducing the inflow of foreign savings;
- At the same time, if the budgetary deficit is not reduced or is increasing, the demand for capital continues to remain high merely to service that debt;
- This would have the effect of driving interest rates upward again . . .

Breaking this vicious circle would call for behavioral and policy changes on a par with those of a cultural nature faced by the Japanese.

Even this change, however, would not be enough. Major changes must also be made *on the investment side* so that more of the available investable capital can be directed to the Third World. Two initiatives have been proposed by the World Bank Group:

- The billion-dollar Multilateral Investment Guarantee Agency (MIGA) which has already been launched by the world bank (though not yet operating).
- The Emerging Markets Growth Fund (EMGF) which is being set up by the International Finance Corporation.

These, respectively, are designed to reduce the political risks for private investors and to facilitate private capital flows by offering diversified portfolios of investment opportunities in Third World enterprises. The response to MIGA is problematic: It will take a veritable sea change to reverse the decline in foreign private investment in the developing countries which fell from $17 billion in 1981 to under $10 billion by 1984 and has not yet recovered from that low level. The EMGF is targeting to raise $50 million. However, the potential is tantalizing great, as can be gleaned from some relevant statistics that indicate the magnitude of the pool of capital which could be tapped:

- More than $2 trillion is being held in the portfolios of pension funds, mutual funds, insurance companies, and credit unions in the industrialized countries. In the past year this pool of funds has been growing at a rate of about 15 percent. Over $100 billion of such funds is estimated to be held by citizens of the debtor countries who moved capital abroad. Professor Richard Gardner of Columbia University has noted that every 1 percent diversion of this increment could yield about $3 billion annual flow.[19]

- About $650 billion in short-term foreign securities is being held by Japanese banks alone, part of which could be made available for investment in developing debtor countries.

The big question is whether the G-7 Governments are prepared to actively encourage the diversion of these funds to the Third World by such measures as underwriting some

---

[19] Cited by Leonard Silk ("The Global Appeal of Capitalism," The *New York Times,* May 23, 1986) in a report on a meeting of the trilateral commission in Madrid, Spain. Professor Gardner also drew attention to a study which showed that the rate of return of a weighted stock index of nine developing countries stock exchanges was more than double that of a similar index for industrialized countries.

of the risks and easing some restrictive regulations, or in some cases, by making capital flight from debtor countries less welcome. Exhortations and placid gestures will not suffice. In any case, it does not appear realistic to expect that the G-7 ministers would support such policies vigorously enough to encourage significant increase in the flow of private capital. Given the magnitude of the requirements of the Third World, particularly of the poorest of the debtor nations in sub-Sahara Africa, the amount of new private foreign investment in the Third World is hardly likely to be "adequate," even to restore per capita income in Africa and Latin America to pre-1980 levels, let alone to enable the citizens of the indebted countries to hope for positive rates of growth.[20]

In the final analysis, over the longer term lowering interest rates to the historic 2 percent level, which is essential for containing and resolving the debt crisis, and keeping them there, requires overcoming the disparities in the growth in productivity. It is not enough to go on a low-calorie diet; a rigorous body building and toughening exercise regime is also mandatory. This calls for commitment to systemic changes, which deal with underlying fundamentals and not merely surface symptoms. Attending post-Tokyo meetings of finance ministers without making commitments to such discipline would be an exercise of very limited

---

[20] "Adequacy" is a relative concept. This is treated in Chapter Three. Sir Shridath Ramphal, Secretary-General of the Commonwealth Secretariat in a speech in May 1986, cites $25 billion as the annual additional net requirements of the developing countries, an estimate based on a study by the U.N. Committee on Development Planning. He also noted that $150 billion net had been transferred from these countries to the rich industrialized countries over the last three years. Apropos the African situation, he drew attention to the *reduction* of net financial flows to these countries of about $7 billion as compared to 1980 to 1982. See "There's No Substitute for a More Democratic World," The *International Herald Tribune*, May 10, 1986.

value. And because to be effective, commitments must also be made in tandem, coordination is an imperative, not an option. However, because achieving the requisite degree of coordination requires more than the periodic G-7 meetings envisaged at the Akasaka Palace, the call is still out for an appropriate framework, a new Bretton Woods which would "impose" a degree of policy discipline that otherwise would not be attainable.

Expanding Funds Available At Concessional Interest Rates

The second approach to lowering interest rates involves measures to enable lending to developing countries to be undertaken at *concessional* interest rates. These take various forms. At one extreme there are many suggestions for "new" financial instruments of international lending that can incorporate such concessionality.[21] The concessionary element hinges on the degree to which donor and recipient

---

[21] See Donald R. Lessard and John Williamson, *Financial Intermediation Beyond the Debt Crisis,* (especially Chapter 4, "Financial Instruments," pp. 49–88), Washington, D.C., Institute for International Economics; September 1985). The list of "most promising candidates" includes 1) investment by nonbank financial institutions in developing country equities, 2) investment by multinationals in projects with a return determined by a "quasi-equity" contract such as sharing of production, revenue, or profit, 3) lending by banks on a stand-alone basis for export-oriented projects whose earnings, if any, could be escrowed for debt servicing, 4) long-term index-linked bonds partially guaranteed by donors endowing a modest guarantee fund, 5) commodity-linked bonds with a yield tied to the prices of major commodities, 6) use of swap markets to match currencies of debt-service streams with that of export earnings, and 7) use of options market to cap interest rates on floating-rate borrowings. The authors note that the fullest exploitation of these new financial instruments requires "important changes in attitudes" including willingness to maintain "a proper degree of financial discipline (and) to pay a realistic price for the risk shifting" to financial markets.

governments assume some of the risks associated with international lending to sovereign borrowers. Thus, governments, parastatal agencies, and international institutions would need to be involved as intermediators or as parties directly engaged in these forms of capital transfer.

This would not necessarily exclude the private commercial banking system from making a contribution by reducing interest rates to debtor countries and thereby accepting lower profits. Involvement of commercial banks on the scale and in the manner assumed during the 1960s and 1970s must be considered a thing of the past.[22] That role, in retrospect, is regarded by all—including the bankers themselves—as excessive, the Baker initiative notwithstanding. But this does not imply a "hands off" policy.

A second form of capital transfer which incorporates concessionality is found in multilateral aid programs such as IDA and bilateral aid programs that generally lend on terms with an appreciable grant element. This high grant feature in IDA has led to suggestions that such funds be directed entirely to low-income African countries. This idea has been realized through the establishment of two new

---

[22] This point is made very lucidly in C. Fred Bergsten, William R. Cline, and John Williamson, *Bank Lending to Developing Countries: The Policy Alternatives,* (Washington, D.C.: Institute for International Economics, April, 1985) p. 14. After reviewing 20 options the authors opt for 5, of which 3 are centered on interest rate reduction. The degree of concessionality is clearly beyond what the private commercial banking community could be expected to provide or could be capable of providing even in normal times, let alone under prevailing conditions. Felix Rohatyn has proposed that if World Bank or United States Government guarantees are forthcoming commercial banks reduce interest rates to Latin American debtor countries by 4 percent and thereby shave $15 billion off their annual debt servicing bill. He estimates their profits would be reduced by $4.5 billion. One modest step in this direction is evident in the Brazil rescheduling when New York creditor banks accepted a reduction in interest rate spread from an average of 2.125 percent to 1.25 percent. Mexico achieved this earlier.

special funding arrangements, the Special Facility for Sub-saharan Africa and the Special Trust Fund, both of which together are devoting about $2 billion annually to assisting low-income African countries. Though the funds thus made available are hardly adequate, it is a welcomed gesture.

Another suggestion that has often been put forward most recently by the United States in IDA 8 negotiations, calls for "a third window" to provide loans on intermediate terms for countries that do not qualify either for IDA or for the harder terms of World Bank lending.[23] This proposal raises the thorny problem of how the criteria for eligibility for borrowing from this "semi-soft" window will be established and maintained and on that ground alone is likely to flounder. Borrowing from IDA's soft window does not post such problems with regard to eligibility and the specific rate to be charged because the criterion is so clear-cut. Eligibility is based on per capita income levels, a criterion easily understood and usually accepted despite the statistical and conceptual fuzziness involved in measuring income or welfare levels in very different societies. Once this is established eligible countries are billed only for an "admin-

---

[23] There is a contentious policy issue implied in the World Bank's exclusion of countries deemed not to be "creditworthy" yet are not able to qualify for IDA since their per capita income average is above the threshold figure. That one-dimensional criterion poses problems since in other respects the country may be very underdeveloped with an income base that is fragile and volatile.

The proposal for an "intermediate" rate has been put forward by Pakistan Finance Planning and Economic Affairs Minister Mahbub ul Haq in his plenary speech before the 1985 annual meeting in Seoul (Press Release, no. 7, p. 5). He suggested the rate be 5 percent and the terms be 30 years with a 10-year grace period as illustrative of what he has in mind as "intermediate terms." He suggested the funds come from direct contributions from the industrialized nations and future SDR allocations. Former Japanese Foreign Minister Saburo Okita has also put forward a similar proposal.

istrative charge." Still problems arise but they are minor compared with what can be contemplated when a decision has to be made as to the "appropriate" rate to charge to which countries.[24]

A variant of this concessionality idea is also incorporated in many proposals to establish a new international refinancing facility that would be designed to encourage continued commercial bank lending at lower interest rates and longer maturities. In effect, the lending banks would be subsidized as well. While the idea merits consideration for some types of lending operations, the main issue revolves around the question: Where are the necessary funds to come from? If public, are these public sources of funds well matched with private institutions as intermediaries? Political considerations would preclude the private institutions being subsidized. If the subsidy is from private sources, the banks themselves, not much can be expected.[25]

Yet another source of capital at lower interest rates is the category that is the ultimate in concessionality, interest-free loans on terms that have a 100 percent grant element and, interest-capital from "special sourcing." This last group refers to the granting of taxing and royalty rights to developing countries. These sources, which are potentially the largest and most reliable source of capital, merit elaboration under a separate heading.

---

[24] Given its ideological predisposition to let the market rule on such matters, it is strange to find the United States arguing for positions that necessitate even more interventionism by politicians and bureaucrats. Apparently, frugality is a more dominant consideration. The degree to which the factor of China's and India's participation in IDA plays a role is difficult to determine.

[25] See footnote 22. Felix Rohatyn's proposal that U.S. banks reduce rates by 4 percent to Latin American debtors would amount to less than a $5 billion cut in bank income, much of it absorbed by a reduced tax bill. But this is fiercely resisted by the private banking community.

THE CAPITAL TRANSFER FACTOR: HOW TO RAISE IT

There is a well-recognized and understandable reluctance on the part of the commercial bankers to lend more than they must to the developing countries. Thus, in 1985, their disbursements to developing countries increased by less than 1 percent. The same attitude is held by private investors who are not tempted to venture into the risky waters of the Third World with the exception of a few such as China, India, Korea, and other newly industrializing countries (NICs). The developing countries thus have to rely principally on ODA sources for any significant additional foreign funds. Yet, ODA has stagnated at the $35 to $40 billion level and is not likely to rise in the near future without some special initiative. The multilateral institutions, including the development banks and the IMF, are able to increase their levels of lending and accelerate their rate of disbursement but can only do so in significantly greater volume when capital increases are authorized. But the totals, helpful as they may be, will be less than spectacular when measured against the need. The situation can be aptly characterized as "a crisis of commitment."[26]

This somber scenario leads to consideration of *innovative* arrangements for increasing the flow of capital, particularly of concessional aid for the poorest countries saddled with heavy debt burdens. The most recurrent suggestion for increasing lending to developing countries at concessional rates takes the form of the Marshall Plan. As early as 1977, Professor Ronald Muller of American University,

---

[26] See *The Report of the Development Committee's Task Force on Concessional Flows*, (Washington, D.C.: World Bank, August 1985). The report describes the situation also as an "aid supply crisis" and forecasts a modest increase in real terms over the next few years of roughly 2 percent annually.

in testimony before a congressional committee, put forward a proposal for a "Third World Marshall Plan."[27] Henry Kissinger has proposed an approach along these lines for heavily indebted Latin American countries. He envisages establishing an international credit facility within the framework of a special agency that would lend for long terms at low interest rates. This arrangement would be akin to the Marshall Plan with a fixed date set for its demise. The Brazilian ambassador to the United States advanced the same idea in a speech in early 1985.

One of the most recent suggestions along the same lines, but with a Japanese connection, was put forward by an American executive, James Robinson of American Express Co. He tied his Marshall Plan proposal to a Japanese contribution of donated, loaned, or invested capital.[28] The New York investment banker Felix Rohatyn has suggested that Japan allocate about $175 billion of new money over five years for Latin American debtor nations. The writer Alvin Toffler has put forward a more specific idea, establishing a "Mexi-Yen strategy" under which $20 billion would be allocated for Mexico alone.[29] Meanwhile, the Japanese gov-

---

[27] "The Transformation of U.S. Banking and Economic Instability: A Systemic Dilemma," *Hearings before the Congressional Committee on Banking, Finance and Urban Affairs*, (April 6, 1977), p. 8. The idea of "a Marshall Plan" pertains more to the theme of how to increase the flow of aid, that is, the additionality aspect rather than the modality aspect, which is secondary. This is so because the Marshall Plan was directed to help European nations in their reconstruction and had clear geopolitical objectives. The outstanding feature of that gesture by the United States was its relative magnitude, about 4 percent of GNP, and its concentration to a small group of countries.

[28] James D. Robinson, "For a Japanese Equivalent of the Marshall Plan," *Washington Post* (May 3, 1986). See also "A Costlier Yen is not Enough," *New York Times* editorial, (April 7, 1986).

[29] Felix Rohatyn has proposed that Japan increase the size of its financial markets and currency and allow them to be used in stabilizing the world monetary system. He suggests that Japan provide growth

ernment has set targets for its aid program of $40 billion over the next seven years, reaching about $9 billion per year by 1992. They are being urged to do better but are having difficulty meeting the present aid targets they have set for themselves. This appears to be a problem with a quick and ready solution.

Another frequent proposal has focused on substantially increasing the allocation of SDRs and doing so in a way that would mainly benefit the developing countries. The G-24 has gone on record repeatedly proposing the issuance of more SDRs and also of allocating a greater percentage to developing countries on a basis that ensures some automaticity and, at the same time, is linked to the need for liquidity. The SDR issue has been given a thorough hearing before congressional subcommittees and in the United Nations, but has not made much headway.[30] On the basis of

---

capital to Latin America through long-term commitments to the capital of multilateral institutions and a five-year commitment of $20 billion per year and interest rate reductions amounting to $15 billion per year, which would total about $175 billion of new capital over the next five years. "The New Chance for the Economy," *New York Review of Books*, (April 24, 1986), pp. 20 and 21.

Futurist Alvin Toffler has proposed "the Mexi-Yen Strategy." This calls for Japan allocating a large part of the $20 billion saved by virtue of the fall in oil prices to an investment program in Mexico that has lost a comparative amount through that drop in oil prices. "Where one nation is sucking in capital and another is losing it, there is always some potential for recycling. Japan has all those yen. Mexico needs them. Japan's future will not be served by international upheavals of the kind implied in a Mexican catastrophe . . . (yet) in 1983 Japan invested only a paltry $121 million in Mexico." *Washington Post*, (March 2, 1986), pp. C1 and 4.

[30] Professor Charles Kindleberger has some pertinent comments to help explain why "the SDR is headed nowhere in particular." He writes: "If the bulk of SDRs were issued free to the LDCs who chose to spend them as claims to real assets rather than as additions to liquidity for rainy days, the developed countries would be unwilling to accumulate them in significant quantities, the scheme would have to be liquidated and the SDR would be 'inside money,' (that is, a credit which must be

present policy, the share of the developing countries could be expected to amount to about $3 billion over the next three years. While the SDR could be a substantial source for expanding the capital flows to developing countries, the prospect for a significant increase is not bright.

The authors of the 1985 Development Committee Task Force's *Report on Concessional Flows* have enumerated nontraditional forms of aid, many of which have been suggested in the reports of several commissions beginning with Pearson (1969), Brandt (1980 and 1983), and most recently Manley (1985). These have a common feature, granting developing countries the rights to levy taxes on international trade and travel, and the rights to royalties on commercial operations utilizing the "global commons," which embraces the oceans, outer space, Antarctica, and areas not under any one nation's jurisdiction. The Brandt Commission proposed a World Development Fund be set up to collect and administer the incomes generated by such royalties and taxes, while others have suggested establishing an authority on the use of the international seabed, another on outer space, and so forth.

It has been estimated, in the case of the seabed, that the rent that could be collected from the rights to drill

---

repaid rather than an asset which is akin to gold or dollars held as reserves). Conservatives would say no link or it will ruin the SDR. Do-gooders, optimists, proponents of the LDCs or however you characterize them would make the link substantial on the ground that seignorage in issuing paper money is large and that on the grounds of equity and morality it should go to the poor rather than the rich . . . With SDRs attitudes are linked in a chain of confidence or infection . . . They will not be forthcoming if others want them and the USA does not. . . . The system is on dead center (so long as) there is no push or force behind the attempt to organize a new international monetary system and the committee of 20 (now the Interim Committee) has practically abandoned the task." "The International Monetary System," *International Money: A Collection of Essays*, (Boston: George Allen & Unwin, 1978), pp. 296–7.

offshore for oil and gas, to fish and to mine for seabed mineral-rich nodules could amount to more than $6 billion per year. At the same time, this could yield an additional benefit in so far as it succeeds in reducing the economic loss from overfishing which arises because of the absence of property rights to ocean fisheries and other common property resources. The potential contribution is constrained by the lack of international agreement on seabed mining and the use of outer space. It appears, however, to be an idea that should be pushed until there is the political will to achieve a more equitable distribution of global income and the recognition that it is advisable to reduce reliance on the whims of parliaments and congresses by an agreement to make such transfers automatic or a matter of entitlement.

A third category of proposals falls under this heading of "special sourcing," the diversion of some percentage of military expenditure to development purposes. The Manley Commission report has proposed that a commitment be made of an additional $100 billion a year for recovery and development. This sum, the report notes, amounts to about 10 percent of global arms expenditures.

> We are not suggesting a naive formula by which the world would decrease its arms spending each year by a 10th in favour of spending for development. But we do advocate that the target for a global budget should, over 10 years, be at least equivalent to current global arms spending.[31]

While the connection between arms expenditure and development aid is not an operational one, the conceptual link is apparent. The dichotomy between the two levels of expenditure is glaring, as can be seen in Charts 8–1, and 8–4 which show the relationship of arms expenditures

---

[31] Michael Manley, *Global Challenge—From Crisis to Co-operation: Breaking the North-South Stalemate* (London: Pan Books, 1985), p. 207. The citation goes on to state, "We should be spending a trillion dollars a year more than now on additional resources to sustain global development and transform the current global crisis."

by the industrialized countries to their budgetary outlays under official development aid (ODA) and for other purposes. In current dollars, between 1960 and 1983, annual military expenditures rose almost $460 billion while economic aid increased about $25 billion, reaching a plateau at between $35 billion and $40 billion per year. In constant dollars in *per capita* terms, while military expenditure almost doubled, there has been no increase in the amount of aid over the past quarter of a century.[32]

The contrast between the aid and the military budgets is particularly striking in the case of the United States, which has been devoting more than $300 billion per year to arms and less than $3 billion to "pure" aid.[33] This situa-

---

[32] Ruth Leger Sivard, *World Military and Social Expenditures, 1985,* (Washington, D.C. World Priorities), p. 23. The aid level in 1960 averaged out at $8.50 per capita (for a population in the developing world of 1.4 billion) while in 1983 the average was $8.40 per capita for a population of 3.6 billion. The report also reveals that some of the increase in the total expenditure can be attributed to military purchases by poor developing countries. The military share of their GNP rose between 1960 and 1982 from 4.8 percent to 5.8 percent. "Much of the development aid that was provided on a bilateral basis appeared to be guided more by military considerations than by economic. Most of the recipient countries had higher average incomes and a higher than average ratio of military expenditures to GNP."

[33] The U.S. administration is currently budgeting $16.7 billion in foreign aid (down from $20.4 billion the year before) with the military component rising from $5.8 billion to $6.7 billion. According to the official record of the Development Advisory Committee (DAC) of the OECD, the United States has been contributing about 0.2 percent, the lowest percentage of the 21 donor countries.

Testifying before the congressional Subcommittee on International Development Institutions of the House Banking Committee, former World Bank President Robert McNamara noted that if the military component in the U.S. aid total were stripped away, and if the geopolitical component with respect to Egypt and Israel were also deducted, only about one third of this 0.2 percent would be counted, making the U.S. contribution to ODA, 0.075 percent. He estimated that only about $2.5 billion, or less than one of every eight dollars in the aid budget, goes to the poorest countries.

Even this overstates the value of the aid in as much as aid is "tied," that is, must be spent in the donor country. In this respect, Canada's

tion is seen to be even more anomalous when it is recognized that the amount of military aid has been increasing as the development aid component has been decreasing. The ironic aspect is that the nonmilitary aid can be said to provide the preferred way to further the security interests of the United States in so far as it improves living conditions in the populace in the recipient countries and provides a greater measure of hope, thus diminishing the chances of unwelcome political changes in the Third World.

As a practical matter, the proposals for diverting such military expenditures to aid and to development purposes are clearly not on today's agenda. Nor is the suggestion to tie aid budgets to savings from future hoped-for reductions in military expenditure. Nonetheless, it is relevant to make the contrast, even if only to indicate how profound a difference could be made in the volume of aid if a small percentage were to be diverted to development. In doing so, it might be noted that there would appear to be an inverse relationship between the size of the military appropriations and the rate of growth of productivity, as can be seen in Charts 8–2 and 8–3, which show the relevant correlations for various countries. A boost to productivity might be regarded as a bonus for reducing military expenditures. The bars in Chart 8–3 depicting the Japanese and American arms spending growth as contrasted with the increase in productivity is eloquent enough especially when it is reinforced by the experience of several other countries.

There is a fourth source of funds that some advocate be tapped for relieving the burden on debt-ridden countries, namely, providing debt relief through "forgiveness." The

---

contribution of about 0.4 percent is overstated since as much as three quarters of the aid is in this tied category and therefore measured about one third its value (as compared to what that same money could buy on the open market under international competitive bidding).

CHART 8-1 Developed Countries' Military Expenditures and Foreign Economic Aid

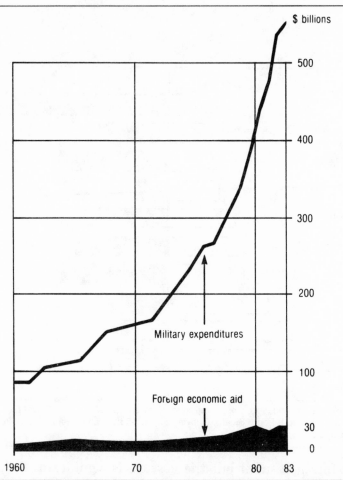

SOURCE: Reproduced, with permission, from *World Military and Social Expenditures* 1985 by Ruth Leger Sivard. Copyright © 1985 by World Priorities, Box 25140, Washington, DC, USA.

CHART 8–2 Military Burden and Productivity (1960–83)

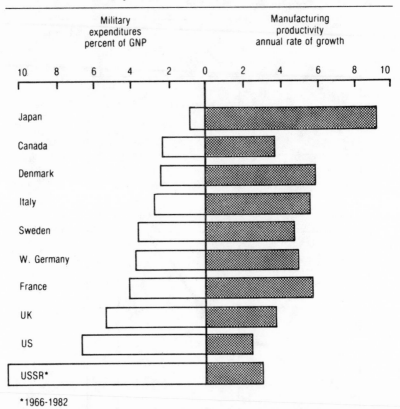

	Military expenditures percent of GNP	Manufacturing productivity annual rate of growth

*1966-1982

SOURCE: Reproduced, with permission, from *World Military and Social Expenditures* 1985 by Ruth Leger Sivard. Copyright © 1985 by World Priorities, Box 25140, Washington, DC, USA.

---

amounts are small but the gesture is significant. Danish banks recently forgave their share of Togo's debt; and at the special United Nations at the May 1986, General Assembly session on Africa's economic crisis, the Dutch Minister of Development Cooperation announced that her country would cancel all payments of interest and principal owing the Dutch government from poor African countries

CHART 8–3   Military Spending and Productivity

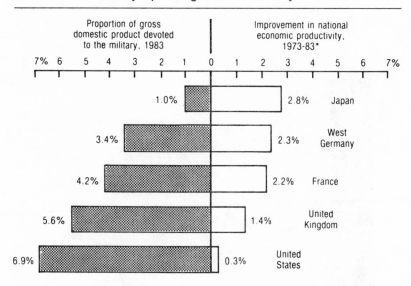

Proportion of gross domestic product devoted to the military, 1983	Improvement in national economic productivity, 1973-83*	
1.0%	2.8%	Japan
3.4%	2.3%	West Germany
4.2%	2.2%	France
5.6%	1.4%	United Kingdom
6.9%	0.3%	United States

*Average annual increases in productivity, measured as Gross Domestic Product per employed person.

SOURCES: Stockholm International Peace Research Institute. President's Commission on Industrial Competitiveness.

for five years, which amounts to a savings of $80 million for the debtors. The Canadian Minister for External Relations likewise has offered a 15-year moratorium which totals about $250 million in debt relief. This is, however, a far cry from the $80 to $100 billion in debt relief and aid sought by the African nations for the years 1986 and 1990.[34]

---

[34] The other nations refuse to regard the assembly meeting as a pledging session. In the Organization of African Unity's report, "African Priority Program for Economic Recovery," (presented to the United Nations General Assembly) the request is for an increase of $45.6 billion in aid and $35 to $55 billion in debt relief in the next five years. The

CHART 8-4   World Military and Other Expenditures of Governments (1983)

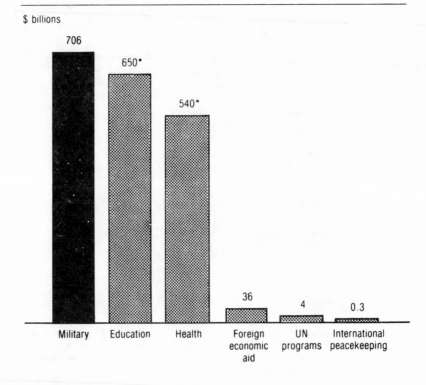

$ billions

706

650*

540*

36

4

0.3

Military   Education   Health   Foreign economic aid   UN programs   International peacekeeping

*Projected

SOURCE: Reproduced, with permission, *from World Military and Social Expenditures 1985* by Ruth Leger Sivard. Copyright © 1985 by World Priorities, Box 25140, Washington, DC, USA.

Organization of African Unity requests the conversion of $15 to $25 billion of government loans to grants and the consolidation of from $20 to $30 billion of nongovernmental debts and interest into long-term loans. The total African debt is estimated at $175 billion and debt repayment at about $25 billion a year from 1986 to 1990.

Congressman Charles Schumer, a member of the House Banking Committee, has suggested the debt burden be shared among debtors, banks, and governments and, as part of that approach, proposed that the banks absorb losses by writing off approximately 30 cents on each dollar of their loans as "nonperforming," stretching out repayment periods and lowering interest rates on the remaining debt. This, he points out, would be "in line with the average discount at which banks are currently reselling some of their Third World debt."[35] Other suggestions are less direct, involving reduction of the real cost of the debt by converting debt to indexed or zero coupon obligations or absorption of debt by central banks at subsidized rates.

In all these proposals for easing the debt burden the common feature is a form of contribution through forgoing payments due in whole or in part. The potential for this form of "aid" is considerable and likely to be realized involuntarily if not made beforehand as a gesture of generosity. This applies particularly to the debt owed by the poorest and smallest of countries. Such debt relief should pose no problems for the banking community because the amounts involved in the case of these countries are relatively small. Forgiving a percentage of debts in the case of the larger debtors could also be arranged without traumatic impact on the bank balance sheets. One way or the other this is the most likely outcome. To balk on the grounds that the precedents are dangerous or invoking reasons of "moral hazard" rings hollow as well as futile.

---

[35] "Ease Up on Debtor Nations," *Washington Post* (March 10, 1986). He also suggests that debtors "be helped as a group, rather than case by case," that " 'sustained growth' replace wrenching economic austerity," that "Third World debt is simply unpayable as structured," and that "what is needed is a creative solution" that would involve capping repayment at 25 percent of exports.

THE ASYMMETRY OF THE ADJUSTMENT: THE ASPECTS OF HOPE & JUSTICE

Goals must be worth striving for and within reach. When the growth of the debt exceeds interest payments and negative net transfers ensue, the debtor countries face a stark dilemma: should they continue to run up an escalator that is going down? Getting off would seem a sensible option if there is little sense of progress and if there is little hope of reaching some worthwhile landing. Under these circumstances one would question whether it is acceptable to set as a goal a return to "normalcy," mid 1980s variety.

Normalcy in today's world can be sketched in terms of some grim statistics:[36]

- More than 800 million people live under the degrading conditions of "absolute poverty," lacking the basic physical necessities of life and, in almost all cases, dignity and hope as well.
- More than 30 million of these people suffer from malnutrition to a point where they are faced with imminent death without the strength to work or study.
- More than 30 million workers in the industrialized countries are officially classified as "unemployed."

---

[36] The figures used are from the World Bank and, if anything, err on the side of underestimation.

For a lucid sketch of "the wretched of the earth," see Michael Harrington, *The Vast Majority: A Journey to World's Poor.* (New York: Simon & Schuster, 1977), pp. 15–17. He refers to a "fourth world" of a billion who live in "a daily agony" and of contrasts where 30 percent of the world's population have 3 percent of its income.

At the same time, it should be noted that the two decades from 1960 to 1980 were a period of unprecedented achievement. The growth rates of the developing countries, taken as a whole, doubled incomes in a little more than a decade, enabling rising per capita incomes and the widespread provision of such basics as primary schooling and health services that drastically reduced infant mortality and extended life expectancy from 42 years to almost 60.

Normalcy can also be described as a profoundly political asymmetric international economic system. Serious questions must arise when the citizens of one group of countries are expected to make draconian sacrifices while in the other they are called on to suffer only some stress. As Professor John Spearos has observed:

> A primary source of debtors' rebelliousness with present remedial measures lies in the assymetry of the situation where "the creditor banks, while asked to reschedule their clients' debts and in some instances to stump up some extra cash, are not required to do anything which adversely affects their bottom line."[37]

This imbalance is reinforced in the case-by-case process on the premise there should be unequal obligations. The assumption is that all the blame lies with the debtor countries whose leaders and citizens took borrowed money for misconceived investments, for extravagant consumption, and for transfer abroad.[38] Recognizing there is some truth

---

[37] "Cheered by the Rich and Tough on the Poor," *Guardian* (June 12, 1985).

[38] Sally Shelton-Colby, "Helping to Ease the Latins' Debt," *New York Times* (March 19, 1985). From the perspective of the developing countries, particularly the heavily indebted ones, serious umbrage is taken when it is argued that the adverse impact on the debtor countries should be ignored since borrowers who want to play the game must recognize the risks and be prepared to pay the price of miscalculations. On this point the observation of a former Brazilian minister of finance, Mario Henrique Simonsen, is germane:

"Witch hunters may argue that rational markets should have anticipated a world recession in the early 1980s since inflation in OECD countries was escalating to intolerable levels . . . Lenders and borrowers were probably prepared to face a normal adjustment shock, like the one of 1975. What rational economic agents could never foresee was the policy mix of the U.S. where tight money was accompanied by loose fiscal policy which led to an unprecedented rise in real interest rates and the value of the dollar. Expectations are based on historical experience rather than the possibility of unorthodox policy experiments." "The Developing-Countries Debt Problem," *International Debt and the Developing Countries: A World Bank Symposium*, ed., G. W. Smith and J. T. Cuddington, (Washington, D.C.: World Bank), p. 120.

in these allegations and that the leaders and people of the debtor countries have to get their house in order, the questions must be asked: However high the cost? *Are the lending bankers blameless?*

The answers would also point to the failings of the prevailing global financial system and to the need for its structural reforms. From the side of the creditors there is virtual silence regarding any real structural reforms to be undertaken by the G-10 governments or the institutions that are integral parts of the global framework within which the debtors and creditors have been interacting. There is an illusion being fostered that summits and G-7 meetings will suffice though their tangible outcomes address but one facet of the present crisis, exchange rate volatility. This lopsided treatment of the diagnostic and the cure is being noted and subjected to criticism as inadequate and unfair.

The main thrust of the critique is, however, directed at the unfairness of the current adjustment process in as much as it is proceeding in a way that increases societal strains in the debtor countries while the creditor banks find that, with time, there is a decreasing danger to their financial viability. The major banks have been able to build up reserves and diversify their portfolios with lessened dependence on the questionable assets represented by the accounts receivable of sovereign troubled borrowers. Yet little tolerance is shown by the banking community with respect to measures that would provide debt relief. The potential political damage being done by the creditors maintaining a hard posture is not an academic issue. These are "costs" that need to be factored into the equation, if not by the banks themselves, at least by their governments, which ostensibly place some value on the maintenance of democratic societies in the Third World.[39]

---

[39] It is difficult to square remarks by U.S. Treasury Secretary Baker's to the effect that debt write-offs pose a threat to fragile democracies in light of the strain that is associated with rescheduling that piles

TABLE 8–1   Effects of Macroeconomic Changes on the Current
Account Balance of All Developing Countries

(billions of dollars)

Type of Change	1984	1990
One percentage point increase in interest rates		
Existing variable rate debt	−2.3	−2.3
Existing fixed rate debt refinanced at new higher rate	0.0	−1.6
New debt	0.0	−4.1
Total	−2.3	−8.0
One percentage point improvement in terms of trade	2.2	4.8
One percentage point improvement in industrial countries' GNP growth		
Without dollar appreciation		
Through terms of trade effect of increased commodity prices	2.2	4.8
Direct terms of trade effect	1.3	2.9
Total	3.5	7.7
With dollar appreciation		
Through terms of trade effect of increased commodity prices	0.0	0.0
Direct terms of trade effect	1.3	2.9
Total	1.3	2.9

SOURCE: World Development Report, 1985

There is another troubling aspect of this asymmetry.
Debtors become alienated when they find themselves in a
situation where their payments increase or decrease in
quantum leaps by virtue of exogenous events unforeseen
and beyond their control. The rise or fall of interest rates
and the appreciation of the U.S. dollar and other factors
seriously affect the conditions of life for millions who have
little or no participation in the process. As Table 8–1 re-

---

the debts ever higher and pushes the figurative light at the end of the
tunnel ever further—and in some cases, out of sight. On this point,
see the article by Sir Shridath Ramphal, "There's no substitute for a
more democratic world." The *International Herald Tribune*, May 20,
1986. He questions the summit declaration that can claim "world economic conditions are better than they have been for some considerable
time"—at a time of Latin America's most acute debt crisis and famine
in Africa. He asks: Are we living in two or more worlds, each with its
shutters down? "Is the 'South' believed to be so marginal to the prosper-
ity of the 'North' that its realities do not compel adjustments or a world
view as seen from a prosperous heartland?"

veals, in 1984 under prevailing conditions, a reduction of 1 percent would improve the total current account position of all developing countries by an estimated $2.3 billion and by 1990 as much as $8 billion. The impact also works the other way.

Under the circumstances it is understandable that the spokesmen for the heavily indebted developing nations have strong feelings about their voices in the international forums resonating in empty chambers, unheeded. At the same time, it is apparent that institutions like the IMF practice an uneven surveillance of economic performance. Peruvian President Garcia and Henry Kissinger, despite their different vantages, join forces on that point. The list of commentators on this issue is indicative of widespread awareness that the dice are loaded to favor one side. In the prevailing debt management process a higher priority is being placed on protecting bank balance sheets than on preserving democratic societies.

There were gyrations of anxiety, euphoria, and the return to anxiety as the debt crisis passed through phases from 1982 to today. Now there is a growing fear that, unless genuine attempts are made to arrive at long-term sustainable solutions rather than make do with short-term expedients, the consequences are unthinkable. There continue to be references to the debt crisis as a "financial time bomb ticking away" suggesting a sense of danger and urgency. Such anxiety is healthy and continues to give rise to a crescendo of proposals for action. This has prompted the investment banker Felix Rohatyn and others to propose the appointment of "an international committee of experts," a group that ostensibly would be free of the tight constraints operating on politicians and be able to consider the wide array of technical and political options.[40]

---

[40] "How to Defuse the World's Financial Time Bomb," *Business Week* (December 16, 1985) Such a group, he suggests, could be made up of such persons as Arthur Burns and Helmut Schmidt. He suggests a pur-

Whatever the form such a "council of wise persons" might take, there is a need for "wisdom," which Barbara Tuchman in her provocative book *The March of Folly: From Troy to Vietnam*, defines as "the exercise of judgment acting on experience, common sense, and available information." As she points out, the historical record is replete with the lack of "wise" judgment as demonstrated by countless examples of the pursuit of policy contrary to self-interest. "Why" she asks, "do holders of high office so often act contrary to the way reason points and enlightened self-interest suggests?"

This global debt crisis, in all its ramifications, provides a testing time. The present approach has been rationalized as "a least bad option." This should not preclude examining other approaches, including some that would modify the rules of the game. This is clearly necessary when the roots of the crisis are deep and systemic and cannot therefore be addressed adequately or fairly on a case-by-case basis, which leaves the framework for this process merely patched at the margin. Certainly, the record of how it has been managed so far is not encouraging, being neither prudent nor equitable in putting off the day when developing countries can hope to grow again. Time may not be on the side of those who count on muddling through without a helmsman, hoping for fair winds. Too late, they may find out that a policy of coping is not enough.

---

pose, namely, "to prepare a conference with the U.S. in the lead along the lines of Bretton Woods with the purpose of recommending changes in the monetary system (in which) the dollar (would) no longer serve as the only world currency." Others have in mind different objectives and composition but the principle is a common one, namely, to broaden the scope of the deliberations in both its geographic and temporal scope so the parochial and short-term will not dominate—as it does in politically constrained forums.

INDEX